D1084786

Bloom's Modern Critical Interpretations

The Adventures of
Huckleberry Finn
The Age of Innocence
Alice's Adventures in
Wonderland
All Quiet on the
Western Front
As You Like It
The Ballad of the Sad
Café
Beloved
Beowulf
Black Boy
The Bluest Eye
The Canterbury Tales
Cat on a Hot Tin
Roof
The Catcher in the
Rye
Catch-22
The Chronicles of
Narnia
The Color Purple
Crime and
Punishment
The Crucible
Darkness at Noon
Death of a Salesman
The Death of
Artemio Cruz
Don Quixote
Emerson's Essays
Emma
Fahrenheit 451
A Farewell to Arms
Frankenstein
The Glass Menagerie

The Grapes of Wrath
Great Expectations
The Great Gatsby
Gulliver's Travels
Hamlet
The Handmaid's Tale
Heart of Darkness
I Know Why the
Caged Bird Sings
The Iliad
Jane Eyre
The Joy Luck Club
The Jungle
Long Day's Journey
Into Night
Lord of the Flies
The Lord of the
Rings
Love in the Time of
Cholera
The Man Without
Qualities
The Metamorphosis
Miss Lonelyhearts
Moby-Dick
My Ántonia
Native Son
Night
1984
The Odyssey
Oedipus Rex
The Old Man and the
Sea
On the Road
One Flew Over the
Cuckoo's Nest

One Hundred Years
of Solitude
Persuasion
Portnoy's Complaint
Pride and Prejudice
Ragtime
The Red Badge of
Courage
Romeo and Juliet
The Rubáiyát of
Omar Khayyám
The Scarlet Letter
A Separate Peace
Silas Marner
Song of Solomon
The Sound and the
Fury
The Stranger
A Streetcar Named
Desire
Sula
The Tale of Genji
A Tale of Two Cities
"The Tell-Tale Heart"
and Other Stories
Their Eyes Were
Watching God
Things Fall Apart
To Kill a
Mockingbird
Ulysses
Waiting for Godot
The Waste Land
Wuthering Heights
Young Goodman
Brown

Bloom's Modern Critical Interpretations

Tennessee Williams's
A Streetcar Named Desire
New Edition

Edited and with an introduction by
Harold Bloom
Sterling Professor of the Humanities
Yale University

BLOOM'S
LITERARY CRITICISM
An imprint of Infobase Publishing

Bloom's Modern Critical Interpretations:
A Streetcar Named Desire—New Edition

Copyright © 2009 by Infobase Publishing
Introduction © 2009 by Harold Bloom

Bloom's Literary Criticism
An imprint of Infobase Publishing
132 West 31st Street
New York NY 10001

Library of Congress Cataloging-in-Publication Data
Tennessee Williams's A streetcar named desire / edited and with an introduction by
Harold Bloom. — New ed.
    p. cm. — (Bloom's modern critical interpretations)
  Includes bibliographical references and index.
  ISBN 978-1-60413-389-9 (hardcover)
  1. Williams, Tennessee, 1911–1983. Streetcar named Desire. I. Bloom, Harold.
II. Title. III. Series.
  PS3545.I5365S8275 2009
  812'.54—dc22   2008049231

Text design by Erika K. Arroyo
Composition by EJB Publishing
Contributing editor: Pamela Loos
Cover designed by Ben Peterson
Cover printed by Yurchak Printing, Landisville, Pa.
Book printed and bound by Yurchak Printing, Landisville, Pa.
Printed in the United States of America

This book is printed on acid-free paper.

All links and Web addresses were checked and verified to be correct at the time of
publication. Because of the dynamic nature of the Web, some addresses and links
may have changed since publication and may no longer be valid.

Contents

Editor's Note

My introduction meditates on Blanche's place in the lifelong relationship of Williams as lyrical dramatist to the great lyrical poet Hart Crane.

Gulshan Rai Kataria considers Blanche together with Maggie the Cat and Myrtle (in *Kingdom of Earth*) as three instances of women whose very essence is sexual love.

In a sensitive Orphic interpretation, Calvin Bedient reads *Streetcar* as a dramatic lyric of mourning for Blanche, while Susan Koprince insists on emphasizing "domestic violence" as the play's center.

"The kindness of strangers" is converted into the benignity of closure by George Toles, after which Philip C. Kolin employs the trope of paper as a key to *Streetcar*'s sense of mere Being.

The absence of African-American characters is scrutinized by George W. Crandell, while Bert Cardullo isolates the placement of Scene 11 in New Orleans on All Souls' Day.

John S. Bak investigates the use of music as metalanguage by Williams in *Streetcar*, after which Rachel Van Duyvenbode uncovers elements of racial strain in *Baby Doll* and in *Streetcar*.

This volume's final essay, by Michael Paller, brings forward the overshadowing background of homoeroticism in *Streetcar*.

HAROLD BLOOM

Introduction

I

It is a sad and inexplicable truth that the United States, a dramatic nation, continues to have so limited a literary achievement in the drama. American literature, from Emerson to the present moment, is a distinguished tradition. The poetry of Whitman, Dickinson, Frost, Stevens, Eliot, W.C. Williams, Hart Crane, R.P. Warren, Elizabeth Bishop down through the generation of my own contemporaries—John Ashbery, James Merrill, A.R. Ammons, and others—has an unquestionable eminence and takes a vital place in Western literature. Prose fiction from Hawthorne and Melville on through Mark Twain and Henry James to Cather and Dreiser, Faulkner, Hemingway, Fitzgerald, Nathanael West, and Pynchon has almost a parallel importance. The line of essayists and critics from Emerson and Thoreau to Kenneth Burke and beyond constitutes another crucial strand of our national letters. But where is the American drama in comparison to all this and in relation to the long cavalcade of Western drama from Aeschylus to Beckett?

The American theater, by the common estimate of its most eminent critics, touches an initial strength with Eugene O'Neill and then proceeds to the more varied excellences of Thornton Wilder, Tennessee Williams, Arthur Miller, Edward Albee, and Sam Shepard. That sequence is clearly problematical and becomes even more worrisome when we move from playwrights to plays. Which are our dramatic works that matter most? *Long Day's Journey Into Night*, certainly; perhaps *The Iceman Cometh*; evidently *A Streetcar Named Desire* and *Death of a Salesman*; perhaps again *The Skin of*

1

Our Teeth and *The Zoo Story*—it is not God's plenty. And I will venture the speculation that our drama palpably is not yet literary enough. By this I do not just mean that O'Neill writes very badly, or Miller very baldly; they do, but so did Dreiser, and *Sister Carrie* and *An American Tragedy* prevail nevertheless. Nor do I wish to be an American Matthew Arnold (whom I loathe above all other critics) and proclaim that our dramatists simply have not known enough. They know more than enough, and that is part of the trouble.

Literary tradition, as I have come to understand it, masks the agon between past and present as a benign relationship, whether personal or societal. The actual transferences between the force of the literary past and the potential of writing in the present tend to be darker, even if they do not always or altogether follow the defensive patterns of what Sigmund Freud called "family romances." Whether or not an ambivalence, however repressed, toward the past's force is felt by the new writer and is manifested in his work seems to depend entirely upon the ambition and power of the oncoming artist. If he aspires after strength and can attain it, then he must struggle with both a positive and a negative transference, false connections because necessarily imagined ones, between a composite precursor and himself. His principal resource in that agon will be his own native gift for interpretation, or as I am inclined to call it, strong misreading. Revising his precursor, he will create himself, make himself into a kind of changeling, and so he will become, in an illusory but highly pragmatic way, his own father.

The most literary of our major dramatists, and clearly I mean "literary" in a precisely descriptive sense, neither pejorative nor eulogistic, was Tennessee Williams. Wilder, with his intimate connections to *Finnegans Wake* and Gertrude Stein, might seem to dispute this placement, and Wilder was certainly more literate than Williams. But Wilder had a benign relation to his crucial precursor, Joyce, and did not aspire after a destructive strength. Williams did and suffered the fate he prophesied and desired; the strength destroyed his later work, and his later life, and thus joined itself to the American tradition of self-destructive genius. Williams truly had one precursor only: Hart Crane, the greatest of our lyrical poets, after Whitman and Dickinson, and the most self-destructive figure in our national literature, surpassing all others in this, as in so many regards.

Williams asserted he had other precursors also: D.H. Lawrence, and Chekhov in the drama. These were outward influences and benefited Williams well enough, but they were essentially formal and so not the personal and societal family romance of authentic poetic influence. Hart Crane made Williams into more of a dramatic lyrist, though writing in prose, than the lyrical dramatist that Williams is supposed to have been. Though this influence—perhaps more nearly an identification—helped form *The Glass Menag-*

erie and (less overtly) *A Streetcar Named Desire*, and in a lesser mode *Summer and Smoke* and *Suddenly Last Summer*, it also led to such disasters of misplaced lyricism as the dreadful *Camino Real* and the dreary *The Night of the Iguana*. (*Cat on a Hot Tin Roof,* one of Williams's best plays, does not seem to me to show any influence of Crane.) Williams's long aesthetic decline covered thirty years, from 1953 to 1983, and reflected the sorrows of a seer who, by his early forties, had outlived his own vision. Hart Crane, self-slain at thirty-two, had set for Williams a High Romantic paradigm that helped cause Williams, his heart as dry as summer dust, to burn to the socket.

II

The epigraph to *A Streetcar Named Desire* is a quatrain from Hart Crane's "The Broken Tower," the poet's elegy for his gift, his vocation, his life, and so Crane's precise equivalent of Shelley's *Triumph of Life*, Keats's *Fall of Hyperion*, and Whitman's "When Lilacs Last in the Dooryard Bloom'd." Tennessee Williams, in his long thirty years of decline after composing *A Streetcar Named Desire*, had no highly designed, powerfully executed elegy for his own poetic self. Unlike Crane, his American Romantic precursor and aesthetic paradigm, Williams had to live out the slow degradation of the waning of his potential and so endured the triumph of life over his imagination.

Streetcar sustains a first rereading, after thirty years away from it, more strongly than I had expected. It is, inevitably, more remarkable on the stage than in the study, but the fusion of Williams's lyrical and dramatic talents in it has prevailed over time, at least so far. The play's flaws, in performance, ensue from its implicit tendency to sensationalize its characters, Blanche DuBois in particular. Directors and actresses have made such sensationalizing altogether explicit, with the sad result prophesied by Kenneth Tynan twenty-five years ago. The playgoer forgets that Blanche's only strengths are "nostalgia and hope," that she is "the desperate exceptional woman," and that her fall is a parable, rather than an isolated squalor:

> When, finally, she is removed to the mental home, we should feel that a part of civilization is going with her. Where ancient drama teaches us to reach nobility by contemplation of what is noble, modern American drama conjures us to contemplate what might have been noble, but is now humiliated, ignoble in the sight of all but the compassionate.

Tynan, though accurate enough, still might have modified the image of Blanche taking a part of civilization away with her into madness. Though

Blanche yearns for the values of the aesthetic, she scarcely embodies them, being in this failure a masochistic self-parody on the part of Williams himself. His *Memoirs* portray Williams incessantly in the role of Blanche, studying the nostalgias and inching along the wavering line between hope and paranoia. Williams, rather than Blanche, sustains Tynan's analysis of the lost nobility, now humiliated, that American drama conjures us to contemplate.

The fall of Blanche is a parable, not of American civilization's lost nobility, but of the failure of the American literary imagination to rise above its recent myths of recurrent defeat. Emerson admonished us, his descendants, to go beyond the Great Defeat of the Crucifixion and to demand Victory instead, a victory of the senses as well as of the soul. Walt Whitman, taking up Emerson's challenge directly, set the heroic pattern so desperately emulated by Hart Crane, which is then repeated in a coarser tone in Williams's life and work.

It must seem curious, at first, to regard Blanche DuBois as a failed Whitmanian, but essentially that is her aesthetic identity. Confronted by the revelation of her young husband's preference for an older man over herself, Blanche falls downward and outward into nymphomania, phantasmagoric hopes, pseudo-imaginative collages of memory and desire. Her Orphic, psychic rending by the amiably brutal Stanley Kowalski, a rough but effective version of D.H. Lawrence's vitalistic vision of male force, is pathetic rather than tragic, not because Stanley necessarily is mindless, but because she unnecessarily has made herself mindless by failing the pragmatic test of experience.

Williams's most effective blend of lyrical vision and dramatic irony in the play comes in the agony of Blanche's cry against Stanley to Stella, his wife and her sister:

> He acts like an animal, has an animal's habits! Eats like one, moves like one, talks like one! There's even something—subhuman—something not quite to the stage of humanity yet! Yes, something —ape-like about him, like one of those pictures I've seen in— anthropological studies! Thousands and thousands of years have passed him right by, and there he is—Stanley Kowalski—survivor of the stone age! Bearing the raw meat home from the kill in the jungle! And you—*you* here—*waiting* for him! Maybe he'll strike you or maybe grunt and kiss you! That is, if kisses have been discovered yet! Night falls and the other apes gather! There in the front of the cave, all grunting like him, and swilling and gnawing and hulking! His poker night!—you call it—this party of apes! Somebody growls—some creature snatches at something—the fight is on! *God!* Maybe we are a long way from being made in

God's image, but Stella—my sister—there has been *some* progress since then! Such things as art—as poetry and music—such kinds of new light have come into the world since then! In some kinds of people some tenderer feelings have had some little beginning! That we have got to make *grow*! And *cling* to, and hold as our flag! In this dark march toward whatever it is we're approaching.... *Don't—don't hang back with the brutes*!

The lyricism here takes its strength from the ambivalence of what at once attracts and dismays both Blanche and Williams. Dramatic irony, terrible in its antithetical pathos, results here from Blanche's involuntary self-condemnation, since she herself has hung back with the brutes while merely blinking at the new light of the aesthetic. Stanley, being what he is, is clearly less to blame than Blanche, who was capable of more but failed in will.

Williams, in his *Memoirs*, haunted as always by Hart Crane, refers to his precursor as "a tremendous and yet fragile artist" and then associates both himself and Blanche with the fate of Crane, a suicide by drowning in the Caribbean:

I am as much of an hysteric as ... Blanche; a codicil to my will provides for the disposition of my body in this way. "Sewn up in a clean white sack and dropped over board, twelve hours north of Havana, so that my bones may rest not too far from those of Hart Crane ..."

At the conclusion of *Memoirs*, Williams again associated Crane both with his own vocation and his own limitations, following Crane even in an identification with the young Rimbaud:

A poet such as the young Rimbaud is the only writer of whom I can think, at this moment, who could escape from words into the sensations of being, through his youth, turbulent with revolution, permitted articulation by nights of absinthe. And of course there is Hart Crane. Both of these poets touched fire that burned them alive. And perhaps it is only through self-immolation of such a nature that we living beings can offer to you the entire truth of ourselves within the reasonable boundaries of a book.

It is the limitation of *Memoirs*, and in some sense even of *A Streetcar Named Desire*, that we cannot accept either Williams or poor Blanche as a Rimbaud or a Hart Crane. Blanche cannot be said to have touched fire that burned her alive. Yet Williams earns the relevance of the play's great epigraph to Blanche's terrible fate:

> And so it was I entered the broken world
> To trace the visionary company of love, its voice
> An instant in the wind (I know not whither hurled)
> But not for long to hold each desperate choice.

GULSHAN RAI KATARIA

The Hetairas (Maggie, Myrtle, Blanche)

It would be appropriate to know and understand here the hetaira's psychological characteristics both in her positive and negative manifestations. 'Hetaira' literally means 'courtesan' and by extension means a companion woman engaged in the service of love. Jung's collaborator Toni Wolff (and other Jungians too), considers her as a woman for whom love is an end for which she can subordinate all familial and social taboos and surmount all physical and material impediments.[1] Her relationship is with the man and really a decisive factor of her life. Lord Byron had none other than a hetaira woman in mind when he said, "Man's love is of man's life a thing apart / 'Tis woman's whole existence." A hetaira is permeated by the essence of love or probably breathes love itself.

She is the extreme opposite and furthest away from the maternal type. She is instinctively oriented towards the individual and relates with him for his own sake and not as a father of her children or for his social status. She gets her fulfillment in interpersonal relationship, by being companion to him on any plan—intellectual, spiritual or sexual—all three at once, but not necessarily all three. Such a woman is often seen in those marriages where procreation is assigned a secondary significance. Elsewhere, in extramarital relationships, she is the 'other' woman, constantly filling the gap which a maternally oriented wife leaves in a husband's psyche, giving him value in

From *The Faces of Eve: A Study of Tennessee Williams's Heroines*. © 1992 by Gulshan Rai Kataria.

7

himself over mere husband or father. Because a hetaira is concerned with the subjective individual aspect in man as well as in herself, she tends to address herself to the shadow side of the individual, to the same extent that a mother will tend to disregard it in favour of social persona. In other words, that part of the psychic life of her man which a mother woman suppresses, ignores or hides (such as his talent for poetry or his fondness for oriental philosophy or cricket, simply because it is not 'useful' for the family) is sedulously tendered by this woman. She cares for his needs, moods and ambitions, and loves him in spite of his weaknesses and failures.

Now a hetaira, like a mother can be of two types: in extreme positive cases she may be *femme inspiratrice*, guiding and motivating the man to higher goals. Ann B. Ulanov says in this context, "In its positive aspects, this type . . . is symbolized for Jungians in the images of the priestess dedicated to the service of love, the love deities, the hierodules, and the woman who inspires men to prodigious feats."[2] Such a woman understands her man: discusses, adds and abets his projects, whets and feeds his appetite, but never stands in the way of his advancement. It is one such woman who stands behind a successful man without taking credit for anything. Further, if/because such a woman operates from outside the marriage, she comes in direct confrontation with the family of the person, the law and society at large not to mention her need for financial independence. The hetaira role thus cannot be played by a weaker woman because of inherent difficulties. The woman remains constantly on the horns of dilemma: if she loves her man and seeks her own fulfillment in giving him fulfillment, she rankles like a wound in conventional societies. If, on the other hand, she accepts the latter's dictates she has to neglect her own genuine nature. It is here that a hetaira finds herself on shaky grounds and tries to change her status of mistress to that of a wife, mistakenly believing that marriage is inevitable for a lasting relationship. Jungians, however, believe that the moment she attempts to give herself a status she ceases to be a pure hetaira. Irene Claremont de Castillejo writes, "The hetaira woman who breaks other people's marriages in order to become the wife herself has not yet learned what belongs to her particular form of relationship."[3] In other words, she has to observe rules of her peculiar relationship and know that the man belongs to her only in a relationship which she has to respect more than her own needs for a legal status. She has to understand what does not belong to her relationship and has moreover "to know when a relationship has become fulfilled and complete."[4] Upon realizing the fulfillment this eros-motivated woman must leave without making demands. The onus on the hetaira is rather heavy.

An unadapted or negative hetaira can become a *femme fatale*. Because of the intimate knowledge of her man's unconscious—his needs, wishes and ambitions—she can lapse into the role of a seductress weaning him away from everything else. De Castillejo remarks, "if so she may lure him away from his real destiny or the practical necessities of outer life, in favour of some illusory anima ambition, and so ultimately ruin him."[5] She might try to keep him tied to her apron-strings, use all feminine wiles and guiles to emasculate his urge for achieving miraculous heights or at least his cherished goals. Her possessive love and inordinate solicitude might make him seek her image in other women and cripple him psychologically. Another characteristic of a negative hetaira woman is her lack of commitment to permanence in outer relationship. She might throw her hands up too soon and walk away to seek and give fulfillment to another man. Such a hetaira is the *puella aeterna*, the eternal daughter, seeking love wherever she can get it. Edward C. Whitmont comments, "Indeed, she may, like her male counterpart, *puer aeternus*, shy away from making any concrete commitment and forever lead a provisory life of emotional wandering."[6] Exhibitionism and egotism are other negative traits in such a woman: for a true hetaira mediates the personal unconscious of her man unobtrusively, quietly, without looking for credit or reward.

Lest the foregoing discussion should create an impression that a hetaira has to be a weak woman or a doormat, it may be repeated that that is not true. The woman has to be brave enough to face the world, work for her own financial independence, and simultaneously bring the best out of her man. She might use her maidenly softness now and alternate it with aggression and wilfulness then, all in the service of the relationship. Secondly, it is not necessary that a hetaira can only be the other woman and not one's wife. In fact, the converse is as true, though rare. Blessed is the man who has a wife with an overlay of hetaira personality in her. And lastly, the traits mentioned above are archetypal. Variations on the archetype are always possible depending upon the secondary personality which might be of the mother or medium.

Tennessee Williams created at least two pleasing and positive hetairas, viz., Maggie (in *Cat on a Hot Tin Roof*) and Myrtle (in *Kingdom of Earth*).

Maggie, the wife of Brick Pollitt, is companion to him at the sexual level. She is a beautiful, sleek, slender and a soft woman, immensely conscious and proud of her looks. Unlike the other heroines of Williams, who are, more often than not, past their prime, Maggie is youthful, lusty, and vivacious. Williams describes her as a "pretty young woman"[7] with a voice that "has range and music," (p. 111) a "gay, charming smile," (p. 113) a woman who has "lovely bare arms" (p. 111), and "giggles with a hand fluttering at her throat and her breast and her long throat arched," (p. 114) and her speech is oddly funny, because her eyes "constantly twinkle and her voice shakes with laughter which is basically indulgent." (p. 113) She has a "bitchy" humour (p. 114), which Williams attributes to her estrangement with her husband for the nonce. In other words, she is a sensual, languorous, and voluptuously appeasing hetaira woman, who has kept herself attractive for the conquest of her alienated husband. (p. 128) She is "Great: the greatest" (p. 172) in bed. She has an intense love for Brick, and she would not look at any other man: "I can't see a man but you! Even with my eyes closed, I just see you. . . . But don't continue my torture. I can't live on and on under these circumstances." (p. 123) Immediately after her marriage with Brick, she tries to obliterate her identity in his love and in his love for football. Brick recalls:

> She went on the road that fall with the Dixie Stars. Oh she made a great show of being the world's best sport. She wore a—wore a—tall bearskin cap! A shako, they call it, a dyed moleskin coat, a moleskin coat dyed red!—Cut up crazy! Rented hotel ball rooms for victory celebrations, wouldn't cancel them when it—turned out—defeat. . . . (p. 172)

Maggie has been presented in the play as a hetaira woman for whom love of the man is supreme. She has sacrificed herself for him in the past and continues to do so when the play opens.

As a hetaira, Maggie is more into the power and allure of sex than into other components of the hetaira. She is aware of the spell she can cast upon men by her bewitching looks and figure. She has exploited them many a time to gain favour, love and attention. She is conscious of Big Daddy's eyes which seem to pry into her person. She flirts with him now and then knowing that the lascivious "Big Daddy harbours a little unconscious lech for me. . . . Way he always drops his eyes down my body when I'm talkin' to him, drops his eyes to my boobs an' licks his old chops! Ha ha!" (p. 113) This charming woman has exercised her powerful beauty in the past and forced Brick to marry her. (p. 172) She has deliberately exercised her charms on Big Daddy to circumvent the danger of being cut off from his inheritance in view of Brick's intemperance with alcohol. She relishes talking about the attentions she receives from men while walking on the roadside. She tells Brick about them:

> They still see me, Brick, and they like what they see. Un-huh. Some of them would give their— . . . Other men still want me. . . . Why, last week in Memphis everywhere that I went men's eyes burned holes in my clothes, at the country club and in the restaurants and department stores, there wasn't a man I met or walked by that didn't first eat me up with his eyes and turn around when I passed him and look back at me. Why, at Alice's party for her New York cousins, the best lookin' man in the crowd—followed me upstairs and tried to force his way in the powder room with me, followed me to the door and tried to force his way in! (pp. 128–129)

She talks of this handsome man as a having a "lech" for her. By way of comment, one may add that her repeated babbling of others' "lech" for her comes from her idea that this way she can excite Brick's jealousy and also his desire for her. Brick who has not been sleeping with his wife ever since his friend Skipper died has made Maggie as nervous as a cat. She has begun to feel that Brick's deliberate casting her aside means her defeat and of her lack of charms, to provoke sexual desire in her man. She, therefore, talks of others' "lech" for her so as to arouse the sexual passion in him. She flaunts her powerful battery—her breasts and her hips—to Brick and says:

> You know, our sex life didn't just peter out in the usual way, it was cut off short, long before the natural time for it to, and it's going to revive again, just as sudden as that. I'm confident of it. That's what I'm keeping myself attractive for. For the time when you'll see me again like other men see me . . . Look Brick! [*She stands before the long oval mirror, touches her breasts and then her hips with her two hands.*] How high my body stays on me! Nothing has fallen off me—not a fraction . . . (pp. 128–129)

Her exhibitionistic use of her sexual lure also sets her up in the hetaira modality. But her exploitation of her sexual charms to gain her selfish ends makes her a powerful and dangerous hetaira.

To a perceptive reader, the animus of Maggie would clearly seem reflected in Big Daddy. Her lust for life, for love, for children, for money, for comfort and for talking, all would reveal her connection with the old man. Her aggressive, indefatigable spirit and strength are much like Big Daddy's who started from a scratch to become the biggest landlord of the Delta, just as Maggie has fought her way up to Brick. Her desperate but spirited attempts at the revival and restitution of her conjugal life are identical with Big Daddy's vigorous zest for life with which he seeks to defeat death. Her talk of others' "lech" for her can be equated with Big Daddy's bragging about his sexual potency, even on his deathbed, "I still have desire for women and this is my sixty-fifth birthday." (p. 155) When Maggie talks of sleeping with another man surreptitiously so that Brick could not cast her off for faithlessness and adultery, she echoes Big Daddy's desire which he vociferously announced to his derelict son Brick:

> All I ask of that woman [Big Mama] is that she leave me alone. But she can't admit to herself that she makes me sick. That comes of having slept with her too many years. Should of quit much sooner but that old woman she never got enough of it—and I was good in bed . . . I never should of wasted so much of it on her. . . .

They say you got just so many and each one is numbered. Well, I
got a few left in me, a few, and I'm going to pick me a good one to
spend 'em on! I'm going to pick me a choice one, I don't care how
much she costs. I'll smother her in—minks! Ha ha! I'll strip her
naked and smother her in minks and choke her with diamonds!
(pp. 157–158)

Thus, Maggie combines in herself the sexuality and aggressiveness of Big
Daddy. Moreover, she delights in Big Daddy's use of four letter words, and
laughs heartily at his jokes. She shares Big Daddy's love for Brick and hatred
for Mae and Gooper, and their little children, whom she calls 'no-neck
monsters.' (p. 109) She indulgently and delightfully reports Big Daddy's
strong aversion of their children to Gooper. Maggie adds, "Well I swear, I
simply could have di-ieed." (p. 110) The rapport between Maggie and Big
Daddy is obvious from her remark:

Big Daddy dotes on you, honey; and he can't stand Brother Man
and Brother Man's wife, that monster of fertility, Mae; she's
downright odious to him. Know how I know? By little expressions
that flicker over his face . . . (p. 112)

Moreover, Maggie's concern at Brick's alcoholism and avoiding sexual
intercourse with her is echoed by Big Daddy. Only she and Big Daddy try
to break into the wall of his composure to elicit the confession from him
about his relations with Skipper. She succeeds only in part, but Big Daddy
succeeds completely.

Being possessed by Big Daddy's animus, the animus of a sexually
aggressive hero and not that of a wise old man, Maggie often acts in an
aggressive and drastic manner. Her actions, when offended or irritated, are
replete with wilfulness and drive for power. Pointing out the negative facets
of the hero animus, Ann Belford Ulanov says, "Negatively, the hero animus becomes unrelated aggression, ravaging her, severing ties both within
herself and outside her in destructive ways."[8] This devastating aspect of
her personality is seen in her destruction of the love affair between Skipper and Brick which threatened her conjugal harmony. She was aware of
their attraction to each other at college. After their graduation Skipper and
Brick decided to tie themselves together under the banner of one team so
that their goings-on together would not be perceived. But with the help of
her differentiated and perspicacious animus, Maggie focused on the problem and saw through the game that was designed to dupe the collective.
She says:

You married me early that summer we graduated out of Ole Miss, and we were happy. Weren't we, we were blissful. Yes, hit heaven together ev'ry time that we loved! But that fall you an' Skipper turned down wonderful offers of jobs in order to keep on bein' football heroes—pro-football heroes. You organized the Dixie Stars that fall, so you could keep on bein' team-mates forever! But somethin' was not right with it!—*Me included!*—between you. (p. 135)

Maggie, his anima since his college days, recalls that even in college they never dated exclusively. It was always double-dating with Skipper and his sweetheart. But Maggie reminisces that every date "was more like a date between you and Skipper. Gladys and I were just sort of tagging along as if it was necessary to chaperone you!—to make a good public impression—." (p. 134) With all these facts of the past in mind, Maggie set out to destroy the relationship which was so far disguised as an idyllic attraction. She stepped in with all her power and challenged their idyllic romance and their hanging on to the adolescent dreams of glory. She destroyed their idyllic Eden by telling Skipper about his homosexual feelings for Brick. Skipper then "made that pitiful, ineffectual little attempt to prove that what I had said wasn't true. . . ," (p. 135) by trying to sleep with her. When it did not work out he thought the charges were true. Skipper thereafter broke down and died. Maggie, the cat, thus achieved her goal and delivered her husband, Brick, from being seduced away. Indeed, Skipper paid heavily for his intrusion into the domain that belonged to the hetaira woman.

But Maggie also overreacted in exposing Skipper. She has not understood what belongs to her realm. As the carrier of Brick's anima, she should have been wary and careful. She lacks the scruples that a finely differentiated hetaira with a sense of psychology and ethics would have. Toni Wolff sounds a note of warning regarding the problematical ethical areas in the hetaira-power over the male. Ulanov explains her warning:

> The Hetaira's relation to the male stimulates and promotes his individual interests, his inclinations, and even his problems, thus effecting his shadow side and the subjective side of his anima. This can be dangerous if she has not learned what properly belongs to the relationship and what does not.[9]

By working on the destruction of her husband's homosexual friend, Maggie inadvertently slighted the shadow side of the former's personality. This was the side that Brick would have hidden from public view. She traces the reasons for his alcoholism, ennui, and disgust with the world to a factor, which for reasons like exposure and scandal, Brick wants to conceal. Even Brick warns her off when she pricks him again and again by the mention of Skipper and their relationship. He says, "Look Maggie, what you're doing is a dangerous thing to do. You're—you're—you're fooling with something that nobody ought to fool with." (p. 133) Brick obviously means his shadow. As his anima, the contents of Brick's personal unconscious were available to her. She committed a mistake, therefore, by telling Brick about having tested and proved Skipper homosexual. She admits her mistake now:

> I've thought a whole lot about it and now I know when I made my mistake. Yes, I made my mistake, when I told you the truth about the thing with Skipper. Never should have confessed it, a fatal error, tellin' you that thing with Skipper. (p. 133)

Maggie is rightly penitent over having trifled with the shadow side of his personality, which as a mediatrix of his personal unconscious she should have avoided.

In fact, by having driven Skipper to death, by declaring and proving him homosexual, Maggie has put Brick also in a predicament where he has begun to feel afraid of being an unconscious homosexual himself. He has deteriorated so badly over the weeks after Skipper's death that he does not like sex being mentioned in his presence. Bernard F. Dukore has made interesting observations:

> To be sure, Brick is afraid that he is homosexual and this fear explains a great deal of the past and present action. He refuses to sleep with his wife. He is disgusted with even the mention of sex. "That kind of talk is disgusting," he says when Maggie describes Big Daddy admiring her body. When his father talks of having pleasure with women, "Brick's smile fades a little but lingers." He advises Maggie to take a lover. This would give him reasons for despising women, a justification for his homosexual fears. Since his close friend Skipper was homosexual, Brick doubts his own normalcy. Maggie realizes that Brick is not homosexual, but although he states that he is not, he inwardly fears that he is . . . thus, he is the one who, in discussing his relationship with Skipper, 'names it dirty' though he unjustly accuses Maggie of doing so.[10]

To avoid the risk of being tested sexually like Skipper, Brick begins to soak himself in alcohol. He uses drink to, what is called in Gestalt psychology, "desensitize" himself. His dissociation from the quotidian reality is thus designed to insulate himself against being hurt. His withdrawal, his nonchalance about Big Daddy's huge property, cash, or his pathological problems can be construed as his desperate attempts to check his neurosis from turning into psychosis. In other words, by swamping his brain with liquor, he is using a kind of defence mechanism to alleviate his ego-injury, his neurotic anxiety.

When Maggie set out to explore and explode the relationship between Brick and Skipper, she was not conscious of the repercussions. Now faced with them, with Brick hitting the bottle, drifting away and lapsing into a state of dissociation, Maggie becomes cautious and nervous. It seems that Brick's state of anxiety has infected her mind and body. In other words, she becomes the 'cat on a hot tin roof' of the title. She admits that she has "gone through this *hideous!—transformation become—hard! Frantic!* . . . cruel!" She adds, "I'm not-thin-skinned any more, can't afford t'be thin-skinned any more." (p. 116) Her use of the word 'afford' probably signifies that now she is aware of the troubles ahead if Brick continues with his intemperate behaviour, which has compelled her—the Cat—to fight a defensive battle. Cat is the symbol of the sensual hetaira, as also of the mystery, jealousy, savagery, vindictiveness and guilefulness associated with the Feminine. The "hot tin roof" of the title not only signifies that a highly sensual woman, believing intensely in man–woman relationship, has been suddenly denied the pleasure of the senses; the denial intensifies her sexuality till it burns in an infrared manner. She really becomes a cat sizzling on a hot tin roof. It also alludes to the troubles under the tin roof on which she stands. There is Big Daddy dying of cancer, there are claimants to his inheritance already in the house clamouring hard to cut Brick and Maggie off from the legacy, simply because Maggie is childless and Brick an alcoholic. On top of it, there is her husband, Brick, indifferent to the tough times ahead, if Mae and Gooper succeed in their designs. Consequently, Maggie is obliged to fight for her husband, and by implication, for herself too. She cannot afford any complacency because the war is on. Nancy M. Tischler defines Maggie beautifully: "She is a scrappy little fighter, spitting at the enemy, purring for the master, clawing for survival."[11] In taking up the defence for her crippled husband, Maggie becomes the amazonian hetaira. On the other hand, she reminds one of the mother-cat carrying her kitten lovingly by the neck, coaxing him back to life, attempting to reconstitute and revive his interest in reality.

But her repeated attempts, her overtures, her entreaties meet with the unruffled 'cool' of the man. Her attempts recoil on herself and the cat on a hot tin roof becomes even more nervous. She notices his detachment which throws her off her balance. She becomes even more catty and tries all the feminine wiles and guiles on him. She envies his coolness and says, "But one thing I don't have is the charm of the defeated, my hat is in the ring and I am determined to win!" She asks, "What is the victory of a cat on a hot tin roof? I wish I knew. . . . Just staying on it, I guess, as long as she can. . . ." (p. 118) Her vigorous spirit coupled with her unflinching determination makes her a real fighter. She proceeds in a cool and calculating manner to break into his composure and elicit the information regarding his neurosis which manifests itself in his dissociation from reality. She tells him about the conspiracy afoot to send him away to Rainbow Hill, where "dope fiends" are lodged. (p. 112) Then she tells him about being repeatedly taunted for childlessness. She reports, "it goes on all the time, along with constant little remarks and innuendoes about the fact that you and I have not produced any children, are totally childless and therefore totally useless." (p. 110) Then she talks of others' "lech" for her and includes Big Daddy and Sonny Boy Maxwell who have eyed her with lascivious desire. But she finds that the mention of these three details fail to move, disturb or pierce the impervious wall of his composure. Then she talks of Skipper and succeeds. Brick suddenly loses his enviable cool and shouts at her. Maggie's delight at finding out the root cause of his troubles is obvious in these lines:

> We mustn't scream at each other, the walls in this house have ears . . . but that's the first time I've heard you raise your voice in a long time, Brick. A crack in the wall?—Of composure?—I think that's a good sign. . . . A sign of nerves in a player on the defensive! (p. 119)

She tells him to cathart, so that the burden is lifted and shared. She wants to extricate him from the whirlpool of detachment and withdrawal. She wants him not to give in to defeat and passivity. Rather, she wants him to fight his way out of the labyrinth of despair and noninvolvement. She enthuses and provokes him to grapple with life. Like a true *femme inspiratrice* she says:

> Laws of silence don't work. . . . When something is festering in your memory or your imagination, laws of silence don't work, it's just like shutting a door and locking it on a house on fire in hope of forgetting that the house is burning. But not facing a fire doesn't put it out. Silence about a thing just magnifies it. It grows and festers in silence, becomes malignant . . . (p. 119)

Like a true hetaira, the carrier of his anima, she wants to share his problems. She smashes his composure and enters into the fortress and advises him, "My only point, the only point that I'm making, is life has got to be allowed to continue even after the *dream* of life is-all-over . . ." (p. 134) She tells him that the only way to protect the inheritance and their interests is by exploiting the love that Big Daddy has for both of them. But Big Daddy would make reservations in his legacy unless they beget a child. For the sake of inheritance, for the sake of future life and comfort they have to make love and have a child. She says, ". . . there is no reason why we can't have a child whenever we want one. And this is my time by the calendar to conceive." (p. 137) She forewarns him of the dangers of his intemperance in drinking—it can cut them out of the legacy which would mean growing old without money. She says:

> You can be young without money but you can't be old without it. You've got to be old *with* money because to be old without it is just too awful, you've got to be one or the other, either young or *with* money, you can't be old and *without* it. (p. 132)

Another danger that she foresees is that Gooper is going to be given the purse and the power of attorney to "dole out remittances" to them, which would mean complete dependence because then he would be able to "cut off our credit wherever, whenever he wanted". (p. 112) She wants him to wake up to the emergency of the situation by reconnecting him to the reality principle. With these facts in mind, it is difficult to agree with Jeanne M. McGlinn who thinks of her as a selfish, self-centered, manipulative and destructive woman who acts out of the motivation to benefit herself.[12] Maggie, though not entirely altruistic, yet acts out of a profound love and concern for her husband. She wants a child not only to protect the inheritance, but also because it would mean making Brick a responsible man once again. Moreover, the begetting of a child would stem the tide of the taunting attacks and also fulfil her—"'cause I'm consumed with envy an' eaten up with longing?" (p. 122) She has not given up hope of emerging victorious. Defeat is not for her. She would rather die or kill herself before facing defeat. She says:

> You know, if I thought you would never, never, never make love to me again—I would go downstairs to the kitchen and pick out the sharpest knife I could find and stick it straight into my heart, I swear that I would! (p. 118)

To seduce Brick back into life, she alternatively entreats, mocks, curses, warns, goads, harangues and even threatens suicide. Like a zealous mother, she tries to plan and provide for his future, like a lawyer she fights for him and like a priestess of love, a hierodule, she invites "the godlike being" (p. 133) to consummate with her, beget a child and save himself.

In order to get perhaps at the deepest layer of meaning in the Maggie–Brick relationship, one has to take recourse to the Sphinx myth. Sphinx the Egyptian deity adopted by the Greeks had a cat's body with face and breasts of a woman. She was the archetype of the all-enveloping and all-deluding mysteries associated with the Feminine. She is the deepest level of the Archetypal Feminine. She, it is said in the myth, would pose riddles and put to death those who failed and rewarded those who succeeded in meeting the challenge posed by her. The riddles of the Sphinx could not be answered by those who denied life. For answering her riddles one was supposed to know life experientially. She was the hetaira of Matriarchy who would question a man's shadow and kill his anima in case he failed. In her all authority of life was vested. Moreover, a Sphinx was housed on an elevated platform from where she shot questions at victims. Maggie is also a "cat"—a Sphinx—on a "hot" tin roof. Both the symbols ("Cat" and "hot") signify lust and sex. The question of the Sphinx in this play, therefore, is whether Brick can answer Maggie's lust in order to save himself. Skipper could not answer her riddle and perished. Brick, too, cannot individuate unless he answers her sexuality. Towards the end of the play when Maggie tells a lie about having conceived, he seems to answer one of her riddles by "keeping still", (p. 195) to save her face, and implicitly affirming her lie. His surrender to Maggie at the end of the play is surrender to the Feminine, which means dropping the ego in order to reconnect with the springs of life. He drops his ego and walks into her arms which hold him "gently, gently with love" (p. 197), in order to rejuvenate and reconstitute him.

Like Maggie, Myrtle Ravenstock (née Kane) in *Kingdom of Earth* is not only central to the play but also a positive hetaira woman. At the beginning of the play, however, she appears maternal—but that is merely a persona to hide her real nature. Her maternal role first.

Myrtle, one discovers, meets her one-lunged husband, Lot Ravenstock, on a television programme, quickly accepts his proposal for marriage in her attempt to bunk from "show business."[13] She wishes to put an end to the life of emotional wandering and the life of a prostitute she has led, to give herself "a quiet and happy married life", (p. 189) to fulfil her dream of "settl'n down somewhere sometime". (p. 209) Her keenness to settle down with a man-with-property in order to have social security, stability and 'decency' blinds her to the future on the conjugal front. She does not pause to reflect on the prospects that her marriage with a sickly man (who unknown to herself is a transvestite and also tuberculoid) would offer her. For both Lot and Myrtle marriage is the most expedient measure: while Myrtle gets the coveted status of a wife, Lot hopes to retrieve his property from his half-brother Chicken. The latter, a mulatto, hated by Lot's mother as a 'nigra' had made Lot sign a document bequeathing all property to himself. Unable to win over Chicken in a straight fight, Lot has now married so that the property passes on to her, a white woman, after his death giving the souls of the mother and son (Lot) eternal peace.

Finding her husband in a desperate situation, Myrtle quickly steps into the maternal role of a nurse. She coddles him with "Lot Baby" and "Sugar", puts his head in her lap, strokes his forehead affectionately and sings him a lullaby:

> "Cuddle up a little closer, baby mine.
> Cuddle up and say you'll be my clinging vine!"
> Mmmm, Sugar! Last night you touched the deepest chord in
> my nature, which is the maternal chord in me. Do you know, do
> you realize what a beautiful thing you are? (p. 135)

She assuages his regret over his failure in bed on their first night by cooing words of endearment, "Baby, last night don't count. You was too nervous. I'll tell you something that might surprise you. A man is twice as nervous as a woman, and you are twice as nervous as a man". (p. 135) His insistent references to his mother, Miss Lottie make her jealous and she tells Lot that she would have none of it. "Now, baby, this mother-complex, I'm gonna get that out of you, Lot, 'cause I'm not just your wife, I'm also your mother and I'm not daid, I'm livin'." (p. 130)

Her new found role of a wife, mother and nurse has also made her decency-conscious, so to speak. An "elegant" blond man for a husband, "a little dream of a parlor" (p. 137), and so much of property have made her rise to the occasion and behave with "self respeck an' decency as a woman!" (p. 178) Her loud protests against indecency stem from her compensatory need to drown her promiscuous past in over-genteel mannerisms and affectations. For instance, she chastises Chicken for carving an indecent picture on the kitchen table, "An' you ought to know it's insulting to a clean-livin' woman who is not interested or attracted to indecent things in life." (p. 164) She complains to Lot against him and his vulgarity, "Decent people have got to be protected, flood or no flood, yes, come hell or high water. I'm going down there and try to phone the police." (p. 167) What one needs to see through is her attempt to disguise her real sensual nature under compulsion from the newly acquired role of a housewife. Jerrold A. Phillips also notes that she tries to "repress her own elemental nature—her sexuality—as she tries to reform her promiscuity to wifely virtue and motherly kindness."[14] It is only when she meets Chicken that she realises that her husband is an impotent child, her house no home, her marriage no security. It is then that she decides to give up all pretence and returns to her own essential nature, which is that of a woman who enjoys giving love and receiving attention from men.

Myrtle is a voluptuous young woman, one who would arouse "curious attention". Williams, her creator conceived Myrtle as "a rather fleshy young woman, amiably loud-voiced . . . wearing a pink turtle neck sweater and tight checkered slacks. Her blonde-dyed hair is set up in a wet silk-scarf, magenta colored. Her appearance suggests an imitation of a Hollywood glamor girl which doesn't succeed as a good imitation." (p. 127) Later when she goes downstairs on instructions from Lot to trounce Chicken and get the papers from his pocket, she changes into a rather flamboyant costume "a sheer blouse sprinkled with tiny brilliants and a velveteen skirt." (p. 156) She says she never wears slacks after dark, which tells about her past life in show-business where she was billed as a 'Petite Personality Kid'. Her confident boast, "I've yet to meet the man that I couldn't handle" (p. 137), and "I'm not scared of that man [Chicken], or any man livin'! No, Sir!" (p. 141) obviously stem from her promiscuous experience with men. Chicken minces no words when he tells her for what he takes her, "You kick with the right leg, you kick with the left leg, and between your legs you make your living?" (p. 147) Even Lot calls her a "whore" (p. 195), when he finds her mesmerised by Chicken and returning to him on one pretext or another. From her assumed mother role she once again returns to her vital self. Jerrold A. Phillips' remarks corroborate these observations, "Myrtle's seven descents also reveal a changing definition of love that occurs during the course of the play. She moves from her sacrificial motherliness to a resumption of her real self."[15]

Being thus in the hetaira modality, Myrtle makes no mistake in recognising Chicken as a powerful masculine figure who will finally bring her emotional stability and deep instinctual fulfillment. In this context it would not be beside the point to recapitulate Myrtle's confession at the first sight of Chicken in the story entitled "Kingdom of Earth" published in *The Knightly Quest and Other Stories* (1966): "The minute I laid eyes on you, the first glance I took at that big powerful body, I said to myself, Oh, oh, your goose is cooked, Myrtle! . . . Well, I said, when somebody's goose is cooked the best way to have it is cooked with plenty of gravy."[16] To Chicken who needs affirmation and love of a woman, she gives the best compliments in the play. She says, ". . . and another thing, I pride myself on is noticin' an' appreciating a man's appearance. Physical. I notice such things about him as a strong figure, in fine proportion. Mouth? Full. Teeth? White. Glist'nin', why, you look like a man that could hold back the flood of a river." (p. 208)

Chicken, a deprived young man, begotten out of wedlock on a coloured woman, has been despised by the neighbourhood and rebuffed even by the white trash (the prostitutes) to stay in his place. "That's how it is with me an' wimmen around here. Talk, suspicion, insult." (p. 206) He is naturally suspicious of Myrtle's gooey words and remains stiff and unresponsive even when passion tears him within. He responds to her only when she volunteers to abdicate the 'kingdom of earth' he is after, and which he fears she will grab from himself. It is only after she writes "All's Chicken's when Lot dies", (p. 200) that he makes love to her on the kitchen table. He is thrilled at having been powerfully desired by a woman. His passionate love-making leaves Myrtle in a daze: "she looks as if she had undergone an experience of exceptional nature and magnitude." (p. 203) He gradually opens up and confesses that he is a mulatto, that he has got a raw deal out of life, and that he holds a woman's love as the highest and the most enviable gift a man could ever have. Nothing could compare with "what's able to happen between a man and a woman, just that thing, nothing more, is perfect." (p. 211) The woman he desperately needed, one who would look up to him for love, protection and satisfaction, he finds in Myrtle. The latter gives him value in himself by praising his physical attributes and declaring his her "saviour". (p. 183) With her head leaning on his shoulder, she says the very words he always yearned to hear:

> I pray for your protection, and right now I feel like that prayer is going to be answered. Go on talking in that deep voice of yours. I don't just hear it. It, it—it gives me a sensation in my ears and goes all through my body—it vibrates in me. I don't even hear the river. (p. 211)

The uncouth youth, Chicken, who acquired the name when he bit off the heads of chickens to quench his thirst with their blood as he perched atop the roof of their house one time when the Mississippi flooded the entire area, finds a woman who pays tribute to his boorish virility. The Mississippi is flooding once again and Chicken with his Herculean prowess seems to her the only one who would save her from this catastrophe. A gratified Chicken promises to save her and requests, "Produce me a son. Produce a child for me, could you? Always wanted a child from an all-white woman." (p. 214) A child from Myrtle will symbolise emergence from a life of deprivation to a life of wholeness, helping him overcome the sense of injury from the society at large. The Kingdom of Earth would then prosper to fruition with both Chicken and Myrtle happy in their garden of love.

The symbols in *Kingdom of Earth* though complicated yet bring us to the core of the play's meaning. The flood recalls the deluge of the Old Testament that washed away Sodom and Gomorrah: only Lot was saved along with his two daughters while his wife turned into a pillar of salt. In a grotesque inversion of these stories, Lot the transvestite here is the weak and corrupt who tries to cheat Chicken through getting married and one who is likely to be washed away by the surging waters leaving the Kingdom of Earth clean. The flood at the same time also symbolises the human passions. Myrtle tells that she is a passionate woman who has been taking pills from a Memphis doctor to restrain her natural inclination to give herself in service of all comers. Her sensual nature is also hinted at in the diagnosis of her asthma which said that she "was living with a cat and had an allergy to it." (p. 171) Cat, as mentioned in the analysis of Maggie, represents the feminine principle—mysterious, playful, jealous and loving. She is probably allergic to cats because she has not entered into a comprehensive relationship with the attributes that cat signifies and has only lived her animal nature. On arrival in Lot's house she tries to repress the latter as well in favour of wifely virtue only to find the inexorable flood of passions rising and asking for someone who would have the strength to tame it. Chicken the "bull of a man," (p. 168) and "a suitable antagonist to a flooding river", (p. 125) rechannelises her sexuality and reconnects her with her essential nature.

The play is suggestively subtitled "Seven Descents of Myrtle". A perceptive reader would understand that each descent takes her closer to Chicken. Her first descent is to the Mississippi delta house, to the Kingdom of Earth, from Memphis. Her second descent is coming downstairs with Lot to the kitchen for coffee: here she tells Chicken all about her past life, giving Chicken a playful little slap on the shoulder, (p. 102) which surprises the latter. She comes down alone during her third descent smelling hot French fries and expresses the wish to be "better acquainted" with each other. (p. 163) Her fourth is on Lot's persuasion to make Chicken drunk and steal away the legal papers about the property from his wallet. This time she sings some old favourite numbers with him and plays on the "mansize instrument", the guitar, which he gives her. She runs away screaming this time when Chicken throws the cat in the water. Her fifth descent to fill the 'hot water bottle' for warming Lot, messes up her life. She has difficulty with heating the water which suggests her attempt to repress her own elemental nature. Chicken furnishes her with fresh rain water from the barrel outside which probably is suggestive of the invigorating freshness she may have from him outside her marital life. Chicken coolly talks of the flood, of Lot's imminent death and her own death by water unless he saves her. Even as she implores him to rescue her, he does not promise safety unless she brings to him their marriage licence. The tables are thus turned on herself: she came downstairs a while earlier to steal away the legal papers but goes upstairs now to bring her marriage certificate, with which she returns in her sixth descent. Her seventh is her surrender to Chicken: she writes as dictated by him. Chicken now consummates with her for he does not fear her as a rival but accepts her as a partner in his kingdom of earth. Number seven, symbolic of perfection, signifies the union of the high with the low, the 'decent' with the boorish, the white with the 'nigra' and archetypally speaking of fire with water. Through each

descent the hetaira modality is progressively constellated till through surrender comes wholeness.

II

In the second part of this chapter a negative hetaira woman, Blanche
DuBois, shall be analysed. 'Negative' here is neither any attempt to deni-
grate her status as an excellent artistic creation of Williams nor is it used in
any moral sense. 'Negative' is merely restricted to the archetypal manifestation of the hetaira where one lacking in emotional centring attracts the
label. While Blanche too is engaged in the service of eros, enjoys giving and
taking of love, hers is not necessarily with someone to whom she is emotionally drawn. A drift characterises the numinous core of her personality. And
that is not all for categorising her as negative: several other reasons shall be
mentioned as exploration and analysis unfolds her inherent personality.

Blanche DuBois, by far the greatest creation of Tennessee Williams, is
the heroine of *A Streetcar Named Desire*. Born into an old agrarian Southern
family of French extraction, she was raised at Belle Reve (meaning "Beautiful Dream") the ancestral mansion outside Laurel, Mississippi. She and
younger sister Stella (and possibly a third, Margaret who died) had the best
of a pampered and comfortable childhood what with all the affluence, black
slaves and courteous attention from gentlemen. Their adolescence, however,
saw the rich plantation going to seed as a price for the "epic fornications"[17]
that the men of the family indulged in, leaving only the house and some
twenty acres of land.

Blanche's downhill journey also seems to begin around this time. She
fell in love with an extremely good looking young poet Allan Grey and
eloped with him. She "adored him and thought him almost too fine to be
human", (p. 140) until one day she discovered his homosexuality. Sexually
innocent then she could not understand that the boy needed her help through
his half-spoken pleas to be saved from his perversion. Shocked and repelled
Blanche accused him publicly precipitating his suicide a few minutes later
by the shore of the lake. The grievous loss and how it came about left a deep
trauma in her psychic life. In close succession to her husband's death came
the deaths of her father, mother, sister Margaret and an old cousin Jesse, each
contributing to her loneliness and fear of death and disease. Stella by then
had left and settled with a Polish master-sergeant Stanley Kowalski, visiting
only briefly for funerals. Blanche who had to pawn the estate to meet the
medical and funeral expenses soon found it slipping from her fingers and had
no means to retrieve it.

It was around this time that her loneliness began to overwhelm her
leading to the beginning of her search for distraction in eros, the opposite

of thanatos. Fleeting intimacies with younger companions seemed to take
the sting out of her loneliness, at least momentarily, and seemed to neu-
tralise the feeling of guilt over having caused young Allan's death. Young
trainee soldiers, young schoolboys and other young (*Evening Star* collector
is one such) boys began to fill her life. Her grief drove her to drink, hysteria and nymphomania. All this was supposed to be anodyne to assuage
the pain and grief of her miserable life. Her physical relationship with
one of her students, her one-night stands with strangers, made her a town
character, leading to her dismissal from school and eviction from the hotel
and town both.

Blanche having lost her all—husband, family, financial security from
inheritance, her job, her youth as also her fair reputation reaches New Orleans
to look up her sister Stella. Her "delicate beauty . . . that suggests a moth"
(p. 117), her fragile nerves and her uncertain manner, show her as a sensitive
woman in a brutal world, in desperate need of refuge. She finds one such
person in those shabby surroundings too—the mother coddled Mitch—but
throws away her chance of finding stability mainly because she cannot anymore commit herself to a man. She thinks the best way to get a man is by
using the trappings of her ante-bellum charm. She sees in Mitch an opportunity to prove her allure and score an easy sexual conquest. She fools the
gullible Mitch by feeding him on magical details about herself. To arouse
his desires, she passes for a coy virginal old-fashioned Southern belle and
does not allow him any other liberties than a kiss. She dupes him regarding
her age and declares herself younger to Stella, tries to fool him regarding her
drinking habits, avoids going out with him until after dark and manages to
avoid being seen in direct bulb-light. She buys a paper lantern to avoid detection of her true age. All these deceptions she considers necessary for fanning
the flames of love in Mitch: she adopts a cool dignified posture calculated
at achieving the desired results. "I want his respect: And men don't want
anything they get too easy. But on the other hand men lose interest quickly.
Especially when the girl is over thirty." (p. 171) She believes reality kills the
romantic spirit, while illusion is necessary to keep the flame kindled. "Yes,
yes, magic! I try to give that to people. I misrepresent things to them. I don't
tell the truth. I tell what ought to be truth." (p. 204)

Blanche's sexuality cannot function as an expression of psychic related-
ness. She remains caught up in the persona reality of her jazzed up and fan-
tasized Belle Reve past. While a true hetaira would meet her lover, naked,
denuded of pretensions, Blanche never tires of game-playing. She continues
to delude and misrepresent things, hiding facts about herself. She cannot
open herself to the relationship as a process, as an exploration, as a continuing communion. She relishes the projections and desires of men to get
affirmation of her own existence. Every relationship for her is an adventure,

a fresh occasion to have her sexual superiority and charms confirmed. She exploits her manners and genteel past as art to gain easy conquests on men.

Her lurid past uncovered by Stanley, coupled with the explanations offered by Blanche herself, points towards the past of a whore, at best "a sentimental prostitute" as Signi Falk calls her.[18] The trauma of young Allan's death, followed by those of several others, compelled her to glut herself sexually as she says, in order to forget the hovering spectre of the tragedy. This indiscriminate indulgence has helped her escape from loneliness and has also alleviated her sense of worthlessness. But it has made her neglect the much needed centring of her emotions through commitment to one person. The biological energies thus gratified have left no scope for emotional maturity. Jeanne M. McGlinn's observation corroborates this point of view. McGlinn regards Blanche sexually immature and inadequate "because of which she avoids adult sexual relationships but actively seeks affairs with adolescents."[19] Blanche becomes, to adapt a phrase from D.H. Lawrence's *The Plumed Serpent*, the "Aphrodite of frictional ecstasy", revelling in the fulfillment of temporary unions. Williams very aptly selected the epigraph for the drama from Hart Crane's "The Broken Tower":

And so it was I entered the broken world,
To trace the visionary company of love, its voice
An instant in the wind (I know not whither hurled)
But not for long to hold each desperate choice.

Early in the play Stella describes Blanche as "flighty" (p. 189), probably alluding to her incapacity to experience love as a relationship. The epigraph does not refer to the "theme of the soul's quest for ideal love in the most unlikely of places—the broken world of actuality," as Leonard Quirino interprets it.[20] The epigraph, on the other hand, clearly points out the gratification that Blanche seeks in the arms of "each desperate choice" to refurnish the broken quality of her life, looking for closeness, perhaps kindness in that physical contact. "I've run for protection, Stella, from under one leaky roof to another leaky roof—because it was storm—all storm, and I was—caught in the centre." (p. 164) It is also for this reason that she does not see herself as a mere prostitute. Her moral vision blurred by her desperate need to be with someone, with ancestors for models who indulged in "epic fornications" with impunity, she moves through the world filling the void in her life with lust. "Yes, I had many intimacies with strangers. After the death of Allan—intimacies with strangers was all I seemed to be able to fill my empty heart with. . . I think it was panic, just panic, that drove me from one to another, hunting for some protection. . . ." (p. 205) It is this need that blinds her to her moral reality. Normand Berlin aptly says, "She cannot see herself a whore because sexual activity was for her a temporary means for needed affection, the only refuge for her lonely soul."[21]

Erich Fromm in his famous book *The Art of Loving* divides human love in five categories: brotherly, motherly, erotic, self and Love of God. Among these erotic love is "the craving for complete fusion, for union with another person." This union is the "souls' union" if the craving matures into caring, mutual respect, tenderness, or flowers into understanding the psychic needs or what Lawrence calls the 'otherness' of the partner. The true union comes if the partners relate with each other's intrinsic nature. Such a relationship becomes an exploration into the infiniteness of finite love. In mystical writing such love partakes of the divine. Only the pure hetairas are capable of such love. However, in the absence of these values, the union is merely physical and the happiness shortlived. Sexual contact in such cases does not touch, much less involve the soul. The contact thus is no better than the mating of animals. In the light of this latter observation, if one looks at the sexual conquests of people like Blanche one is struck by Fromm's telling observation, "Since they experience the separateness of the other person primarily as physical separateness, physical union means overcoming separateness."[22] Each new affair brings freshness, intensity and exhilaration along with an illusion that the new love will be different from the earlier one. Blanche has been chasing this mirage in ever new affairs, even in the brief one-night-stands because only physical contact seemed to her the antidote to her pathetic existence. For her the conquests have to go on, so that she goes on living without getting time to reflect on her life. The mere thought of being alone with herself frightens her, because it would mean confrontation with her own sordid reality. Sex in the name of anxiety of aloneness, gratification of vanity, expiation of guilt, or seeking refuge (or "protection" as she calls it) are prompted by a desire to seek in the world of romance that which is hopelessly bleak all around herself. She flirts with Stanley, Mitch and the *Evening Star* collector boy almost simultaneously. Among them she pursues Stanley for the gratification of her vanity because he poses a challenge she has not had before. The "gaudy seed bearer", (p. 128) she has for a brother-in-law, feels insulted by her pose of superiority and decides to put her in her place by making "her recognise that she is the same as he, a sexual animal."[23] So her customary hope of seeing him wilt before her flamboyant manners, apparel and charm bounces back leaving her badly shaken. He piece by piece unravels her past and confronts her with the reality she sought to deny in herself. She had always been on the brink of lunacy but finds herself even closer to it. The second hope was in Mitch. She hoped that overwhelmed by her charms he would rebel against the stories of Stanley and would not desert her. Her hopes of protection, because it is all that she seeks in him, a house, "a cleft in the rock of the world that I could hide in!" (p. 205), bounce when despite her hopes and probably fervent prayers he does not come on her birthday party. He was the man who had "stopped that polka tune that I had caught in my head", (p. 201) the tune which played when Allan committed suicide, the tune that always haunted her, that tune now comes back. She finally realizes to her dismay that she has lost her reputation, a place to go to, and what is worse, her charms. This realisation, painful as it is, coupled with the rape, sends her reeling into a world of shadows, from which she was never really far away.

Elsewhere in this chapter it was pointed out that the dominant archetype of the hetaira is The Great Father to whom the former relates as a *puella aeterna* (or eternal daughter). True to the archetype, Blanche seeks mainly one thing from her lovers—"protection". She sees them as refuge, even though "leaky", (p. 164) from the "panic", (p. 205) "the storm", (p. 164) all around. She sees Mitch as a sanctuary where she can take rest. "I want to rest! I want to breathe quietly again! Yes—I want Mitch . . . very badly! Just think! If it happens! I can leave here and not be any one's problem. . . ." (p. 171) She no longer wants journeys because "travelling wears me out." In other words, journeys on the streetcars named desire, the abnormal sexual activation since adolescence, have cloyed her now. She needs a cosy nook to squirm herself into because more than physical aggrandisement she requires the protection and security of a home. Mitch fits into her requirement like one made to order: he has a big heavy frame which promises to protect her and he is tender and mother-complexed which assures her compassion. Leonard Berkman's words aptly sum up her need, "It is specifically the intermingling of sex with compassion that Blanche longs for; sex without compassion that she cannot accept."[24] She genuinely thanks God for Mitch who seems to her as "the poor man's paradise" where she can have her "peace" (p. 205) from the cruel world.

Blanche's ambivalent attraction towards Stanley and her attempts to fight it down also require discussion. In the very first scene together, Blanche regards Stanley's half-naked torso with awe as he changes his T-shirt in front of her. Roger Boxill comments, "It is because she is torn between attraction and repulsion, that she thinks she is going to be sick. The 'Varsouviana', echoing the guilt she bears for the suicide of her young husband filters through the dialogue."[25] She flirts with him, sprays him with her atomizer, asks him to button up her blouse prompting Stanley's blunt remark, "If I didn't know that you was my wife's sister I'd get ideas about you!" (p. 138) Some hours later, however, she violently criticises him as 'primitive', 'sub-human', 'apelike', 'madman', 'brute' (Scene IV). What, however, betrays her reaction formation (a Freudian term which means you criticise something bitterly in others that you yourself desperately want) are two speeches in this very scene. The first reads, ". . . I saw him at his best! what such a man has to offer is animal force and he gave a wonderful exhibition of that! But the only way to live with such a man is to go—go to bed with him! And that's your job—not mine!" (p. 161) The speech barely conceals an intense wish. The next speech repeats the motif in the previous one a trifle more vehemently, "I am not being or feeling at all superior, Stella. Believe me I'm not . . . A man like that is someone to go out with—once-twice-three times, when the devil is in you. But live with! Have a child by?" (p. 162) Both speeches showing Blanche's strong hatred of Stanley's animalism are indeed only in the nature of subterfuge to disguise her own immense need of raw passion and sexuality. It is borne out by the fact that she too would like to settle down with a "wolf" (p. 146) from the pack of Stanley. The latter, however, is not the kind to understand the psychological reason for Blanche's virulent attack against himself. He can only understand that the latter is trying to ruin his marriage by prompting Stella to get away and that he must pay back, eye for an eye, by destroying the chances of her marriage with Mitch. In any case, her attempt to break Stella's marriage because she cannot get Stanley would be considered, according to Jungian psychology, an obvious deflection in her hetaira personality. A woman who breaks or attempts to break others' marriage has not understood the limits within which a hetaira is to operate: breaking homes is a negative trait. Roger Boxill, however, has a different opinion as to why Stanley destroys Blanche's marriage with Mitch. Adducing evidence from the early drafts of the play he writes, "In retrospect neither his uxoriousness nor his protestation of friendship for Mitch rings true. Stanley's underlying motive for warding off Blanche's only suitor, we are bound to conclude, has been to remove the obstacle in the way of keeping his 'date' that he has had with her from the beginning."[26] Boxill's opinion finds support in how Stanley is portrayed in the Stage Directions. "Since earliest manhood, the centre of his life has been pleasure with women . . ." (p. 128), which implies that he is not a faithful husband and that he is a liar too. He denies rape which is "a greater lie than any Blanche ever told.[27]

At another level the encounter between Stanley and Blanche can be seen as a clash between two contrary ontologies. Mythically, Stanley is Pan, the Greek god of all enveloping cosmic energy manifested in human terms through sexuality and libido. In several mythologems, based on stories and depth experience of the psyche, Pan is deemed to have a duplex nature—he is the god of erotic ecstasy, libidinal virility, art, creativity and transformation on the one hand, and on the other, of violence, rape, nightmare, alienation and madness. Stanley in *Streetcar* represents the chthonic principle and is characterised by fire. In comparison Blanche is in the modality of nymph who archetypally embodies grace, delicacy and elegance and is characterised by water. Their ambivalent attraction leading to abrasive encounter is thus always on the cards. A fuller discussion would clarify these points.

Stanley Kowalski is the primal blacksmith of the flaming "red hot" (p. 141) milieu, The Elysian Fields ("Stanley" or "Stone-lea" suggests the Stone Age man and Kowalski is Polish for "smith").[28] He is the rough hewn lord of his house, immensely proud and possessive of his things: his liquor, his bathroom, his game, his team, his wife, his child, "everything . . . that bears his emblem." (p. 128) He quotes from Huey Long's 'Every Man is a king', and believes rather intensely in it. He believes it is his right to flaunt his brutal life force through all kinds of barbarism including smashing things, bellowing at people, hitting his wife and insulting others. Williams describes him and his friends as "men at the peak of their physical manhood, as coarse and direct and powerful as the primary colours." (p. 143) He gives Stanley Capricorn as his birth sign and gives him animal habits. Boxill's recapitulations of Marlon Brando as Stanley show that brutish force and fire as also sexual attractiveness was combined by him in his lively portrayal of the character. "The first Stanley had the face of a poet, the body of a gladiator and the vocal placement of a whining adolescent. Brando's performance was a mosaic of sexual insolence, sullen moodiness, puckish good humour and terrifying rage. His slurred delivery and loutish stances added to the grammar of acting."[29] Audiences still remember the tiger-like suddenness with which Brando, in the birthday party scene smashes plates, stalks out onto the porch, shouts while continuing to pick his teeth and lick his fingers.[30]

Blanche, however, is not the youthful but an aging nymph ("A gargoyle" as Henry Popkin, "a witch" as Nancy M. Tischler call her). Her name means "white woods", like an "orchard in spring" which is ironic because she knows she has lost her youthful vitality and looks. Like her ironic name she has an ironic birth sign, Virgo or the virgin, with the background of a whore. She is fond of water which refreshes her, makes her a "brand new human being." She frolics for long hours in the bathroom, soaking her frayed nerves in hot water. Her "hydrotherapy" is necessary for her probably to wash away the feeling of guilt as also the stains of her promiscuous life. While locomotive journeys wear her out she views the prospect of voyage on the Caribbean with Shep Huntleigh with pleasure, "I can smell the sea air. The rest of my time I'm going to spend on the sea. And when I die, I'm going to die on the sea." (p. 220) Before her last journey from the Elysian Fields, she questions Stella from the bathroom, "Is the coast clear?" As Eunice and Stella assist her to dress, Blanche treats them like handmaidens in the service of a water nymph. The climax of her fantasies is also connected with the sea. She hopes, "And I'll be buried at sea sewn up in a clean white sack and dropped overboard into an ocean as blue as . . . my first lover's eyes!" (p. 220) Water which dominates her lively fantasies has always dominated her life. Water principle which manifests itself through drift, dependence and buoyancy, has kept her on the move, to one lover from another, to one leaky roof from another, without allowing her to experience the much needed cathexis to her emotions, to find time to introvert and see her psychic life as it really is.

No discussion of *A Streetcar* can be complete without a sideways glance at the character of Stella, who in Jungian terms is a typical mother woman wallowing in the bliss of animalistic life, much as Serafina before Rosario's death. Stella unlike Blanche, lives in the present and does not raise her eyebrows over the quality of her sordid existence. What matters more to her is the security and sense of fulfillment in the love of Stanley. Emerging from the cocoon of plantation life, Stella adopted her husband's way of life with equanimity. Blanche is intrigued by her stolid indifference over life with Stanley, "Is this a Chinese philosophy you've cultivated?" (p. 158) Like a tolerant mother woman she casually observes that Stanley is the smashing type, that a house in which men are drinking violent things do happen, that men and women have to get used to each other's ways of life. She gets up with a smile to fix the things in the house, stow away the beer bottles, and clear the mess the poker players made, and be ready for him when Stanley returns home. She forgives Stanley for hitting her because "he was as good as a lamb when I came back", (p. 157) and because he promised never to play poker again in the house. Her absolute acceptance of Stanley on his word is seen when she wakes up next morning: "Her face is serene. . . . Her eyes and lips have that almost narcotized tranquillity that is in the faces of Eastern idols." (p. 156) That Williams wanted Stella to be passive, physically and imaginatively static, is understood from a note he wrote to Elia Kazan, the first director of the New York Production, "I think her natural passivity is one of the things that make her acceptance of Stanley acceptable. She naturally 'gives in', lets things slide, she does not make much effort."[31] For Stella, passive by conditioning in a house in which the elder Blanche dominated, taking things as they came has been a way of life. It is for this reason, she is cool and peaceful and sits with her "little hands folded like a cherub in choir!" (p. 123) unruffled by things that could have shaken anyone else. Her contentment with her lot stems from profound satisfaction at the sexual level, "But there are things that happen between a man and a woman in the dark—that sort of make everything else seem—unimportant." (p. 162) Like Serafina, she too is proud of the potency of her husband and believes that "Stanley is the only one of his crowd that's likely to get anywhere," (p. 146) because he has the "drive" (p. 147) in him. She is proud of his physical attributes, his captaincy of the bowling team and his status at the plant. She tells Blanche of course, that Stanley comes from "a different species" (p. 124) than they have known.

Stella has, if one considers her affluent plantation background and compares her with Blanche who cannot get away from her view of herself, made a radical compromise with life. She does not complain against the ramshackle two-room apartment or meagre income of Stanley. It is she, rather than Blanche who claims, "I'm very adaptable—to circumstances", (p. 150) who has adjusted with the sweeping winds of change and thus found contentment. The climax of her rejection of the past and acceptance of the new comes when she has to choose between Stanley the rapist and Blanche who needs love and attention. She chooses Stanley and lets Blanche slip away into insanity. In this process she, as Bigsby says, "opts for the future over the past, for potency over sterility. And if that also means accepting a world bereft of protective myth and cultural adornments this is a compromise which she has the strength to make. Blanche cannot and is broken."[32] Stella, thus, in spite of her seeming indolence and passivity, must be seen as a more practical and sane woman. Her categorical rejection of Blanche derives from her need to "go on living with Stanley", (p. 217) because nothing to her is greater than marital bliss.

And finally it would be wrong to consider her, like Elia Kazan did, as "Stanley's slave."[33] She may not have succeeded in monopolising her husband's love, but has certainly been able to extract his dependence on herself. He loves and needs her which is seen in his hollering as he finds her gone with Blanche to a neighbour's to spend the night after the fracas of the poker night. He kneels to her and carries the sobbing Stella inside the bedroom. Some time later when he finds her upset over Blanche he reassures her, "Stell, it's gonna be all right after she goes and after you've had the baby." (pp. 195–196) He cares for her, in spite of his arrogance and loud mouth.

In every conceivable way Stella offers a contrast with the character of Blanche and helps as a foil in bringing it out. In another essay C.W.E. Bigsby pays a profound tribute to Stella when he says, "The real hero of the play, therefore, is Stella, for she alone is prepared to offer the necessary comfort and understanding. Like Connie Chatterley she discovers a genuine fulfillment based on sexuality but, more significantly, she thereby stumbles on the urgent need for that tenderness and compassion which, to both Williams and Lawrence, is the key to the human predicament."[34] In the world of *A Streetcar*, in other words, she is the only sign of humanity because both Stanley (too bestial) and Blanche (too delicate) with their mutual sparring row and vehement antagonism present a bleak vision of life. And Williams wanted people to believe that love is the only answer in this world bristling with anger and discontent. He believed that "the only satisfactory thing we are left with in this life is the relations—if they're sincere—between people, love being "the closest we've come to such a satisfying relationship."[35] Stella is a woman committed to dependence on her man in family relationship: to her everything else is secondary.

Maggie, Myrtle and Blanche have been grouped under the hetaira category in view of eros as the driving force of their life. Their fulfillment lies in the giving and receiving of love. While the positive ones, Maggie and Myrtle, are fortunate to find men they could love, whose psyches they could mediate, whose shadows they could penetrate into without resistance: they have in the process stabilised, their emotions have found apt cathexes, and their lives acquired a meaning. Made in the hetaira modality Blanche has been unfortunate in losing her blue-eyed, adorable, lover-husband simply because she did not understand him and his needs. She has been trying to give meaning to her life by indulging with younger boys or softer men in the vain hope of finding another Allan she could adore, and thus have a fulfilled existence. That path, however, has led to moral degradation, at least in the eyes of society at large. Inability to find one more Allan despite desperate search, makes her depend on "the kindness of strangers," and finally even in the public asylum.

NOTES

1. Toni Wolff, "Structural Forms of the Feminine Psyche", trans. Paul Watzlawik (Zurich: Students Association, C.G. Jung Institute, 1956), p. 6.

2. Ann B. Ulanov, "Descriptions of the Feminine", *The Feminine in Jungian Psychology and in Christian Theology* (1971; Evanston: North Western Univ. Press, 1978), p. 203.

3. Irene Claremont de Castillejo, *Knowing Woman: A Feminine Psychology* (1973; New York: Harper and Colophon, 1974), p. 66.

4. Wolff, p. 7.

5. De Castillejo, p. 65.

6. Edward C. Whitmont, *The Symbolic Quest: Basic Concepts of Analytical Psychology* (1969; New York: Harper and Colophon, 1973), p. 179.

7. Tennessee Williams, *Cat on a Hot Tin Roof* in *Cat on a Hot Tin Roof* and *The Milk Train Doesn't Stop Here Anymore* (1955; Harmondsworth: Penguins, 1969), p. 109. All subsequent refs. to the text are from this edn.

8. Ulanov, "Descriptions . . . ," p. 205.

9. ibid., p. 204.

10. Bernard F. Dukore, "The Cat Has Nine Lives", *Tulane Drama Review*, 8 (Fall 1963), p. 97.

11. Nancy M. Tischler, "A Gallery of Witches", *Tennessee Williams: A Tribute*, ed. Jac. Tharpe (Jackson: Univ. Press of Mississippi, 1977), p. 501.

12. Jeanne M. McGlinn, "Tennessee Williams's Women: Illusion and Reality, Sexuality and Love", ibid., pp. 517–518.

13. Tennessee Williams, *Kingdom of Earth: Seven Descents of Myrtle*, Vol. V, *The Theatre of Tennessee Williams* (1967; New York: New Directions; 1975), p. 143. All subsequent refs. to the text are from this edn.

14. Jerrold A. Phillips, "Kingdom of Earth: Some Approaches", *Tennessee Williams: A Tribute*, p. 352.

15. Phillips, p. 353.

16. Tennessee Williams, "Kingdom of Earth", *The Knightly Quest and other Stories* (New York: New Directions, 1966), p. 161.

17. Tennessee Williams, *A Streetcar Named Desire* in *Sweet Bird of Youth, A Streetcar* and *Menagerie*, ed. E. Martin Browne (1947; rptd. Harmondsworth: Penguins, 1976), p. 140. All subsequent references to the text are from this edn.

18. Signi Falk, "The Profitable World of Tennessee Williams", *Modern Drama*, 1 (December 1958), p. 158.

19. Jeanne M. McGlinn, p. 513.

20. Leonard Quirino, "The Cards Indicate a Voyage on *A Streetcar Named Desire*", *Tennessee Williams: A Tribute*, p. 80.

21. Normand Berlin, "Complementarity in *A Streetcar Named Desire*", *Tennessee Williams: A Tribute*, p. 98.

22. Erich Fromm, *Art of Loving* (1957; rptd. London: Unwin Paperbacks 1978), pp. 48–49.

23. McGlinn, p. 514.

24. Leonard Berkman, "The Tragic Downfall of Blanche DuBois", *Modern Drama*, 10 (Dec. 1967), p. 254.

25. Roger Boxill, *Tennessee Williams* (New York: St. Martin's Press, 1987), p. 82.

26. Boxill bases his argument on Vivienne Dickson, "*A Streetcar Named Desire*: Its Development Through the Manuscripts", *Tennessee Williams: A Tribute*, pp. 154–71.

27. Bert Cardullo, "Drama of Intimacy and Tragedy of Incomprehension: *A Streetcar Named Desire* Reconsidered", *Tennessee Williams: A Tribute*, p. 150.

28. Leonard Quirino, p. 79.

29. Boxill, p. 88.

30. ibid.

31. Tennessee Williams to Elia Kazan in Toby Cole ed., *Directing the Play* (Indianapolis, 1953), p. 306, rptd. in C.W.E. Bigsby, *A Critical Introduction to the Twentieth Century American Drama*, Vol. II (London: Cambridge, 1984), p. 65.

32. Bigsby, p. 66.

33. Elia Kazan, quoted in Bigsby, p. 65.

34. C.W.E. Bigsby, "Tennessee Williams: Streetcar to Glory", in Harold Bloom, ed. Tennessee Williams's *A Streetcar Named Desire* (New York: Chelsea 1988), p. 47.

35. Bigsby, "Streetcar to Glory", p. 47.

CALVIN BEDIENT

There Are Lives that Desire Does Not Sustain: A Streetcar Named Desire

Tennessee Williams thought of himself as the Dionysus of modern American theater. He was more its Orpheus, I think, and what he could not bring back from the underworld, intact, was simplicity, unity, and purity—Apollonian virtues. With respect to persons, his Eurydice was a compound of his mother (Edwina) and his sister (Rose). Hades was his father (Cornelius), a virilized Dionysus, drunken and wanton.

How to get the women up without exposing them to Hades' death-bearing wrath? Indeed, how to escape the whole male community's vengeance for what looks like an incestuous compassion—for a melting complicity with women?

In Williams's play *Orpheus Descending*, Val, the snakeskin-jacketed hero, befriends two older married townswomen. One is a visionary primitive painter who believes that the Son has looked down on her from the sky and put his hand to her bosom; her husband sees her placing Val's hand there in imitation. The other, Lady, is a storekeeper maternally linked with food (her pet scheme is a confectionery, which on the stage, so Williams instructed, is "shadowy and poetic as some inner dimension of the play" [*Tennessee Williams: Four Plays*]); *she* becomes pregnant by him and is shot by her malignant, invalid husband, who is "death's self" (141). Eventually, the townsmen torch him alive as a menace to local decency. So it is that the

From *Confronting Tennessee Williams's* A Streetcar Named Desire: *Essays in Critical Pluralism*, edited by Philip C. Kolin. © 1993 by Philip C. Kolin.

play plays with the fire of nostalgia for the legendary union of mother and son. But this antisocial passion is forbidden; it offends the territorial rights of husbands. It is the serpent after it has left Eden.

Williams kept writing variants of this plot, trying to get it right. How to exorcise his own guilt both for being so attached to the family women and for hating them for it? If *A Streetcar Named Desire* is one of his stronger plays, the reason, in part, is that here Orpheus is missing. A more or less minor character, Mitch, has the opportunity to lead the heroine, Blanche DuBois, out of her hell but muffs it. He is still too much of a boy, and too much a bungler, to be a hero. Blanche herself innocently directs this mother's boy to the "Little Boy's Room" soon after meeting him (296); his friends tell him that he needs a sugar tit; he carries a carnival statuette of Mae West upside down (some way to treat a lady); and his relationship to the regenerative sparagmos of the torn-apart god is a mock one: He works at the "precision bench in [a] spare parts department" (292). In this play, there is no one with whom the playwright could want to identify. To put it quite another way, he'd almost rather be Stanley Kowalski, Blanche's ultimate destroyer (though she has done most of the work of destruction herself), than Blanche. He keeps his balance; the snakeskin jacket, Orpheus's sign, stays in the closet.

Eurydice, then, is left to the mercy of her brother-in-law, Stanley, who rapes her in order to show her which sex is the master sex. There is some Dionysus in him: his sign is the Goat, he drinks, and he's a *"gaudy seed-bearer"* (265). But when he finds it convenient, he respects Apollonian law (though his rape violates it), and he is offended by what he takes to be Blanche's immoralism. In all, he acts out the playwright's own would-be potent vengeance against his castrating mother and sister. He is the Phallus through which going ahead is possible. How condemn him without cutting out one's own chance for an escape from women? How, on the other hand, condone his brutality?

Here, Williams is suspended between wanting to forgive his mother (who is more Blanche than Blanche is, a monster of Southern gentility, affectation, and affectless garrulity) and wanting to uproot her from his psyche. The play is more an elaboration of his quandary than its catharsis. The ending, in fact, is crushing. To cart the mother/sister away to a grim mental institution (Williams's sister was placed in several such institutions) is not a true purgation; on the contrary, it only darkens the guilt. So one leaves the theater or closes the book circumspectly, as if afraid to hurt further something already squashed. This something is a Eurydice who was not delivered from bondage but brought forward only to be sent back even more shattered, more hopeless, than before.

Blanche gets ground up between the mills of Williams's compassion and his condemnation. What is there to condemn? Primarily, the power of seduction—the archaic, maternal glamor that makes those seduced by it feel weak. It is against this unmanning seduction that Stanley declares his independence. His loudness, his drinking, his buddy system, all defend him against it. Who do women think they are, coming over one with their ball-busting pretensions to fragility, their contempt for a man's necessary, pushy virility? Turn the mother-woman out of the house. Slip your hand into your wife's blouse as she sobs luxuriously over the defeat of sisterhood and feminine sanctities. (Does she not secretly rejoice in the triumph of a harsh masculine order? After all, women, too, must fear the mother's seduction.) In sum, be a man.

The action of *Streetcar* consists of a masculinist rout of female abjection. Now, this is veritably *the* story of patriarchy. How well did Williams understand his own complicity in it? He is reported to have summed up the moral of his play as follows: "If we don't watch out, the apes will take over" (Quirino 88). But what Stanley really represents, in his brutish fashion, is the patriarchal order, and this order, in *its* fashion, stands as a bulwark against the primitivism of feminine abjection, the pull of the archaic mother. Because he is a speaking being, because he believes in "civilization," the playwright himself must oppose the abject identity-threatening corporeality that the mother, in her archaic guise, represents; more, he must fear the abyss on the far side of abjection—what Julia Kristeva calls "the archaic 'Thing,' the elusive preobject of a mourning that is endemic with all speaking beings" (*Black Sun* 152). Everyone buys into the "legal fiction known as symbolic activity," Kristeva adds, in order to "lose the Thing" (*Black Sun* 146). Only suicides and the depressive dumb or those who use words without any belief in them keep a kind of faith with the encrypted fantasy of the mother as the guarantee of her offspring's omnipotence.

Williams's plays stage ritual reenactments of the sacrifice of either the archaic mother or a mother-sodden son—the sort of sacrifice on which Western culture is based. I would argue that it was this very thing that helped ensure his power over his audiences. While the famed "poetry" of his theater uttered incest, his plots burned it at the stake.[1]

In the 1970s, Kristeva announced with revolutionary jubilation that theater in the United States was turning less resentful of "the ever-present constraints of power" in society. Instead, it was offering a "supple subjectivity, finding its catharsis in the deepest psychic clouds, . . . abreacting its death and its catastrophes." "The remaking of language," not communal interplay, had become its subject—the "reconstruction of the subjective space experienced by our modernity." This was accomplished, for instance, through "the silent theater of colors, sound and gestures," with its inclusion of the symbolic (that is, concepts) within the "semiotic" (that is, prelinguistic sensory phenomena) ("Modern Theater" 131–32).

Williams himself considered his words and thoughts subalterns to "the color, the grace and levitation, the structural pattern in motion" of his theater live. "*Dynamic*" was his mana-word for the stage (*Where I Live* 69). *Streetcar* is not only pervaded by snatches of music; it was originally called *The Primary Colors*, and the stage directions disclose the significance Williams placed in the stage colors. As if heeding Burke on the sublime, he sought strong hues reminiscent of Gauguin's and Van Gogh's aesthetic fundamentalism (i.e., primitivism). Did he hope thus to scare off the fainting moth of Blanche's real (as well as pretended) neurasthenia? Color Stanley green and scarlet, color Blanche scarlet and white: the two meet at a bloody intersection, as if in a painting in which the wildest colors had a "date with each other from the beginning" (402), in the words Stanley addresses to Blanche just before he rapes her.

Still, like the other Broadway playwrights, Williams did not contribute to the "most advanced experiments in writing"—those which, in Kristeva's words, "address themselves uniquely to the individual unconscious" ("Modern Theater" 131). In his list of the "dynamic" properties of his theater, he included "the quick interplay of live beings"—in other words, character. His own theater is, for all its "levitation," conventional or, to use a more honorific word, classical. Where he lived, the community still harried and brought down beautiful (that is, feminine) souls, urging the dogs of coarse sublimity against them.

As a boy, Williams himself was laughed at for his Southern gentility in St. Louis after the family moved there from Clarkesdale, Mississippi. Gangs of schoolboys followed him, calling "Sissy!"—or so he remembered. And he had been shocked by the "ugly rows of apartment buildings the color of dried blood and mustard"—depressive Van Gogh. It was in one such building that he lived.

"I am glad that I received this bitter education," he said, "for I don't think any writer has much purpose back of him unless he feels bitterly the inequities of the society he lives in" (*Where I Live* 59–60). But in Williams, social inequity is not a burning subject. *Orpheus Descending* and *Streetcar* (to stay with the two plays already compared) focus, instead, on the fragility of, respectively, an ingenuous and a disingenuous poetry of being, the false hope that the soft, mother-remembering soul can be spared from sacrifice.

To vary an earlier statement, Williams's plays enact the all-but-ritual purgation of abjection from the community. They would do for the audience and the playwright what his guitar does for Val, the hero of *Orpheus Descending*. "It washes me clean like water when anything unclean has touched me" (*Tennessee Williams: Four Plays* 50). In his foreword to *Sweet Bird of Youth*, he wrote:

> If there is any truth in the Aristotelian idea that violence is purged
> by its poetic representation on a stage, then it may be that my cycle
> of violent plays have had a moral justification after all. . . . I have
> always felt a release from the sense of meaninglessness and death
> when a work of tragic intention has seemed to me to have achieved
> that intention. . . .
>
> I would say that there is something bigger in life and death
> than we have become aware of (or adequately recorded) in our
> living and dying. And, further, to compound this shameless
> romanticism, I would say that our serious theater is a search for
> that something that is not yet successful but is still going on.
>
> (*Three by Tennessee*, xii)

If Kristeva's piece on the new American theater leaves Williams covered by
its avant-garde dust, her analysis of the "theological" sacrifice of the body
in *Revolution in Poetic Language* points one to the cultural centrality of
Williams's "tragic intention." More, *Powers of Horror: An Essay in Abjection*,
her brilliant supplementation of Freud's (neglectful) discussion of incest, and
Black Sun, her study of depression and its secret allegiance to the encrypted
mother-Thing, help us to a view of the coherence and etiology of the ills in
Streetcar, hence to an understanding of the play's jangly, if truthful, failed
catharsis.

I shall leave the relevant arguments of *Revolution in Poetic Language*
aside in this essay in order to concentrate on abjection and melancholy. To
take up, first, the most difficult and unfinished of Williams's suggestions
about serious modern theater, namely that it intimates "something much
bigger in life and death than we have become aware of." Is this mysticism? If
so, it is a mysticism of dread.[2] Williams brooded over "an underlying dread-
fulness in modern experience." He intuited "something almost too incredible
and shocking to talk about." But for that very reason, it is the one necessary subject, the one unavoidable truth. So Williams faulted Proust for not
quite daring "to deliver the message of Absolute Dread." The atmosphere of
Proust's work is "rather womb-like" (*Where I Live* 46).

Dread: life outside the maternal shelter? Life as a malady of grief,
of death, because the disappearance of my omniscient beginnings, of my
autoerotic fusion with the mother, "continues to deprive me of what is most
worthwhile in me" (*Black Sun* 5). Dread, then, as the sensation of standing
on the slippery lip of a depression (*Black Sun* 6):

> The child king becomes irredeemably sad before uttering his first
> words; this is because he has been irrevocably, desperately separated
> from the mother, a loss that causes him to try to find her again . . .

first in the imagination, then in words . . . if there is no writing other than the amorous, there is no imagination that is not, overtly or secretly, melancholy.

If this universal fatality of being a child seems, all the same, a *modern* malady, that may be due to the erosion of theological support for the symbolic order—the disappearance of consolatory myth. "As if overtaxed or destroyed by too powerful a breaker," Kristeva writes in "The Malady of Grief: Duras" (*Black Sun*), "Our symbolic means find themselves hollowed out, nearly wiped out, paralyzed" (223)—which leaves more and more people prey to the mother-Thing, something prior to language and imperial enough to make a mockery of it, something maintained by jealously kept affects. A preobject, then, that keeps us from an attachment to objects, from the extroverted paths of desire, and that makes love implode into death, death into love.

Williams committed himself to the *truth* of unbearable anxiety. Blanche, accordingly, feels "a sense of disaster closing in on her," and she cries out: "Something has happened!—What is it!" (237). Near the end of the play, Williams assigns her a "*look of sorrowful perplexity as though all human experience shows on her face*" (407). She is the Mona Lisa of dread, the fragility and terror of the "I" exiled from the womb but still inside the mother-space where objects form in grief that this space should exist at all. Why does the world open if it then wants to fold up again? What a catastrophe should it revert back! *Let it do so!* No, *prevent it*!

What checks regression is, in Kristeva's view, the powerful horror of abjection: fear of the mother as murky and suffocating materiality, as mortally unclean. It is the (would-be) clean and proper "I" that conceives this dread of its own annihilation in mother-filth. Yet a lost maternal utopia nonetheless beckons to the fundamentally wounded, deficient, empty—that is, to everyone. Williams's "poetry" is, as already indicated, his wooing of it, the sign of his seduction by it.

What does Blanche herself have to respond to it with? She has "poetry" too—much to Stanley's contempt. But it is largely kitsch. Even to her, it is too little a thing to have. She also has alcohol, which she pours into the bottomless mug of her emptiness, betraying the presence in her of a little girl deprived of the breast. She has, in addition, the memory of the family estate, Belle Reve, but, splashed by several recent deaths within its walls, it has become hideous with abjection. Most of all, she has that involuntary fidelity to the mother-fantasy whose sign is an inability to feel desire. At most, she can only feel a desire for desire, or fake it.

Despite the play's title, Blanche is one of those whose lives, in Kristeva's words, "are not sustained by desire" (*Powers of Horror* 6). (In any case, in the play the streetcar named *Desire* is a poor, rattly thing and but leads to the cemetery). Desire is an object-seeking energy that exceeds our (necessary) narcissism; it is the "drive toward the other" (*Powers of Horror* 33). Blanche's narcissism lacks this sort of redirection, this egress from its self-absorption. If desire is abjection with its back turned, Blanche is too abject, too frightened at the shadowy borderland of subjective identity, to experience it. Her question is not "Whom shall I love?" but "How can I be?" As for her genteel idealizations, they are superficial, the glitter on a black body of water in which she is always about to drown.

To relax from the tensions and to escape the disgusts of abjection, Blanche takes long hot baths (these, however, are ambiguous, for they make her squeal with pleasure like a child as well as leave her feeling clean, purged of her fascination with the archaic mother). She also has her makeup and her fashionable or pretentious clothing, by which she treats herself as a mannequin, a static artifact—something as sculptural, faultless, bloodless, and seductive as the mother-idol that she has set up in a buried temple. By turning herself into an attractive *thing*, she both emulates and keeps a heartless distance from the fantasy of an inseparable (incarcerated) mother that her crushed omnipotence has fabricated.

How sedulously she seduces others! As if to keep from being seduced herself, to preserve herself intact and ready for the incestuous consummation that will restore her omnipotence. Far from committing her to others, her seductive airs cocoon her in a habit of make-believe. She will thus stay young, stay close to childhood! "For these last few remaining moments of our lives together," she says to Mitch, after a date that went poorly, "I want to create—joie de vivre. . . . We are going to pretend," and so on (344). Is not Blanche always in her last few moments, always pretending? Otherwise, she would have to say to life what she thinks men say to women who do not "entertain them"—"no dice!" (341).

Wherever she is, Blanche is already in a play; her existence in Williams's work is thus a sort of doubling of what she already is—an actress on a stage emptied of everything except the shadows of her fancy. Is she perhaps always playing to one hidden audience—a face blind, deaf, sublime, monumental as an Easter Island statue?

Given to continual self-creation and self-concealment, Blanche imitates her author. And, like Williams, she had a promiscuous interest in men, particularly young men: boys or boy-men (Mitch). For a homosexual male, other men can be loved as Narcissan reflections, or else as the Phallus the mother appealed to in asking the father-world to come and admire what *she* has produced, her child. But Blanche? Her psychology is more or less consistent with that of *feminine* depression as Kristeva presents it in *Black Sun*; to a depressed woman, eros is maddening, shattering. Virile Stanley is thus anathema to Blanche, like an alarm clock viciously clattering at the ear of Sleeping Beauty. If she pursues boys, it is doubtless because she can rule them, make toys of them, or use them as mirrors to her vanity. Any Prince Charming who calls her away from the mother *appears* only to wake her up. The youth who comes collecting for the newspaper (Blanche: "It would be nice to keep you, but I've got to be good—and keep my hands off children" [339]) is no more than a phallic statuette to match Mitch's plaster-doll Mae West, part of a Barnum and Bailey world.

Did Blanche really love her boy-husband, Allan Grey? All too desperately! All too idealistically! Evidently, she wanted a life above the flesh (Stella "she thought him almost too fine to be human!" [364]). A life with that idealistic, if also regressive, being, *a poet*. But what was her aim—to *forsake* or to *recoup* the mother-Thing? The chance for recuperation consisted in the fact that her amorous idealization was trellised on an androgyne: "There was something different about the boy," Blanche says, "a . . . softness and tenderness that wasn't like a man's" (354). So her union with Allan was not a true break with the mother. Moreover, the boy seemed uncertain as to what he "needed" from Blanche, whether a liberation from, or an access to, his own encrypted Thing. She therefore had the power to destroy him, and she does.

First, Allan fails *her* by compromising his already equivocal status as the Phallus that can save her from the archaic engulfing mother. In having sex with an older man, Allan perhaps shows his own need for a father-rescuer. If Allan himself is not the Phallus, then is he not one with the abjection that the Phallus opposes with its law, its symbolizations, its dedication to form? "You disgust me," she says to him (355). Whereupon he shoots off the back of his head at the edge of darkened Moon Lake, as if in proximity to the nondifferentiating mother-matter from which his personal identity—terrified and unsure, both hating and loving its source—once arose. This lake is sister-water to Blanche's baths, her drinks, the perfume that she sprays like *eau de mysticism* even on Stanley's red-blooded American maleness.

Once Allan dies, Blanche, it seems, can no longer desire; the experiment of getting outside herself fails. The only one who possesses her, and whom she wants to possess, precedes her—is "the impossible within" (*Powers of Horror* 5). But an attempt to disavow this impossible love can lead a woman "on a feverish quest for gratification" (*Black Sun* 77). Blanche's promiscuity has been of this desperate kind. Perhaps she might have said with Carol, a character in *Orpheus Descending*: "The act of love-making is almost unbearably painful, and yet . . . to be not alone, even for a few moments, is worth the pain and the danger" (*Tennessee Williams: Four Plays* 75).

What keeps her from being pathologically depressed is hysteria, the same that makes her cast about nervously for new, satisfying (at last satisfying!)

fictions about how happy life can be *out here*, in the father's sociosymbolic order. But this effort, being frantic, is no good. Besides, how can the social order compete with the sacred crypt in the ruined garden of her loss? Especially if that order consists not of a beautiful aristocratic dream (*belle rêve*), but of a rowdy bunch on a street ironically named Elysian Fields?

In addition to dread, hysteria, and a lurking melancholy, Blanche illustrates guilt. For Williams, "guilt is universal" (*Where I Live* 109):

> I mean a strong sense of guilt. If there exists any area in which a man can rise above his moral condition, imposed upon him at birth and long before birth, by the nature of his breed, then I think it is only a willingness to know it. . . . Below the conscious level, we all face it. Hence guilty feelings, and hence defiant aggressions, and hence the deep dark of despair that haunts our dreams, our creative work, and makes us distrust each other.

If the play flags Blanche's guilt in her history with Allan, Blanche is guilty, too, over the loss of Belle Reve, and this suggests that she *wanted* to free herself of the estate because it had become synonymous with the mother's lethal legacy of abjection, in particular the body's corruptibility. Protesting overmuch, she denies responsibility for its loss: "You're a fine one to sit there *accusing* me of it!" she says to Stella, who, however, hasn't said a word (261). "I stayed . . . and fought for it, bled for it, almost died for it!" (260). So, it was that important to her. "You came to New Orleans," she adds, "and looked out for yourself!" Blanche's tag for Stella—"Stella for Star" (250)—points to her sister's ability to detach herself and gain distance from the beautiful dream of her maternal and earthly origins. Blanche herself may have preferred to stay within the dream, until it turned to blood, "the struggle for breath." "Death is expensive, Miss Stella!" "The loss—the loss" of which Blanche murmurs is perhaps not just the estate, which was made over to its mortgagees, but the dream of a maternal sphere stronger than death. Which is to say that, for Blanche, *abjection*, with its horror and repulsion, had begun to dominate over the compelling mysticism of the Thing.

Still, in her ambivalent revolt against the mother, Blanche is a divided woman, part fluttery surface and part inner crypt in which lives an impossibly retained empowering mother. Over against the Southern decadence of the DuBois males (epic fornicators), Blanche poses as an immaculate Southern belle, complete with perfect manners, enchanting graces, pure principles, spotless dresses, a fresh-scented body, and clean hair. A drink is splashed on her white skirt; she shrieks. Mitch comes to call in his work-clothes; she scolds. Ironically, her constant pretence to purity makes her appear all the more unclean to others once it lies exposed. A woman free of the deathly crypt? Rather, a whited sepulcher.

Blanche can affect to make light of death: "You've got to dive where the deep pool is," she instructs certain phantasmatic suitors, "—if you hit a rock you don't come up till tomorrow" (91). But, really, she already belongs to death, and when a blind Mexican woman comes to the door with gaudy tin funeral flowers (the antithesis of Stanley's gaudy maleness), Blanche treats it as a sign of doom. She entertains a wistful fantasy of eating something unclean and sinking to the bottom of the sea—of giving in, after all, to a fatal abjection. The unclean edible? "An unwashed grape" from the Dionysian French Quarter, symbol of an intoxicated unselving. But she dreams of being "buried at sea sewn up in a clean white sack" (410). The sack is a fantastic protection from the Great Unclean that must, nonetheless, be re-entered. The ocean reclaims her own. She is death; but outside of her—that, too, is death.

Blanche attempts to stay afloat, not through love, but through seduction—a *glamor* of the surface. To seduce is neither to desire nor to love. Rather, as Jean Baudrillard says in his brilliant book on seduction, it is to challenge the autonomy of sex itself, to provoke desire only to deceive it, to show it as deluded about its power. To seduce is to appear weak so as to render others weak; to avoid the question of truth; to disappear in "the flickering of a presence" (one of Williams's early titles for the play was *The Moth*). It is not to attach any meaning to what one does, for "what destroys people, wears them down, is the meaning they give their acts."[3] It is to turn one's body into a "pure appearance, an artificial construct with which to trap the desire of others"; it is to maintain a spectacular immortality through makeup, stylish clothes, gestures that gild the self-made idol.

Seduction, then, makes a mockery of the seriousness of the law, of productivity, of meaning. It is a theater in which only one player, Narcissan, is lighted, a softening paper lantern over the bulb. Why, even death must hesitate to break up this thespian's act, so mesmerizing is she, so polished.

A seductress whose style is antiquated and wearing thin, Blanche camps, in both senses, in southern coquettish refinement. (Unseen by Mitch, she rolls up her eyes when she protests her devotion to "old-fashion ideals" [348]. She plays him for a chump.) Her life-apart-from-meaning is moonshine, the moon itself pitted, cold. She's a Scarlett O'Hara in the wrong century (so it was natural that Vivien Leigh should play *her*, too). Besides, she drinks too much, and, though she is only thirty, she worries about aging.

If her game succeeds with Mitch for a while, it is useless against Stanley, who represents a "serious" male mentality—the ethic of production and above-board relations. (He is even suspicious of Hollywood glamour, which is hardly even American.) Stanley has his goaty sex—an industrial machine for producing both pleasure and a son (it must be a son). He has his work. And he has his competitive homosocial diversions with the boys (bowling and poker). Everything else is Mardi Gras tinsel and witchcraft (Blanche: "I cannot imagine any witch of a woman casting a spell over you." Stanley: "That's—right" [279]). Stanley has the a- or prehistorical sensibility of a hard-hat industrial worker of the north (never mind that he lives in New Orleans, of all the wrong places). A radical democrat, he sneers at the cloud Blanche trails after her, which is half rice powder and half dying star-fall of southern gentility.

To interest Stanley, as Blanche says, a woman would have to "Lay . . . her cards on the table" (279). But when Blanche wants to "kibitz" in the men's poker game (290), she's stone-walled. For, like masculine work, poker must not be contaminated by seduction—by feminine allure, by mother-magic. Its rules are transparent, are willingly adhered to, and lack imprisoning internalization. (Poker is serious: Stanley orders Mitch to get even his male ass off the table.) Poker supplements strict social law without falling into the feminine domain of obscure enchantment.[4] It is a deliverance from the law's guilt—an arbitrary ceremonial, a smoke-filled reprieve from meaning.

In poker, no one is allowed to be larger than the game. Masculine democracy, a cards-on-the-table sternness, restrains competitiveness. Unlike seduction, which is hieratical, hierarchical, poker is compatible with democracy and capitalism. Seduction is played with a trick deck. Only the seductress (or seducer) is allowed to win. Queen of Hearts, Queen of Diamonds (really rhinestones), Blanche flirts and sparkles. The role of the others is but to succumb. But Blanche secretly fears death, the Queen of Spades, hence the desperation underlying her airy ways.

To Blanche, Stanley is like death: He is nonseducible. Paradoxically, his primitive life force is death to her, because she cannot turn it into a game, her game. It is intolerably real. Stanley is male sun to her feminine mists. He is the only man around who will not let her say, without choking: "You may think you can crack me with desire, but, instead, I will make you bow to *appearances*." Fascinated as she is with so pure an opposite to herself, and envious as she is of her sister's pregnancy—to have a baby, to rejoin one's mother through one's child!—she cannot bear Stanley's phallic definiteness, his loud *finis* to her illusions. "The first time I laid eyes on him I thought to myself, that man is my executioner!" (351).

To be triumphant, a seductress must strangle her own psychology, neutralize fantasy. An advocate of seduction, Baudrillard disdains psychoanalysis for suppressing it and bringing upon itself the return of seduction through the Lacanian "imposture" (57). Blanche, however, is psychological, infested with guilty hallucinations. She's unable to exchange psychology for artifice. Finally, she loses her ability even to play with fictions. She becomes their pathetic plaything.

Even if Blanche were not up against the age's hostility to seduction (ours, Baudrillard says, is "a culture of the desublimation of appearances"), she is hopelessly fragile, afraid of being deserted, afraid of the future, afraid of the past, afraid to love, afraid of crowds, afraid of light, afraid of death. Afraid and guilty. She is, as well, the victim of male pride and paranoia. The men around her feel castrated by her Della Robbia blue; but the satiny scarlet in her history makes a whore of her (Mitch: "You're not clean enough to bring in the house with my mother" 390). Males are terrified of the possibility of being taken in by a mother-prostitute. The two elements must be kept distinct. With men, Blanche is at once fire and ice; dry ice. Even as she flirts with a man, she lays a prohibition on his genitals. Then to discover that, with *other* men, she has played the harlot!

Stanley takes his vengeance. It is, deep down, vengeance against the frightening mother. As Kristeva says, a virile man has to cross "over the horrors of maternal bowels" (*Powers of Horror* 53) to appropriate archaic maternal power. And here is Blanche, Miss White, attempting to dismiss Stanley's sexuality as apish. To Stanley, Blanche perhaps has a double significance: She is both the Phallic Mother and the abjection (the feminizing abjection) he fears in himself. She is the possibility that the phallus, at least his, is nothing. So she must be shown up, put down.

The opposite of the "quicksands" (354) into which Allan sank is phallic form, the law. Stanley is Allan's *positive* opposite. Many who have written on the play equate Stanley with sensuality alone, but Williams makes him dual; he represents the sociosymbolic order (in which he is, though a worker, a "king" [271]), as much as he does the bullying Phallus. In fact, the two are related, as the play illustrates. If the available alternatives are the Phallus or depression, abjection or the law, then Stanley makes the right, the only viable, choice. As phallic "one-eyed jack" (286), he defeats Blanche, Queen of Clubs, the Phallic Mother; that is, in a retrospective arrangement, the omnipotent archaic mother before the actual mother is found to be wanting in (masculine) potency.

This defeat recapitulates the violence against the mother-remembering *soma* on which every system of signs is founded. Of course, that Stanley triumphs over his fears in the swaggering conviction that Blanche wants to be mastered by him makes him repugnant. But what he stands for, even as he breaks it, is the social law and its accouterments: desire, objects, productivity.

The catastrophe arises from the collision between, on the one hand, the law and the violence that motivates it and, on the other, lawless seduction, which is itself a reach for power, in other words, between a "masculine" and a "feminine" assertion of strength. What seals it is the actual fragility of Blanche's hold on the world of objects. Each character is what the other must expel in order to keep going, to keep up the pretense of success in life.[5]

I suggest, then, that the play sacrifices Blanche, or "feminine" abjection, however reluctantly, in favor of the transparent social system. When the cards are down, the playwright prefers identity-sustaining law to the engulfing archaic mother.[6] He thus injures and humiliates part of himself, the unspoken part of every speaking being, hence, as I noted before, a final effect of sickening pain. "Is it not by signifying hatred, the destruction of the other, and perhaps above all his own execution," Kristeva asks, "that the human being survives as a symbolic animal?" (*Black Sun* 181).

What price survival? *A Streetcar Named Desire* both wins and loses its own game of seduction. "Violence," Williams said, "is purged by its poetic representation on stage" (*Where I Live* 109). Again, poetry utters incest; but just for that reason, the plot itself must oppose it. No poetry in the plot itself, only "realism."

What kept Williams from the avant-garde route was his need to purge "universal guilt." He used classical plot as a ritual for ridding the symbolic order of contaminants. But is Stanley's "deliberate cruelty" the same thing as a necessary social violence? Blanche calls such cruelty "the one unforgivable thing" and adds that it is "the one thing of which I have never, never been guilty" (p. 397).[7] Characteristically, she protests too much. She was cruel to Allan as, in turn, Stanley is cruel to her. Blanche shows contempt for a fake seed-bearer, a failed protector against the Phallic Mother, and Stanley shows equal contempt for the cock-teaser, Blanche. Of course, this parity between them, such as it is, does not excuse the cruelty of either. The question is: How *much* violence can be justified in keeping at bay the castrating Phallic Mother?

Williams's play does not attempt an exact measure. It has, thanks to Blanche, a wincing core that says any violence is too much. This makes for "serious" theater indeed. Yet for all that she represents "poetry," Blanche is not in any assured sense a positive heroine who offers a needed corrective to the unpoetic patriarchy. In *Orpheus Descending*, the symbolic order is mistaken in its enemy; Val, the snake-youth, is genuinely wholesome. By contrast, Blanche represents the deadly drag of the historical and, even more, archaic past. All the same, she is inescapable; she is the heart of abjection and the heartless depression in everyone. Williams understands that without condemning it. It is this that makes *Streetcar*, for all its heavy symbolism, a profound and powerful work of mourning—a stunning contribution to the modern literature of grief.

NOTES

1. On poetry as an utterance of incest, see Kristeva, *Desire in Language* 137.
2. "Those in despair are mystics—adhering to the preobject, not believing in Thou, but mute and steadfast devotees of their own inexpressible container" (*Black Sun* 14).

3. Baudrillard, *Seduction*; see especially "The Ecliptic of Sex" and "The Effigy of the Seductress."

4. For Baudrillard's discussion of poker and other games, see *Seduction* 132 ff.

5. "The abject has only one quality of the object—that of being opposed to *I*. If the object, however, through its opposition, settles me within the fragile texture of a desire for meaning, . . . what is *abject*, . . . the jettisoned object, is radically excluded and draws me toward the place where meaning collapses. A certain 'ego' that merged with its master, a superego, has flatly driven it away" (*Powers of Horror* 1–2).

6. Kenneth Tynan said that "when, finally, [Blanche] is removed to the mental home, we should feel that a part of civilisation is going with her. There ancient drama teaches us to reach nobility by contemplation of what might have been noble, but is now humiliated, ignoble in the sight of all but the compassionate." Tynan takes Blanche's impassioned speech on behalf of art at face value. I suggest that Blanche hollows culture out, betraying, as she does, a fundamental opposition to being conscious. See Tynan (263).

7. I take Britton J. Harwood's point (133) that Blanche's cruelty seems to burst from her and so to lack deliberation. Still, in uttering her words, she intended to hurt. Conversely, it is not clear that Stanley means to be cruel, as opposed to giving Blanche what he thinks she probably wants.

Works Cited

Baudrillard, Jean. *Seduction*. Trans. Brian Singer. New York: St. Martin's, 1990.

Harwood, Britton J. "Tragedy as Habit: *A Streetcar Named Desire*." *Tennessee Williams: A Tribute*. Ed. Jac Tharpe. Jackson: UP of Mississippi, 1977. 104–15.

Kristeva, Julia. "Modern Theater Does Not Take (A) Place." *Sub-Stance* 18/19 (1977).

———. *Black Sun: Depression and Melancholia*. Trans. Leon S. Roudiez. New York: Columbia UP, 1989.

———. *Desire in Language: A Semiotic Approach to Literature and Art*. Ed. Leon S. Roudiez. New York: Columbia UP, 1980.

———. *Powers of Horror: An Essay in Abjection*. Trans. Leon S. Roudiez. New York: Columbia UP, 1982.

———. *Revolution in Poetic Language*. New York: Columbia UP, 1984.

Quirino, Leonard. "The Cards Indicate a Voyage on *A Streetcar Named Desire*." *Tennessee Williams: A Tribute*. Ed. Jac Tharpe. Jackson: UP of Mississippi, 1977. 77–96.

Tynan, Kenneth. *Curtains: Selections from the Drama Criticism and Related Writings*. New York: Atheneum, 1961.

Williams, Tennessee. *Where I Live: Selected Essays*. Ed. Christine R. Day and Bob Woods. New York: New Directions, 1978.

———. *Tennessee Williams: Four Plays*. New York: New American Library, 1976.

———. *Three by Tennessee*. New York: New American Library, 1976.

———. *A Streetcar Named Desire*. The Theatre of Tennessee Williams. 7 vols. to date. New York: New Directions, 1971. Vol. 1: 239–419.

SUSAN KOPRINCE

Domestic Violence in
A Streetcar Named Desire

Until the 1970s the problem of domestic violence was virtually ignored in American society. Wife-beating was considered a "family matter" rather than a crime or a serious social issue. Women were typically expected to deal with the problem themselves, to keep it behind closed doors. It is no surprise, therefore, to find that the subject of domestic violence has also been ignored by literary critics—even in a drama like Tennessee Williams's *A Streetcar Named Desire* (1947), where Stanley Kowalski actually strikes his pregnant wife, Stella. Although acknowledging Stanley's capacity for violence, critics have tended to focus on the man's sensuality and animal magnetism—on his brutal, Lawrentian passion.

If we view *A Streetcar Named Desire* from a modern sociological perspective, however, we discover—perhaps somewhat shockingly—that Stanley Kowalski is not just a charming, sensual man prone to occasional outbursts of violence. He is a batterer—a man whose aggressive masculinity and desire for control are perfectly consistent with the profile of an abuser. Stanley's wife, Stella, likewise matches the sociological profile of the battered woman; for she is essentially a submissive, self-deprecating wife who tolerates and excuses her husband's behavior. If readers recognize that the Kowalskis are trapped in a cycle of domestic abuse, they can better understand the couple's actions throughout the play. Indeed, the battering cycle

From *Southern Studies* 7, nos. 2 and 3 (Summer/Fall 1996): 43–55. © 1995 by Southern Studies Institute.

even helps to explain Stanley Kowalski's most brutal act of violence: the rape of Stella's sister, Blanche DuBois.

Because Williams published *A Streetcar Named Desire* long before domestic violence became a topic of public discussion in America, he was certainly not familiar with modern-day sociological profiles of batterers and their victims. But Williams knew the subject of domestic violence firsthand, having observed spousal abuse in his own family. As Williams's brother Dakin points out, their father, Cornelius Coffin Williams, would frequently return home intoxicated and fly into a rage against their mother, Edwina. Once in 1933 Edwina "ran into the bedroom and locked herself in. [Cornelius] broke down the door, and in doing so the door hit her and broke her nose" (qtd. in Spoto, 18–19). During another drunken outburst in 1937 Cornelius brutally beat his wife—an episode witnessed by Williams's emotionally fragile sister, Rose, who became hysterical (Spoto, 57). Edwina did not leave her husband during those early years of abuse. "I just stood by and took it," she said (Leverich, 66).

In *A Streetcar Named Desire*, Williams makes use of his personal knowledge of domestic violence, creating in the character of Stanley Kowalski the image of a prototypical batterer. According to modern sociologists, batterers tend to exhibit the following traits: 1) they are hypermasculine, using aggressive behavior as verification of their manliness; 2) they believe in male superiority, viewing women as sexual objects to be dominated; 3) they resort to both physical and psychological abuse in an effort to control their spouses; 4) they are extremely jealous and possessive, fearful that their mates will ultimately leave them; and 5) they have a dual personality—proving to be charming and generous on some occasions but cruel and vicious on others. How many of these traits actually fit the character of Stanley Kowalski? The answer, as we shall see, is *all of them.*

There is no doubt that Stanley Kowalski is hypermasculine. Formerly an army officer, he is now a travelling salesman who has considerable freedom on the road. Not only is he captain of his bowling team, he is a rough-talking, heavy-drinking poker player who enjoys late-night parties and male camaraderie. As Williams suggests, Stanley is also the perfect embodiment of male sexual power:

> Animal joy in his being is implicit in all his movements and attitudes. Since earliest manhood the center of his life has been pleasure with women, the giving and taking of it, not with weak indulgence, dependently, but with the power and pride of a richly feathered male bird among hens. Branching out from this complete and satisfying center are all the auxiliary channels of his life, such as his heartiness with men, his appreciation of rough humor, his love

of good drink and food and games, his car, his radio, everything that is his, that bears his emblem of the gaudy seed-bearer. (264–265)

Like most batterers, Stanley believes in male superiority. He views women as sexual objects—"hens" who have been placed on earth solely for the male bird's pleasure. Indeed, when he meets women, "He sizes [them] up at a glance, with sexual classifications, crude images flashing into his mind and determining the way he smiles at them" (265). Stanley especially believes in male dominance within the institution of marriage. He is completely in charge of the Kowalski household, calling all the shots and expecting his wife's acquiescence. If Stella ever tries to stand up to him, Stanley growls, "Since when do you give me orders?" (275). During an argument with Stella in Scene Eight, in which he hurls his dinnerware to the floor, Stanley even warns, "Remember what Huey Long said—'Every Man is a King!' And I am the king around here, so don't forget it!" (371).

Stanley's macho need for control leads him to abuse Stella both emotionally and physically. On the night of his poker game with his buddies, Stanley reaches out and whacks his wife loudly on her thigh, embarrassing her in front of her sister and the other men. "It makes me so mad when he does that in front of people" (290), complains Stella—suggesting that this humiliating behavior is not uncommon. Stanley's emotional abuse of Stella also includes intimidation, especially through violence directed at household objects; e.g., the slamming of doors, the throwing of dinnerware, the hurling of a radio out the window. Blanche Dubois remarks that Stanley must have been born under the sign of Aries:

Aries people are forceful and dynamic. They dote on noise! They love to bang things around. You must have had lots of banging around in the army and now that you're out, you make up for it by treating inanimate objects with such a fury! (328).

The primary example of *physical* abuse against Stella occurs in Scene Three, when drunk and angry, Stanley first tosses the radio out the window and then charges after his pregnant wife and strikes her. There is the sound of a blow offstage; Stella cries out and then says in an unnaturally high voice, "I want to go away, I want to go away!" (303). It is crucial to understand that this attack on Stella is not an isolated event but part of an established pattern of abuse. According to domestic violence expert Murray A. Straus, "When an assault by a husband occurs, it is not usually an isolated instance. In fact, it tends to be a recurrent feature of the relationship" (qtd. in Swisher, 7). The Kowalskis' neighbor, Eunice, makes it clear that Stanley has *previously* abused Stella when she scolds him by saying:

You can't beat on a woman an' then call 'er back! She won't come!
And her goin' t' have a baby! . . . You stinker! You whelp of a Polack,
you! I hope they do haul you in and turn the fire hose on you, *same
as the last time!*" [italics added] (306).

Incidentally, research shows that pregnant women are especially vulnerable to spousal abuse, for pregnancy places an added strain on the marriage. As Dawn Berry, author of *The Domestic Violence Sourcebook*, notes,
"Battering often escalates when something changes in the violent home, and
pregnancy—especially the first—may trigger an increase in abuse" (59). A
recent article in the *Journal of the American Medical Association* even reported
that "as many as 37 percent of all obstetrical patients may be abused while
pregnant" (qtd. in Berry, 69). Disturbing as Stanley's attack upon Stella is,
therefore, it is not highly unusual.

Batterers also tend to be inordinately jealous—"both of other men and
of anyone or anything else that takes a partner's attention away from them—
family, friends, work" (Berry, 36). Stanley Kowalski certainly displays such
jealousy. He doesn't openly worry that Stella will run off with another man,
but he is extremely resentful of her attachment to her sister, Blanche, believing that Blanche's very presence in their home has seriously interfered with
his marriage to Stella. In Scene Eight, after abruptly arranging for Blanche
to leave New Orleans, he tells Stella:

When we first met, me and you, you thought I was common. How
right you was, baby. I was common as dirt. You showed me the
snapshot of the place with the columns. I pulled you down off them
columns and how you loved it, having them colored lights going!
And wasn't we happy together, wasn't it all okay till she showed
here? (377)

The batterer's greatest worry, in fact, is that his mate will ultimately
leave him. As Berry observes, "Abusive men have a terrible fear of abandon-
ment and become desperate when they feel they could lose their partner."
Despite their macho exterior, such men are indeed "vulnerable and dependent" (36). Stanley's fear that Stella will abandon him is clearly revealed in
Scene Three of the play, when Stella flees upstairs to Eunice's apartment
after her husband has struck her. "Stella! . . . My baby doll's left me," cries
Stanley, who then begins to sob uncontrollably (305). He stumbles desperately outdoors, bellowing his wife's name, and when Stella comes down to
him, "He falls to his knees on the steps and presses his face to her belly,
curving a little with maternity" (307). Numerous critics, including director
Elia Kazan, have pointed to Stanley's vulnerability—"his sudden pathetic

little-tough-boy tenderness toward Stella" (Kazan, 377). It is important, however, to recognize this vulnerability for what it really is: simply another component of the batterer's basic temperament.

Despite his violent nature, Stanley is at times an appealing—even charming—character (especially as portrayed by Marlon Brando in the original Broadway production and in the classic film version of the play). He is handsome, unaffected, and down-to-earth; and his attachment to Stella is genuine. Yet according to domestic violence experts, it is common for batterers to exhibit a dual personality—"a Dr. Jekyll-and-Mr. Hyde aspect to their character" (Berry, 38). They can be charming and generous on some occasions and cruelly vicious on others. Unaware of the violent side of such men, outsiders might even regard them as friendly, successful, and well-liked. This "Dr. Jekyll-and-Mr. Hyde aspect" particularly describes Stanley Kowalski, a man who is alternately charming and cruel, alternately tender and brutal. Reviewing the original Broadway production of *Streetcar*, Irwin Shaw pointed to Stanley's dual personality:

> He is so amusing in a direct, almost childlike way in the beginning, and we have been so conditioned by the modern doctrine that what is natural is good, that we admire him and sympathize with him. Then, bit by bit, with a full account of what his good points really are, we come dimly to see that he is . . . brutish, destructive in his healthy egotism, dangerous, immoral, surviving" (qtd. in Cardullo, 168).

Just as Stanley Kowalski matches the profile of a batterer, so does Stella Kowalski fit the profile of the battered woman. Although not as easy to categorize as their batterers, abused women share a number of important characteristics: 1) they exhibit "a low self-esteem that is usually related to repeated victimization" (Flowers, 12); 2) they hold traditional views about women's roles in the home; 3) they tend to accept things as they are, believing that they have little control over their own lives; and 4) they often cope with their situation through the mechanism of denial (Walker, 31).

Stella Kowalski's low self-esteem is suggested throughout the play. Not only does Stella allow her husband to control her (director Elia Kazan referred to her as "compulsively compliant" and as "Stanley's slave" [Kazan, 374]), but she even permits her sister, Blanche, to boss her around. "Stand up," orders Blanche in Scene One, shortly after her arrival at Elysian Fields. "You hear me? I said stand up! [Stella complies reluctantly] You messy child, you, you've spilt something on that pretty white lace collar! About your hair—you ought to have it cut in a feather bob with your dainty features" (255). In Scene Five, when Stella brings her sister a bottled coke, she confirms her own position of inferiority by saying, "I like to wait on you, Blanche. It makes it seem more like home" (333).

In *Battered Women, Shattered Lives*, Kathleen Hofeller argues that the low self-esteem of battered wives may also be shown in their selection of a marriage partner—their tendency to "'marry down' by choosing men who come from lower socioeconomic groups than they" (80). This is the case with Stella Kowalski, who has given up her genteel Southern heritage—effectively turning her back on all that Belle Reve represents—in order to marry a crude working-class man like Stanley. Blanche exaggerates the difference in socioeconomic background by portraying Stanley as a "survivor of the Stone Age! Bearing the raw meat home from the kill in the jungle!" (323). "You can't have forgotten that much of our bringing up, Stella, that you just *suppose* that any part of a gentleman's in his nature!" (322). Stella loves Stanley, of course, and is drawn to his vitality and sexual charms. She may even have wanted to escape from her decadent aristocratic milieu. But the fact remains that she *has* "married down" by becoming a Kowalski. Even Stanley admits that when Stella first met him, she saw him for what he really was: "common as dirt."

Battered wives tend to have traditional ideas about the home; i.e., they believe that the man is in charge of the household, makes all the key decisions, and that their own role is to be nurturing and compliant. As one expert suggests, such women "may exemplify society's old image of ideal womanhood—submissive, religious, non-assertive, accepting of whatever the husband's life brings. . . . The husband comes first for these women" (qtd. in Flowers, 12). With her upbringing as a Southern belle, Stella Kowalski has been particularly conditioned to embrace this traditional notion of womanhood. Stanley makes all the decisions (e.g., he is the one who speaks about communal property and the Napoleonic code; he is the one who controls the couple's finances, not even giving Stella an allowance); and Stella plays the part of the placid, submissive wife. Indeed, when Tennessee Williams viewed a rehearsal production of *Streetcar*, he advised director Elia Kazan to tone down Stella's vivacity, reminding him that her key quality is passivity, or in Williams's words, a "narcotized tranquility" (Kazan, 374).

Like a typical battered wife, Stella accepts her relationship with her husband as it is, even telling Blanche that "I'm not in anything I want to get out of" (314). Cleaning up the mess after the poker night, Stella says:

> He promised this morning that he was going to quit having these poker parties, but you know how long such a promise is going to keep. Oh, well, it's his pleasure, like mine is movies and bridge. People have got to tolerate each other's habits, I guess. (314)

In a note to Elia Kazan, Tennessee Williams wrote of Stella: "I think her natural passivity is one of the things that makes her acceptance of Stanley acceptable. She naturally 'gives in,' accepts, lets things slide, she does not make much of an effort" (qtd. in Kazan, 374).

Stella also copes with her situation by denying that there is a real problem in her marriage. On the morning after the poker night, when Blanche asks her how she could have returned to Stanley following such abuse, Stella remarks, "You're making much too much fuss about this. . . . it wasn't anything as serious as you seem to take it" (312). She blames Stanley's conduct on the drinking and the poker and adds, "He was as good as a lamb when I came back and he's really very, very ashamed of himself" (312). Like many battered women, Stella is genuinely in love with her husband. She puts up with his abuse because she doesn't want to lose him, and because she feels helpless to change the way that he treats her.

During the 1940s, Freudian psychologists such as Helene Deutsch portrayed the battered woman as a masochist who provoked her husband into abusing her, secretly enjoying the pain he inflicted upon her (Pleck, 158–159). Tennessee Williams may have been influenced by this theory, to some extent, for on the morning after the poker party Stella tells Blanche: "Stanley's always smashed things. Why, on our wedding night—soon as we came in here—he snatched off one of my slippers and rushed about the place smashing the light bulbs with it" (312). "And you—you *let* him?" asks an incredulous Blanche. "Didn't run, didn't scream?" "I was—sort of—thrilled by it" (312), responds Stella. Experts today, of course, totally discount the notion that a battered woman invites or enjoys the violence that is inflicted upon her; and indeed, during the play itself we see that Stanley's violent actions do not "thrill" Stella at all, but instead cause her considerable emotional pain. She cries after Stanley hits her in Scene Three and again after he viciously clears the table in Scene Eight. It is more likely, therefore, that Stella's comments about the wedding night violence are simply part of her complicated process of denial.

In a landmark study entitled *The Battered Woman* (1979), Lenore E. Walker developed a cycle theory of domestic violence in order to explain why many women remain in abusive relationships. According to Walker, the battering cycle "appears to have three distinct phases, which vary in both time and intensity" (55). These are: 1) the tension-building phase; 2) the acute battering incident; and 3) the period of loving contrition. The first phase may include verbal attacks or minor episodes of violence, while the second phase involves more serious battering—"the uncontrollable discharge of the tensions that have built up" (59). The third phase is characterized by loving, contrite behavior on the part of the batterer. Realizing he has gone too far, he becomes kind, attentive—even remorseful. Suddenly he is pampering his wife, giving her presents and pleasurable sex. The woman wants to believe that the batterer is truly sorry for his abusive behavior and that he will never harm her again. But during this third phase, claims Walker, "the battered woman's victimization becomes complete" (65); for the batterer's contrite behavior simply ensures that the woman will remain in the relationship and that the cycle of violence will begin anew.

If we apply Walker's theory to *A Streetcar Named Desire*, we can clearly identify in the play the three specific phases of domestic violence. Phase One—the tension-building phase—begins shortly after the arrival of Blanche DuBois at the Kowalskis' apartment and includes intimidating remarks by Stanley ("Since when do you give me orders?" [275]; "You hens cut out that conversation in there!" [294]), as well as humiliation of his wife (the slapping of Stella on her thigh), and minor acts of violence (the abrupt unpacking of Blanche's trunk, the throwing of the radio out the window). Phase Two—the acute battering incident—occurs on the poker night when a drunken Stanley loses control and strikes his pregnant wife, forcing her to seek shelter with her neighbor. Phase Three—the loving contrition stage—takes place immediately afterwards when Stanley persuades Stella to return from Eunice's apartment and then carries her off to their bedroom. The following morning, in fact, we learn that Stanley was "as good as a lamb" and "very, very ashamed of himself" (312), and that he has given Stella not only a night of enjoyable sex, but ten dollars "to smooth things over" (318).

This cycle of violence is then repeated in the play, the second time with more dire consequences. In Scenes Seven and Eight, we again witness Phase One—the tension building phase—when Stanley and Stella argue over what should be done about Blanche, and Stanley seizes Stella's arm, then violently throws his dinnerware to the floor. "My place is cleared! You want me to clear your places? [Stella begins to cry weakly. Stanley stalks out on the porch and lights a cigarette]" (371). During Phase Two the acute battering incident occurs, yet this time the violence is not directed at Stella, who has gone to the hospital to have her baby, but at her surrogate, Blanche DuBois, whom Stanley rapes.

As domestic violence experts have noted, "there is a strong correlation between marital rape and battering" (Flowers, 13). The rape itself is a brutal act "most often committed out of anger or power, with the idea to humiliate, demean, or degrade the wife" (qtd. in Flowers, 13). In *A Streetcar Named Desire*, Blanche represents everything in Stella's past that Stanley despises. He wants to humiliate the "Hoity-toity" Blanche and bring her down to his level, but he also wants to humiliate and control Stella, separating his wife further from her genteel Southern heritage, pulling her further down off the columns of Belle Reve. As experts on domestic violence have noted, batterers sometimes "*[direct] violence toward other family members*" (italics added) in order to intimidate their spouses and control them (Flowers, 15). This is precisely what Stanley Kowalski has done near the conclusion of *A Streetcar Named Desire*. The rape allows him to destroy Blanche, who is subsequently sent to a mental asylum, but it also allows him to inflict tremendous *psychological abuse* on Stella, who cannot be certain what really happened that terrible night and who must live with her guilt about institutionalizing her sister. "I couldn't believe [Blanche's] story and go on living with Stanley" (405), Stella tells Eunice, again resorting to a strategy of denial. "What have I done to my sister? Oh, God, what have I done to my sister?" (416).

At the end of *A Streetcar Named Desire*, we witness once again Phase Three—the loving contrition stage of the battering cycle. After Blanche is led away to a mental institution, Stanley soothes Stella with affectionate words and sensual caresses: "Now, honey. Now, love. Now, now, love. [He kneels beside her and his fingers find the opening of her blouse] Now, now love. Now, love. . . ." (419). Just as he reconciled with Stella after the violence of the poker night, so does Stanley try to make peace with her at the conclusion of the play, once more employing sex as a way to pacify and dominate his wife.

It should be noted that the domestic violence found in the Kowalski home is not pictured as unique, but as part of a general atmosphere of marital conflict. The Kowalskis' neighbors, Steve and Eunice Hubbell, are shown to have a tempestuous marriage as well, echoing, on a minor scale, the violence found in the Kowalski household. During one altercation, Eunice throws something at Steve and he responds by striking her. She shrieks "You hit me! I'm gonna call the police!" (326). But later Steve leads Eunice back home from the Four Deuces, and Williams makes it clear that the couple has reconciled:

> Steve and Eunice come around corner. Steve's arm is around Eunice's shoulder and she is sobbing luxuriously and he is cooing love-words. There is a murmur of thunder as they go slowly upstairs in a tight embrace. (330)

The Hubbells' conflicts aren't taken seriously by the other characters in the play. Blanche and Stella "laugh lightly" (327) after Eunice threatens to summon the police, and Stanley agrees that it's "much more practical" for her to have a drink than to call in the authorities. Williams's characters thus reflect the prevailing attitude toward spousal abuse in the 1940s—i.e., the notion that domestic violence is not a crime, but merely a family matter that should be handled within the privacy of the home.

Previous critics of *A Streetcar Named Desire*, like the characters in the play, have tended to make light of the domestic violence. Most have viewed the Hubbells as comic foils to the Kowalskis, claiming, like Roger Boxill, that the "row between the upstairs neighbors . . . suggests that the Kowalskis' quarrel need not be taken so seriously" (qtd. in Kolin, 108). Many critics have pronounced the Kowalskis' union a successful one, a happy marriage that is interrupted—and threatened—by the intrusion of Blanche DuBois. Alan Ehrlich, for instance, argues that "in *A Streetcar Named Desire*, the established environment is simply a happy marriage—the couple lives in 'Elysian Fields'" (128). John Roderick claims that Stanley and Stella have a "sexually healthy," successful marriage which is able to withstand conflict because, as Mitch tells Blanche, "There's nothing to be scared of. They're crazy about each other" (Roderick, 116).

Even the most contemporary criticism of *Streetcar* tends to promote the notion that the Kowalskis' marriage is a happy one. In his 1993 essay "Birth and Death in *A Streetcar Named Desire*," Bert Cardullo maintains that "before Blanche's arrival, [Stanley] and Stella enjoyed . . . an intimate, happy marriage, and in this could be said to have achieved a degree of civilization, of humanity, unequaled by the DuBoises of Belle Reve" (168). Mark Royden Winchell, in "The Myth is the Message, or Why *Streetcar* Keeps Running" (1993), likewise argues that "As politically incorrect as it may be, the Kowalski household embodies a patriarchal vision of home as Heaven. There is not enough potential conflict here for either tragedy or farce. Not until Blanche enters the scene" (136).

If we are familiar with current theories on domestic violence, however, we must look at the Kowalskis' marriage in a much less sanguine light. We must recognize Stanley Kowalski for the batterer that he is—a man who is controlling, jealous, and violently aggressive. We must identify Stella as his submissive, accepting wife—the woman who, to echo Edwina Williams's phrase, just "stands by and takes it." Most of all, we must recognize that during the 1940s there was no real help for women like Stella Kowalski. There were no hotlines, no shelters for battered women, no social programs for these victims and their abusers. To borrow the words of director Elia Kazan, "Stella is doomed. . . . She has sold herself out for a temporary solution. She's given up all hope, everything, just to live for Stanley's pleasures" (373). Surely, for her this is not "home as Heaven." Indeed, in all probability Stella's situation will worsen, especially with the added strain of a new baby in the family. Stanley's violence against her will continue—and escalate— and there will be no way out for her. Trapped in a cycle of domestic abuse, Stella Kowalski will be alone and at risk, unable to leave the husband who abuses her, unable to count on social remedies—unable to depend, perhaps, even on "the kindness of strangers."

NOTES

1. To date, no articles have been published on *A Streetcar Named Desire* which focus on the issue of domestic violence. Herbert Blau, in his essay "Readymade Desire," mentions that Stella and Eunice "appeared on the scene before the battered woman syndrome gained public attention" (24), but he doesn't pursue the subject. Sandra M. Gilbert and Susan Gubar, in *No Man's Land*, claim that *A Streetcar Named Desire* "dramatizes the dynamics of the battering of women" (50), but they don't explore the topic in detail, arguing instead that the play is an indictment of heterosexual desire. Even Anca Vlasopolos, in her provocative feminist essay "Authorizing History: Victimization in *A Streetcar Named Desire*," focuses on the victimization of Blanche, not of Stella.

2. For a discussion of the batterer's profile, see, for example, Flowers, pp. 12–15 and Walker, p. 36.

3. Philip C. Kolin, in "Eunice Hubbell and the Feminist Thematics of *A Streetcar Named Desire*," refers to Eunice's apartment as "a safe house from Stanley's terrorism" (115). But Stanley, of course, knows exactly where to find his wife and how to compel her to return to him. In reality, there are no "safe houses" for Stella.

4. According to Kathleen Hofeller, spousal abuse is frequently linked with alcohol consumption:

> . . . but most experts agree that alcohol itself does not actually cause the violence. Instead, being drunk is used as an excuse. Since society allows a person to disavow his behavior while drinking, a man can claim that he simply didn't know what he was doing, and that he shouldn't be responsible for what happened. His wife may tell herself that he really is a good man, and that alcohol, not her husband, is the problem. Unfortunately, even if a man does stop drinking, it does not necessarily mean that the violence will end (91–92).

WORKS CITED

Berry, Dawn B. *Domestic Violence Sourcebook*. Los Angeles: Lowell House, 1995.

Blau, Herbert. "Readymade Desire." Kolin, *Confronting Tennessee Williams's Streetcar*, 19–25.

Cardullo, Bert. "Birth and Death in *A Streetcar Named Desire*." Kolin, *Confronting Tennessee Williams's Streetcar*, 167–180.

Ehrlich, Alan. "A Streetcar Named Desire Under the Elms: A Study of Dramatic Space in *A Streetcar Named Desire* and *Desire Under the Elms*." *Tennessee Williams: A Tribute*. Ed. Jac Tharpe. Jackson: University Press of Mississippi, 1977. 126–136.

Flowers, R. Barri. "The Problem of Domestic Violence is Widespread." *Domestic Violence*. Ed. Karin L. Swisher. San Diego: Greenhaven Press, Inc., 1996. 10–21.

Gilbert, Sandra M., and Susan Gubar. *The War of the Words*. New Haven: Yale University Press, 1988. Vol. 1 of *No Man's Land: The Place of the Woman Writer in the Twentieth Century*. 2 Vols.

Hofeller, Kathleen. *Battered Women, Shattered Lives*. Saratoga, CA: R & E Publishers, 1983.

Kazan, Elia. "Notebook for *A Streetcar Named Desire*." *Directors on Directing*. Ed. Toby Cole and Helen Krich Chinoy. Indianapolis: Bobbs-Merrill, 1963. 364–379.

Kolin, Philip C., ed. *Confronting Tennessee Williams's A Streetcar Named Desire: Essays in Critical Pluralism.* Westport, CT: Greenwood Press, 1993.

———. "Eunice Hubbell and the Feminist Thematics of *A Streetcar Named Desire.*" Kolin, *Confronting Tennessee Williams's Streetcar,* 105–120.

Leverich, Lyle. *Tom: The Unknown Tennessee Williams.* New York: Crown Publishers, 1995.

Pleck, Elizabeth. *Domestic Tyranny: The Making of American Social Policy Against Family Violence from Colonial Times to the Present.* New York: Oxford, 1987.

Roderick. John M. "From 'Tarantula Arms' to 'Della Robbia Blue': The Tennessee Williams Tragicomic Transit Authority." *Tennessee Williams: A Tribute.* Ed. Jac Tharpe. Jackson: University Press of Mississippi, 1977. 116–125.

Spoto, Donald. *The Kindness of Strangers: The Life of Tennessee Williams.* Boston: Little, Brown, 1985.

Swisher, Karin L. Introduction. *Domestic Violence.* San Diego: Greenhaven Press, 1996. 7–9.

Vlasopolos, Anca. "Authorizing History: Victimization in *A Streetcar Named Desire.*" *Theatre Journal,* 38 (1986): 322–338.

Walker, Lenore E. *The Battered Woman.* New York: Harper and Row, 1979.

Williams, Tennessee. "A Streetcar Named Desire." *The Theatre of Tennessee Williams.* Vol. 1. New York: New Directions, 1971. 7 vols. 1971–1981.

Winchell, Mark Royden. "The Myth Is the Message, or Why *Streetcar* Keeps Running." Kolin, *Confronting Tennessee Williams's Streetcar,* 133–145.

GEORGE TOLES

Blanche DuBois and
the Kindness of Endings

In any case it may be time to stop apologizing for "humanism," even
though it connotes a desire for a realm, and a proneness to the kind of
error without which a certain species of human could not live.
—Frank Kermode, "Endings, Continued"

Every fictional plot contains hints and traces of the stories it has excluded
or resisted in order to assume its present shape. As Elizabeth Bowen noted
in discussing the writer's craft, it is imperative that "alternatives to the plot"
be felt up to the last moment—"it is indeed in this that suspense consists."
The alternatives to the plot constitute, among other things, the potential
for disorder in the story's unfolding. The pressure for events to turn out
differently lies behind every unfortunate reversal, every new challenge to a
stable outcome. Whatever interferes with the characters' completing their
business in the way that the storyteller foresees belongs equally to the real
plot and one or more possible opposing plots. Readers naturally count on
such lines of resistance to keep the narrative unsettled, permeated with the
threat of further conflict until a final point of balance is reached. One of the
most formidable tasks in plot construction is surely the finding of a resolution that seems less arbitrary and provisional than the invariably misleading
moments of stasis within the body of the story. If the reader, viewer, or
listener comes to regard balance and stability as untrustworthy—as clear

From *Raritan* 14, no. 4 (Spring 1995): 115–143. © 1995 by Rutgers University.

indications that new narrative tensions are being generated to undo them—how is it that the equilibrium posited in an ending achieves a recognizably different status? What, beyond enervated convention, do endings draw upon to persuade us that the tensions belonging to any difficult story have been sufficiently answered for?

How gratifying—and in some sense, how improbable—it is that so many demanding narratives manage to find adequate closure, causing us willingly to halt at the place where the stories terminate and, from that privileged vantage point, to try to see the final sense of things. Somehow we are persuaded that the vanquished alternative plots, which have been the source of so much frustration, curiosity, or distress during our reading (in the case of theater and movies, our viewing) of the narrative, have lost their power to effect further meaningful changes. They are held in check by the ending's capacity to seal everything in. Endings confer a kind of liberty that life stubbornly denies us: to come to a full stop that is not death and discover exactly where we are in relation to the events leading up to a conclusion (a conclusion free of time). In what William Gass has termed the "kindly imprisonment" of the literary, endings offer the implicit assurance that only those elements circumscribed and rendered significant by the shape of the story need concern us. Here, the ending tells us, is the last segment of a hypothetical total experience that "tells." And because it is the last, we are tempted to seek out in it the story's moment of highest elevation and authority. Whatever fails to connect with the story's closing pattern of illumination, we typically assume, can be safely left out of account. The frame that the ending imposes on the story's action and language secures everything within its borders for a necessarily limited range of intentions.

With traditional mimetic narratives, we judge the strength of an ending by the kind of clarity it brings to the events of the plot, without undue coercion. If an ending seems to be straining to align the conflicting forces of the narrative, it is commonly felt that there are defects in the narrative structure, arising perhaps from the storyteller's lack of control or a confusion about what the story is capable of expressing. Inferences of this sort suggest our underlying confidence—in the face of postmodernist and poststructuralist skepticism about unity and coherence—in the logic of the storytelling process: the process whereby a series of imagined experiences can unite and illuminate each other, finally forming an integrated whole. Do we not perhaps believe, in spite of ourselves, that even unfinished stories (say, Charles Dickens's *The Mystery of Edwin Drood*) inherently possess a "true plot," which can be discovered in tantalizing outline behind the flawed, incomplete versions that artists frequently leave behind? Moreover, why do many of us spend so much time rethinking the plots of plays, movies, novels whose endings bewilder or fail to satisfy us—trying, for example, to isolate the places where a plot betrayed its inner logic, and proposing alternate schemes and images of order that honor the story's "real" proclivities?

It is in the nature of endings to effect a transformation of circumstances or character understanding: an ending is, of necessity, a moment of poise in which some situational factor, however ambiguously, makes a turn and fulfills itself, if only by being locked in place. (Even a concluding violent gesture attains poise, a Grecian urn stillness and arrestedness when nothing follows from it.) An ironic narrative structure, of course, might gradually reveal why various anticipated changes will never occur, so that its ending merely folds back on its beginning and reproduces its circumstances (as in Chekhov's "The Darling"). But such an outcome is transforming in its decisive insistence that a certain pattern can only repeat itself. What has changed is our understanding of why further development, under this set of conditions or with a character of this sort, is not possible.

"Stories begin," Geoffrey Harpham proposes in his valuable study, *On the Grotesque*, "with something that means too much." The unencompassably diverse preliminary trails of the narrative cannot yet be converted into a reliable significance. Events and their agents seem potentially freer of an informing purpose and direction than they will as the narrative proceeds. Because we do not know at the beginning of any but the most formulaic stories where or how to concentrate our gaze, we tend to look everywhere at once, giving roughly equivalent weight to a large number of impressions. In the midst of such pleasurable confusion, one readily imagines the story's endpoint as a point of magical convergence for the rapidly shifting preparatory views: a fixed position, as I noted earlier, from which to see how initially disparate things finally belong together. The back-and-forth, tension-inducing motions of narrative compel our interest, in part, because we await yet another demonstration of story's power to subdue chaos. The promised land we approach, by however circuitous a route, will reward us with a sense of things set within fitting limits (limits that fit).

Narratives that are unwilling or unable to plot a felicitous way out of themselves can scarcely avoid leaving the reader or spectator where she began—"with something that means too much." Instead of experiencing the resonant moment of binding together that an achieved form seems (inexplicably, sometimes almost mystically) to impart, one finds that the form is strangely at odds with the story's abounding desires, and can neither contain them nor "know" itself. A story's characters and incidents suddenly reveal themselves to be as dishearteningly prey to paralysis and indecipherability as their time-molested counterparts in life. The absence of an ending often seems to infect every prior development in a narrative's progression, as though the effort to build around this palpable hole proved as demanding (and deforming) as the human drive to repress death. Broken or insufficient form, in effect, does not know (in some cases, does not wish to know) what belongs to it. Like Aschenbach in *Death in Venice*, it confuses categories, is out of phase with its own needs, and denies until it is too late the nature and force of its actual intentions. Aschenbach, of course, seems doomed from the outset, and perhaps the betrayal of form can only be viewed as a similarly vast chain of contaminations (and misreadings), winding all the way back to the beginning, and gesturing toward a still earlier moment of "blinding."

Ideally, endings clear a space for us where vital questions assume such inviting shapes that we feel drawn to reflect on them. It seems in the presence of certain scenes (and, of course, not only final ones) that only this configuration of elements enables us to face particular problems of existence in a manner that will lead us somewhere. But how do we proceed? The contemplative space generated by an ending's "momentary stay of confusion" positions us both near and far away from the story's reality at once. As we approach some sort of desired understanding under the imperious sway of narrative law, the adamancy of form declares the expendability of our own witnessing. This double awareness is the inescapable burden of taking fiction to heart. Endings make room for us while being chasteningly fickle, and dismissive of our presence. "This is where the universe distills, if anywhere," they seem to say, "but, of course, you cannot stay here. You are too encumbered with things that don't concern us." We attain our experience of balance in endings because form appears tantalizingly close to transmuting the full burden of our living into something spare and light, psychically containable, like a tiny, quivering bird cupped within the suddenly ample space between our hands. But the idea of ourselves that a compelling narrative form manifests and seductively encloses cannot survive for long apart from a story's special atmosphere (where there is so much purposeful activity, economy of attention, and such concentrated effort to make a maximum of sense inside fixed limits). Characters, unlike us, act within a time that is already complete, where everything worth saving has been preserved—"washed free," as Henry James puts it in his preface to *The Spoils of Poynton*, "of awkward accretion" and aimless succession. The weight of our concerns cannot touch the characters, finally, in their impervious ceremonies, their "sacred hardness." Their intensely legible fates, however embroiled in chaos and terror, are at least safe from anything we can do, except misunderstand them. (Perhaps that is injury enough.)

Stories that deny closure seem to stain art with life's fearful excess (or equally fearful lack) of meaning. Whatever unresolved stories fail to bring forth at the level of form, there can be little doubt that they reflect a truth about confusion—that it is in the nature of things to stay confused—that well-ordered narratives cannot "know" in the same way. Fictions that inspire no belief in endings often mirror our encumberedness too faithfully, and with too much show of effort. The punishment and glory of achieved form is to banish us at last, like Adam and Eve, from a garden of narrative harmonies, where our relations to things (and the words that name them) somehow have attained greater clarity and purity of definition. No such banishment is felt in a story whose completed design does not hold us, arrest us, bring us to a stop. We remain, in Frank Kermode's formulation, with our desire for a realm apart unanswered. Instead, with Derrida's bracing negative freedom, we can move backward or forward in the wilderness of discourse, declare endings beginnings, and formlessness the only true form. Yet in a narrative site where all paths are reversible, and where flowers and weeds no longer argue their differences, can there be gain or loss, in the ways that gain or loss count in story?

An ending is minimally an act of leave-taking, a conscious going out from a space that "encloses," then releases us. What ceremony has been prepared to mark our departure? What last provisions has fiction dispassionately left for us to gather and carry out into the night? And as we look back, what shape already fading in the distance do we commit to memory? Endings, in addition to saying "yes" or "no" to our primitive "once upon a time" wishes, invoke a framework of permanence whose measure we take as the narrative closes its doors on us. Without such a place as endings grant us (no more real than godhead, and no less essential) we seem denied our best chance of "arriving," and remain sunk as deeply as ever in the mire of "flawed words" and ungracious circumstance.

* * *

[Blanche] who has never spoken an honest word in her life is allowed, indeed encouraged, to present her life to the audience as a vocational decision, an artist's election of the beautiful, an act of supreme courage, the thorny way.
—Mary McCarthy, "A Streetcar Called Success"

Arguably the best classroom for one interested in the construction, emotional dynamics, and audience reception of endings is the theater. The experience of directing a play, in particular, requires one to move, as far as one's imaginative sympathies can be stretched, inside an ending, to treat it quite literally as a living thing, and to test its reality moment by moment with one or more actors. Mounting a production of a dramatic text provides a swift, salutary release from the radical epistemological doubts that deconstructive theory, in its most grandiose moods, claims is the outcome of all sophisticated transactions with literary language. A director's primary obligation, surely, is to help actors clarify and coordinate the intentions of the words

and actions they must perform onstage, so that they can make choices which
will sustain a living connection with character from the actors' first to last
appearance.

Within the rehearsal process, one has the eerie sensation of moving, by
slow degrees, closer and closer to the reality which the play's language longs
to reveal. In a room containing some makeshift props, taped floor markings,
and nondescript chairs and tables, actors not uncommonly achieve a form of
acute clarity that is also, paradoxically, a partial trance, as they imaginatively
endow the specific space-time continuum of the play's world with felt life.
In the early stages of the rehearsal process, performers seem to be looking
at their lines as something they must see beyond in order to discover (or
uncover) their characters. They attempt to piece together as much relevant
social and psychological background information as possible from the hints
and suggestions contained in the dialogue and playwright's notes, in order to
construct a plausible character history. Gradually, however, they are drawn
back to the unavoidable requirements of the words they have been given to
speak. It becomes clear, if an actor connects with the conditions on which
her character's life depends, that the lines are not a barrier to be overcome
in order to find the meanings that she must communicate. The truths the
actor seeks to express seem, rather, to lie "out in the open," on the suddenly
charged surface of her speech. Theater's remarkable power to reclaim a usable
common speech (that is to say, speech that is both ordinary and held in
common) contends with one's hard-earned experience of language as unend-
ingly duplicitous and at too great a distance from what it names. "Knowing
one's lines," which begins as a mechanical effort to remember the order of
alien word sequences, eventually comes to signify more perilously intimate
acquisitions: knowing the words that belong to you; knowing their private
and public value; knowing the feeling that accompanies each word as it is
spoken; knowing the effect one's words will have on another person if their
meaning is taken in.

If a group of performers can learn to handle the individual words and
actions of a play with so much care and reciprocal awareness, it follows that
their potential illumination of the ending depends on a fuller engagement
with its manifold elements than is possible for a reader. The pressure of the
alternative plot(s), for example, is part of the force field that the actors create
and dwell in onstage. What one character gains for herself, however briefly,
through an act of assertion, is nearly always at the expense of an adversary,
fellow-striver, or a forgotten victim, whose losses are similarly an expression of life-energy, seeking an outlet. The simple act of rising from a chair
may be rendered exceptionally difficult, in a performed scene, by the psychological atmosphere generated inside a room. Finding the right purpose
for speaking a four-word line (or finding a character's strength to break a

silence) may be the solution to the problem of how to leave one's chair. But such problems, which arise everywhere in the staging of a play and provide the spectator's moment-to-moment sense of the resistance that actions and intentions continually face, are only dimly perceptible in the printed text. When one reads it is the large patterns of conflict which are likely to compel one's attention. During the rehearsal process, every scene's action is of necessity broken down into smaller and smaller emotional units. Getting from "here" to "there" (which may be no more than a distance of two lines and a single movement) requires a thorough investigation of all the forces (social, physical, psychological) arrayed onstage for that interval, in their multiple impingements on each character's desires.

I find it disheartening that so much recent commentary on closure programmatically insists that "strong" endings are reductive and reifying in their implied teleology and naive faith in a higher order. The metaphors that most readily convey how endings work (and I have already invoked many of them) suggest all sorts of worrisome connections to oppressive mindsets of earlier centuries, replete with patriarchal chain mail: "binding," "freezing," "locking in," "fixing," "sealing," "settling." Such terms misleadingly suggest that there comes a moment in a narrative's development when closure is achieved by simple fiat. One thinks of a stern factory owner suddenly and without warning announcing that he is shutting down operations, then proceeding to lock out his workers. His only explanation is a vague statement about "painful necessities" or "difficult choices." Or, in the case of happy endings, an estate owner "benevolently" determines what conditions are appropriate for the comfort and satisfaction of his family and servants, and imposes them as inalterable laws. In contrast, subversively "throwaway" endings, which expose the arbitrary, fraudulent means by which so-called stable meanings are generated, have, by similar analogy, associations with brave revolutionary acts of overthrow and repudiation. By granting narratives no authority to resolve their conflicts or to ground us in a field of momentarily lucid moral recognitions, a critic may well imagine that he is somehow putting himself at risk in a struggle with the faceless powers of institutions. And, of course, why shouldn't the authority of endings to privilege certain kinds of truth or insight not be interrogated? My chief concern is that the supposedly natural equation of endings with confinement and cultural stasis deprives us of the questions (indeed, the curiosity) to learn more about how endings actually make claims upon us, and about what sorts of significance they might successfully embody.

In place of "locking" and "fixing" metaphors to characterize an ending's appropriate tasks, perhaps we would do well to consider the force field image that I have drawn from theater. In a force field, even dominant narrative values and assertions are obliged to live in the midst of unsubdued opposition.

What a meaningful dramatic ending finally manages to "say" only makes sense in a context where the saying is hedged on all sides by resisting or partially comprehending presences, whose different stakes in the outcome are given their due. A clear resolution may well posit a moral/political alignment of forces which in this instance takes precedence over other possibilities, but the pressure exerted by everything the ending excludes in order for it to hold sway is what gives any memorable act of closure its tense, fluttering life. As Robert Harbison has observed about the turbulence somehow marshalled and held together in an El Greco canvas, "ways of seeing and feeling multiply more quickly than they can be suppressed." Closure's privileged act of vision is like the banquet in the Psalm, laid out before one's enemies. And the banquet becomes rich to the extent that many unlikely guests find their way in. Other realities are honored by being brought as close as their dispositions allow to the central table, rather than being driven out or forgotten. It may be true that in our avidly monstrous century, what a Mark Strand poem calls "the academy of revelations . . . gets smaller every year." We have come "to see ourselves as less and do not like shows of abundance, descriptions we cannot believe" (although the endings characteristic of television, movies, and popular fiction might suggest otherwise). "The idea of being large is inconceivable," Strand's poem rather largely asserts. And endings that might bring "whole rooms, whole continents to light, / like the sun," are "not for us." But within this diminished realm of no-longer-sovereign ends, the small thing, as in a lyric poem, still contrives ways to become large in the beholding, and the imagination seeks and secures its continents of light in the cracks of perishable circumstance.

I would like to look closely now at both the obviously significant and the more easily passed over details (physical and verbal) that form part of an especially well-known ending in American drama: scene 11 of Tennessee Williams's *A Streetcar Named Desire*. My principal rationale for selecting this play to test out some of my notions of how endings work is my experience directing two productions of it over a twelve-year period. My reader's knowledge of the ending will be supplemented at every point by my recollected efforts to make a living reality of it in another medium. I am also counting on readers who have their own reasonably well-established sense of the play's ending (and the larger context in which it operates) to set against mine. My aim is not to oppose traditional readings of Blanche's significance as the play's "difficult" protagonist, but to show more fully than has been previously attempted how Williams's ending, through a complex series of perceptual/emotional revisions, constructs our final sense of her. The scenic elements I have chosen for analysis will establish the force field within which the ending must struggle to impose its shape, clarity, and modes of inwardness. I would also like to demonstrate how the bits of dramatic narration which seem to dwell on the periphery of the scene's dominant concerns crucially affect our ability to grasp what the conclusion gathers together.

Scene 11 begins by restoring a setting that has become intolerably private—through Stanley's rape of Blanche—to its prior status as a public space, one that flexibly accommodates a range of ordinary activities and divergent attitudes. What this place continues to make room for (card games, the packing of a trunk, demands of a newborn infant, the habitual visit from Eunice, the upstairs neighbor) quickly turns the rape we have just witnessed into something buried. The familiar social/domestic picture has been drawn like a curtain over an event that might have had the power to wrench it apart. The shocking image of violation still quivers in the air, but because no one onstage is prepared to accept that a rape transpired here or consider the difference it has made, it is somehow undermined. Visually we have returned to the scene of a crime, but it is as though the crime has not survived the cleaning of the rooms and the moving of the furniture back to comfortable old positions. Blanche, whose own memory is torn and scattered, a psychic ruin, must try to locate herself in an environment from which nearly all traces of her occupancy have been eliminated. For her sister Stella as well as her sister's husband, the return to marital contentment takes precedence over everything related to Blanche. Their home, notwithstanding the large adjustments to an infant son, seems to aspire to something like its original lax and easygoing character, with both Stanley and Stella reclaiming its earlier routines almost self-consciously, as a way of healing even the smallest pieces of their lives of Blanche's long, infecting visit.

The stage picture which confronts us as the scene opens does not strongly invoke the fact of Blanche's imminent departure. And the first lines that are spoken, by the men at the poker game, certainly make no concessions to it. Stella's silent packing of Blanche's things occurs on the opposite side of the stage from the ongoing card playing, a seemingly minor event on the periphery of the main action. What the poker game casually asserts is that, for all intents and purposes, Blanche has already gone away. The men do not need to wait for her physical removal from their midst to have their regular time together playing poker. Instead of treating Blanche's forceful seizure by the representatives of a state mental hospital as a private family tragedy (to be concealed from general scrutiny), Stanley has decided, with the tacit consent of all the play's characters, to make it a public occasion. It is arguably neither vindictiveness nor guilt which prompted this choice of "endings" for his defeated adversary. Stanley's poker game is not a place where any acknowledgment of Blanche's condition or fate is looked for. The game is conceived as a neutral space of business, where the winning and losing of hands is the sole matter at issue. When Mitch and Eunice briefly interrupt the rhythm of the game with, respectively, a small outburst of feeling and an allusion to callousness, Stanley—with more bewilderment than defensiveness—wants to know "what's the matter."

Stanley has no further need to think about Blanche. She has been exposed and dealt with in the manner that "women of her sort" must be. Nothing could persuade him that his sexual victory over her was a rape, or something that she had any will (or right) to oppose. Her continual flirtation and baiting, her hypocrisy, her long history of promiscuity (including sexual involvement with her students), her repeated attempts to turn his wife against him, and her conscienceless efforts to deceive Mitch about her past so that he would be caught in a marriage with her—all, in his mind, justly condemn her to the punishment she now suffers. Blanche has no grounds for appeal in the social theater Stanley presides over; there is no positive category left for her to occupy. Mitch and Eunice's short-lived protest against Stanley's lack of concern (the sheer force of his indifference) is weakly reflexive rather than reasoned. Eunice would like others to join her in conventional, though not unfelt, expressions of sympathy for Blanche, but as she soon advises Stella, nothing is gained by taking Blanche's side or believing her crazed accusations of rape. "Life has to go on," she insists, implying that one's life will only progress satisfactorily if one takes things at face value, protects one's own position, and avoids difficult questions. Mitch, whose violent repudiation of Blanche on the night of her rape was a strong secondary cause of her mental breakdown, cumbersomely and self-pityingly seeks exoneration. To the extent that he can blame Stanley for Blanche's present torment and show himself sensitive by comparison, he can perhaps recover his preferred sense of his own nature: decent and honorable, temperate, tenderhearted in his dealings with others.

It would be wrong to suggest, however, that this is Mitch's conscious strategy, or a sufficient explanation of his helplessness and confused remorse. Mitch appears utterly lost in this gathering. Since he has by no means gained control of his feelings for Blanche, or come to terms with the destruction of their relationship, he is "sleepwalking" through the game that he has senselessly agreed to join, and the ordeal which will follow it. Mitch irrationally hopes that others will be able to define his role for him here, as they have so often managed to on less onerous occasions. In this he resembles Stella, who can barely look at her sister or form thoughts about her agreement to have her committed. She longs to stand behind someone else's greater strength, whether it be Eunice's or Stanley's, and to withdraw her share in the decision-making. She desperately wants Blanche to be gone, but won't allow herself to own this feeling, nor any of the resentment that Blanche's attacks on her husband and prolonged demands on her have fomented. In one sense, Blanche's apparent insanity is almost a relief to her. It gives her permission to surrender her sister to the proper authorities and have them treat a problem that is now clinical rather than familial or personal. Blanche's disappearance into madness means that her wearisomely complicated attitudes no longer count as a real position. A thoroughly broken Blanche ceases to confront Stella with her passionately articulate skepticism about the life Stella has settled for.

The main line of dramatic tension in the scene (which the entrance of the doctor and matron powerfully focuses) has to do with Blanche's manner of leaving her sister's home. In order to make her way out, she must pass through the room in which Stanley, Mitch, and the other poker players are gathered. If she must be seen by these men, is there a way for her to withstand their scrutiny without being further abased and humiliated? Williams creates a situation in which it seems, not only to Blanche but to the spectator, that everything depends on her surviving her walk through Stanley's half of the two-room apartment. What it is possible for her to achieve (or express) under these final circumstances is severely restricted. She cannot escape the status of victim, on many fronts, nor avert the plans which have led to her committal. Blanche is prey to multiple delusions and incapacitated by dread and uncertainty about what is being done to her. In contrast to Stanley, who exudes confident authority as he continues to win at cards ("Luck is believing you're lucky"), Blanche, from the moment of her last timid entrance, seems already to have yielded to some great emptiness. She has been stripped of nearly all the makeshift resources that she has formerly used to maintain her life in this alien realm. The strength that remains to her is employed in selecting articles of clothing to wear and demanding explanations of "what's happening" from Stella and Eunice that neither will give. They instead attempt to soothe her with "hushes" as her voice briefly rises beyond the limit of permissible female noise in the face of the men's concentration on their game. Eunice is urged by Stella to compliment Blanche on her appearance as a means of pacifying her and alleviating her suspicions until the doctor and hospital matron arrive.

There is nowhere Blanche can turn for answers. Because she has been judged mad, it appears sound policy to insulate her from all meaningful social discourse. Conversation with her is mediated by the understanding that she is not capable of being spoken to as an equal. Any communication of substance must be hidden from her. The language that is heard by others when she speaks is regarded as rambling, and is held in bounds by Stella and Eunice's practiced forbearance. Since she has shown a willingness to believe that Shep Huntleigh, a creature of fantasy, may be coming to rescue her, whatever else she asserts is taken as a similarly dismissable misreading of her situation. None of the characters who have known Blanche, however much they wish to spare her further shame and injury, is able to be her advocate in this closing scene. And she gives every appearance, initially, of being too exposed, terrorized, and disconnected to represent herself as anything but a lost soul. Blanche's single extended speech in the scene is a fantasy of swallowing death in the form of an unwashed grape. This fatal bit of uncleanness can't be expelled; she carries the taste of its darkness in her mouth as she sails upon an ocean where everything else is bathed in light. Finally, a double absolution; the accidental stain is covered over by an immaculate white sack into which her body is sewn before being cast into an equally pure sea. Barring such a deliverance, Blanche is unable to bear witness to any of the positive values that she has claimed allegiance to at earlier stages of the play. She cannot find words or gestures that can be separated from the uncleanness inside her, or from the more insidious pestilence outside, that no one but she, for whatever reason, will acknowledge.

The problem for Williams's ending to resolve then is this. How is the meaning of Blanche DuBois's defeat to emerge for the spectator as something distinct from the pathos of her final infirmity? Does the ending require us to see Blanche as significantly more than a hyperbolized, almost abstract Victim, whose private mind (or serf-hood, if you will) no longer matters? It is astonishing how many readers of *Streetcar* (including some of my colleagues and many students male and female) continue to see Blanche's rape as an action she has invited or inwardly consented to or, even more dismissively, as an example of her creator's homosexual wish-fulfillment, which hardly addresses women's experience at all. In each of these readings, what is rejected is the play's power to edify us, on a plane beyond that of demystified, culturally constructed values. My contention is that the ending takes a number of competing values into simultaneous account and then, in the manner of plotting Blanche's exit, gives her unexpected authority where she previously had none. Out of this momentary enlargement, Williams creates a final effect that is densely intermingled and cathartic.

The palpable weakness of Blanche's mental and physical state as she is led out of the play makes her character difficult to assess, in Charles Altieri's words, as "a model of the capacities for action one gains by an alternative stance." Stanley's method of reading Blanche would have much in common with the ideological formula that makes success in actualizing power on the social battlefield the least artificial measure of a character's real value. What positive transformation does a character undergo in the course of a narrative, and is she more capable as a result of it to effect, at least potentially, significant change in others? In Stanley's view, imagination and spirit (in their very weightlessness) count as nothing in themselves; they prove their value in relation to practical action. If no real world link is demonstrated, Stanley would dismiss references to "refinement," "high ideals," and "sensitivity" as masks or screens by which a once privileged class tries, desperately and emptily, to reassert its "natural" superiority. Stanley builds a consensus in the world of the play around his own notion of what Blanche's ethereal, idealizing nature represents, and no one on stage, including Blanche, is able to show concretely what Stanley's crude but plausible depiction of her leaves out. Altieri has written cogently about the difficulty of explaining the poetic imagination's alternatives to social and material constructs in precise, analytic ways. "We do not come to believe in these powers [generated through imaginative activity] because some argument is made on their behalf; rather, we are invited to participate in the states they make available. Our measure of power is simply the degree to which the resulting modes of self-reflection engage us in new dimensions of ourselves and the world." He suggests that the "wisest rhetorical strategy" for making ideals tangible forces for the reader or spectator is to "work with contrasts: while it may be impossible to persuade others directly of one's claims about values, it often happens that clarifying what one opposes, or what happens when the prevailing values are left in place, opens the way for the audience to try out the identifications necessary to support one's own position."

The ending of *Streetcar* attempts to recover Blanche's value through the total isolation of her voice from the somehow untenable community that requires her elimination. Williams deprives Blanche, however, of one crucial advantage that similarly scape-goated romantic outsiders in literature traditionally possess: a lingering awareness of what their rejected positions are truly worth. Blanche has largely internalized the language of her oppressors. She fears not only their persecution but also their authoritative judgment, as though they may have correctly divined that her entire means of revealing herself to others is fraudulent. When she flees back into the bedroom after seeing the doctor and matron for the first time, Stanley comes after her with the odd demand that she provide a "ladylike" excuse for her panic. He asks her if she's forgotten something, and she seizes upon this explanation of her behavior as though it would make her more creditable in the eyes of the assembled group. ("Yes! Yes, I forgot something.") As she continues to resist the efforts of the matron to lead her outside, Stanley intervenes again, proposing that what she has forgotten is the paper lantern she had used to cover the bare light bulb in her room. Otherwise, "you left nothing here." He brusquely tears the lantern off the bulb and Blanche "cries out as if the lantern were herself." It is not the light of available reality that Blanche, here or ever, declares her affinity with, but the worthless wrapping used to conceal it.

Stanley's casually violent gesture recalls the rape and, less malevolently, repeats the realist's inalterable lesson: those who live entirely in dreams will perish. He shows her, however harshly, the difference between alluring shadows and stubborn actualities. The torn lantern in Stanley's outstretched hand is his final, wordless verdict on what her "inventions," "obfuscations," and "magic" amount to. And Blanche, at this juncture, has

no conviction that the sharply exposed illusion (one last attempt to unde-
ceive the dreamer) can be conceived otherwise. She does not know how to
reassert the value of enchantment, or even to see it as a value worth restoring. In an earlier confrontation between Blanche and Stanley (immediately
preceding the rape) Blanche attempts to name certain qualities in herself
that might be worthy of respect.

> But beauty of the mind and richness of the spirit and tenderness
> of the heart—and I have all of those things—aren't taken away, but
> grow! Increase with the years! How strange that I should be called
> a destitute woman! When I have all of these treasures locked in
> my heart.

The painful irony of this effort at self-definition is that Blanche herself, yet again, barely recognizes what is exemplary, distinctive, or valid
about her spiritual possessions. Stanley, of course, believes that what she
refers to is part of her "act" as a refined and virtuous lady. He sees her posture of delicate softness as a strained, neurotic attempt to evade the force of
her own appetites, her capacity for aggression, and the meaning, for good
or ill, of her troubled history. She uses her tricks of language, in his view,
to establish false conditions for her acceptance as a woman continually in
quest of "ideals."

Blanche's sad eloquence about attainments for which there is no reliable
public measure or demonstrable proof is riven with doubt even before she is
challenged. One feels she cancels her declaration of private faith in the act
of uttering it, and immediately follows it with a pitiful, transparent lie about
Mitch's repentant return and pleas for forgiveness. It is a brave esthetic decision for Williams to have Blanche most unerring in her appraisal of her own
inner powers at precisely the moment she is least equipped to draw on them
or make them effectual. The skepticism that causes her to lose touch with
her treasures in the act of summoning them in her own defense is paradoxically the most persuasive sign that they genuinely belong to her. In the film
version of *Streetcar*, Williams gives Blanche an additional line in her last
meeting with Mitch that speaks directly to the problem of Blanche's understanding of imaginative truth. Replying to Mitch's charge that she has never
been "straight" with him, she says: "A line can be straight, or a road. But the
heart of a human being?" Every lived encounter is a test for those present to
find the mind and heart and soul of another fugitively flickering in faces,
words, and actions. It is never a case of seeing all, it is a case of seeing more,
and to that end one strives to loosen what is securely fixed in one's own manner of perceiving enough to catch glimpses of whatever is there, struggling
to be made clear.

Blanche is as careless and damaging in her words and judgments as the other characters in the play, but she is still, for Williams, the imagination's chosen emissary and prophet. From the outset, she inhabits a language so resilient and expressive that it transfigures her demeaning situation into something estimable, something allied to beauty. As the play progresses, her imagination moves, by slow degrees, further outward (chiefly in her relationship with Mitch), making itself increasingly vulnerable to the force of another's loneliness and his starved, blundering quest for love. Blanche also reopens herself to the terrors of her own past and begins to shed what is false in her gentility (the part that Stanley calls "airs"), which has made so much of her conduct deviously self-serving. She embodies the creative imagination in both its blind and clairvoyant states. At times it seems to disconnect her from everything, hiding her from the light, as it were, and aspiring to a realm that seems stiflingly enclosed and remote. Equally often, however, it furnishes a flame to see things by that is stronger, more searching than the natural light claimed by others. Williams conceives the imagination's approach to higher knowledge as painfully intermittent. Like a figure in Christian allegory, imagination threatens to be destroyed by the illusions that encircle it the closer it gets to truth. And often what it most deeply intuits proves least communicable.

The final scene presents the imagination, as Blanche embodies it, with its most severe trial, since the world of the play seems at all points closed off to further influence by her. The pressure of the alternative plot, which one might call Stanley's plot, to control and designate the play's meanings does not fully abate at any stage of the scene's action. The trajectory of this plot, which draws its vitality from Stanley's unbroken assertions of his position and from the levelling force of his disbelief in Blanche, carries us to the following implied end: "lugubrious cant will not change man's nature or the necessities that arise from it." The poker players might be said to sit gathered, however dimly or uncomfortably, around the table of this understanding. When Blanche faces them as a group for the last time, she does not seek any further acknowledgment from them. She says, rather: "Please don't get up. I'm only passing through." This statement is a plea that her presence be the occasion for nothing more from them. If it were possible, she would pass through altogether invisible. She means what she says when she urges them not to notice her. Their residual awareness could only partake of the glare of exposure. Her phrasing also suggests her sense of how negligible (and effaceable) her passage through their realm has been: "I will soon be gone without a trace."

When Stanley asks Blanche if she's forgotten something and then requires her to identify and claim it if she is to remain even a few moments longer in his house, we are invited to consider whether there is any space on stage that might still reflect her, or disclose some forgotten sign of her being.

What Stanley finds to give her, as we have seen, is the paper lantern, whose original purpose had been to create an alternative atmosphere of beauty, but which cannot convey anything about beauty when that atmosphere is lacking. It is an object which traces beauty's flight ("an instant in the wind") back to darkness. Stanley's offer to return the lantern to her precipitates the ending's single episode of violence, when the extremity of Blanche's suffering becomes fully visible. The hospital matron forcibly prevents Blanche's escape, pinning her to the floor as she writhes in terror and wails like a stricken animal. It is a moment of tragic prostration that is strangely not accompanied by an increase of vision. One sees enough to set one's consciousness on fire, but still one does not know.

It is here that Williams positions the appearance of the doctor as a character, that is to say, as something other than a nameless functionary of the state hospital. His task, in its official outline, is to remove Blanche as expeditiously as possible from the Kowalski household. If her treatment elsewhere will be harsh and unsparing, the doctor must attempt (for her family's sake and the sake of appearances) to screen the more shocking forms of hospital procedure from view. Williams's doctor emerges as someone larger and more humane than the strict requirements of his office demand, but at no point does his response to Blanche part company with his professional objective: how to lead her out. Nevertheless, because of what she sees in him at the moment when he removes his hat and looks at her, she will recover enough self-awareness to walk with dignified composure away from the site of suffering. What is it precisely that she takes hold of in this brief, crucially significant exchange, and how does it open out for the spectator as an event with more than ironic weight (i.e., Blanche's misconstruing of her executioner's intentions)?

The doctor's decision to remove his hat and thus place himself open to view is a gesture which both echoes and makes restitution for Stanley's tearing the lantern from the light bulb. Instead of exposing Blanche and further shaming her, his action serves to expose his own person to her in a way that validates her capacity to judge it. He grants her the tiny freedom to trust the face he shows her or reject it, and makes it seem as though her choice of how to regard him matters. All of the great plays that I know of ultimately center, as this one does, on one or more exalted moments of seeing and being seen. This shared emphasis suggests to me that what the mystery drama may be best equipped to illuminate is the mystery of seeing others momentarily in their wholeness, without impediment or distortion. For the most part, we are not at all clear about where we are in relation to what we see; we are in a false position. We are not present to ourselves, given all that we need to shield from a too trying consciousness, and find it next to impossible to be fully present to others.

Laying claim to the reality we occupy (in either a fretful or tranquil daze) means redeeming the absent present, becoming fully awake to what lies directly in front of us and knowing how deeply and transiently we are bound to it. One recalls Emily's memorable cry to her "restored" mother in *Our Town*, following Emily's return from the dead to relive her twelfth birthday: "Oh, Mama, just look at me one minute as though you really saw me . . . just for a moment now we're all together. Mama, just for a moment we're happy. Let's look at one another." A true occasion for seeing in drama is frequently discovered in conditions that seem very far away from it: in death, in madness, in memory loss, in separation, in a fit of rage. It is as though we come closest to recognizing others (in both their separateness and their potential to meet us where we openly need) in our struggles to overcome absence. Let us say that I am in such terrible straits that nothing, literally nothing, seems to be there for me; how do I find my way back to connectedness, to visibility? Sometimes another person can arrest my sense of absence from life by remembering that I exist, and making that memory tangible through their quality of attentiveness. I come to believe once more (through another's belief) that I am situated, openly, within my life, that I belong to a world that actually contains me. I am sustained by finding myself at home in another's gaze. And once revealed in this other being's sight, where there is room for me to remember myself, I can turn back to my separateness and not be annihilated by it.

Blanche has not been visible, in this sense, since Mitch declared his love for her. Just prior to this avowal, she has revealed to Mitch how she drove her young husband to suicide by her refusal to see him as a homosexual ("I saw! I know! You disgust me. . . ."). She speaks of the light in her world having been turned off: "and never for one moment since has there been any light that's stronger than this—kitchen—candle." Mitch slowly moves forward and joins her in this light, humbly acknowledging that he is mindful of her suffering, values the person revealed in it, and offers to meet her on the ground of common need, where they are equals. Blanche accepts his pledge of love and achieves a moment of transcendence; she sees God (in the only form that makes sense to her) reflected in another human face. There is no sequel to this act of clear beholding, however, until the end of the play. Blanche is exiled from the island of light as soon as she enters into it. It is as though she is consumed by the completeness of her self-surrender. Everyone who looks at Blanche in the play's third act either tries to avoid seeing her (so they will not have to know her as something less than they would have her be) or stares at her (as one rendered transparent in her defilement, who has forfeited the right to any look that does not objectify). Mitch, for example, comes to believe that she owes him something, sex at the very least, for the mistake he made in loving her.

Blanche beholds a possibility for rescue, at some level, in the doctor's granting her the right to scrutinize him freely, and in his willingness to meet her gaze and return it. To test him further, she pleads with him faintly to take her side against the matron, still no doubt counting on betrayal as the likely outcome of his (or anyone's) finding her, this time in the hiding place of madness. ("Ask her to let go of me.") The doctor cannot easily avoid raising false expectations in his response to this request. Blanche is reminding him that he is here as someone with authority, and that it lies within his power to lessen the terror of her external situation—indeed, to actively befriend her. Falsity would enter their just-formed relationship from the moment that he encourages her to believe that she has nothing further to fear from him. His spontaneous, humane gesture of acknowledgment becomes calculated and self-serving as soon as it implies the security of a future tense. The doctor's taking notice of her soul (while allowing her to search out his) is an unexpected mercy, but in its poignant discreteness and unrepeatability does not constitute safe ground.

Is there a way for the doctor to comply with Blanche's request to stop the matron from hurting her without misrepresenting his alliance with this enemy? The matron and he, after all, are together in their efforts to remove her from the scene. If Blanche interprets the loosening of the matron's grip as evidence of the doctor's granting her a measure of real freedom, can he honorably refrain from showing her (letting her know) how things really stand? She is, in fact, still signed over to him, and must submit to his control, one way or another. If she were to attempt another escape, he would no doubt allow the matron to do what she must to restrain her. As he offers Blanche his arm, then, and "draws her up gently" to her feet—is he soliciting her faith in a cunning fiction ("I am a gentleman whose time and intentions await your bidding") or surrendering himself innocently to her need, in mysterious obedience to the vision of her that has, however briefly, possessed him? Does the spectator, in consequence, perceive the doctor as a masked adversary, at one with the asylum whose orders he faithfully executes, or as someone beneficently blinded to the irony of the protector role he rises to? Protection is all that Blanche knows how to ask for, in this world that has gradually reduced itself to pure threat. Perhaps the doctor cannot help but answer her plea—mute, fathomless, unevadable—because it is the only way he can stand apart from the agony that presses in on her from every side. To become the person she is looking for ("the gentleman I was expecting") may, in fact, be the simplest course of action for him to follow, as though he has entered a situation where goodness, for once, is more manageable than any form of cruelty or self-absorption.

I spend so much time on the doctor's possible suppositions about Blanche and the human effect of what he conceals or divulges because his function at play's end can so easily be construed allegorically. The allegorical impulse in a writer like Williams is commonly assumed to coexist awkwardly with his mimetic impulse. In my view, the two dimensions of the doctor's presence beautifully accommodate each other, and we stand to lose much by emphasizing one at the expense of the other. Part of the doctor's meaning is assuredly supplied by Emily Dickinson's vision of death as the courtly suitor in "Because I could not stop for Death—." One thinks immediately of the gently erotic fashion in which the poem's speaker is eased away from the scenes of her life (strangely cleansed of personal attachment) in a carriage ride resulting from Death's "kind" stopping. The prevailing mode of utterance in the poem is summed up by the word surmise in the final stanza. The speaker sees herself in this carriage ride through a kind of a temporal veil, which allows her to register without protest (indeed, with a barely stressed quickening of pulse, akin to slow arousal) the last stages of her graceful departure from life. The journey out seems at once both safely concluded and ongoing. She reports back to us with the amnesiac calm of one who has lost her bearings, but not fearfully. If an ultimate darkness awaits her, she is no more in haste to find out than her driver is to conclude their trip. She seems gratefully relieved of the necessity of taking on any more desire or knowledge than the pleasing prospect of the moment affords. And, of course, she is and is not alone in her journey—"The Carriage held but just Ourselves— / And Immortality."

Blanche's calm walk out of her all-too-earthly prison house, blind to everything but the doctor's arm that she tightly clasps, has a quality of trance and uncanny serenity much like the tone of Dickinson's speaker. The image that Blanche projects in her last moments is of one who has stepped free of the traps that have been laid for her in an endless terrible dream. Having wakened briefly to her true situation, she has willed herself somehow into a still deeper sleep, where she eludes the powers of night by becoming one with them. The doctor picks up death's carriage reins, as it were, for his silent ceremonial exit with Blanche, marking the point at which her consciousness (as a communicable state of being) is erased. The length of her visible walk away from us, out of the world of the play, is designed to make her choice of blankness palpable, as though a final adjustment of her Della Robbia blue jacket has turned her into an effigy, lifelessly wrapped in robes of love. But before this Ovidian mutual transformation of doctor and woman fixes them both as emblems, Blanche speaks her final words, and with them reclaims the play as her own—something only her vision is large enough to encompass.

Can one possibly hear freshly a line that is so well known as to have acquired the immobility of something carved in stone? What remnant of its original work and power to cast a spell can still be found in the act of speaking it? "Whoever you are—I have always depended on the kindness of strangers." The first thing to be said about this remarkable declaration is that it comments on Blanche's much-maligned quality of dependence without the slightest suggestion of weakness. Every other line that Blanche has spoken in the scene is clouded over with tentativeness, distraction, or fear. As we have seen, her assertions repeatedly come back to her unopened, like mail sent to the wrong address. It is as though she were soliciting compliments for the cracked trinkets and shredded garments of a madwoman. She has been regarded, as we have noted, as one who is now merely impersonating herself—an actress failing to establish her role's reality. Her last statement, however, reaches its destination. It is directed not only to the person of the doctor, in all his dimensions, but to the spectator of the play, who seems adroitly summoned and taken into account by Blanche's salutation: "Whoever you are."

In its stunning brevity, Blanche's summation of who she is exhibits what virtuosity in art so often aspires to: openness, certitude, rightness with least effort. It is an utterance which achieves a freestanding authority. All by itself it confers the indelible sense of completeness—allied to the sacred stillness reaching out from the heart of Greek tragedy. The atmosphere it engenders transfigures the onstage action, lifting it (for the length of the line's saying and full absorption) "high above all sorrow."

What does this line that "makes" the *Streetcar* ending manage to express, and to whom? Consider the hard wit that the construction of this peculiar challenge just avoids releasing. In its intense readiness to puncture solemnity, coiled laughter holds the merely piteous dimension of the words in check. The line also moves Blanche swiftly and persuasively from a private realm of diminished, radically alienated presence to a public realm where language knows its audience, and addresses everyone's sense of the occasion. We are meant to hear Blanche's speech as public and private expression simultaneously. Those seated or standing nearby who have not been kind are brought into focus as potential listeners, but the impact of this richly self-possessed statement derives from our awareness that Blanche is not choosing to use her words against anyone. Our conviction that the line is not vulnerable in the manner of Blanche's usual speech rests on the firm implication that the pain she has endured (as well as inflicted) is, at this juncture, beside the point. She has found a way to account for her actions—her very life, if you will—that is not dependent on the powers gathered in this room, nor on any sense of her defeat at the hands of those powers. "I have always depended" (and not been disappointed in my dependence) on strangers. Strangers are what one must rely on, after all. If those you know well cannot be trusted in relation to anything they've revealed to you, one can only relate to the withheld kindness that dwells strangely in the shadow of their actions. The stranger invoked—as human potential—embodies the hope that something else, something further, different, better may emerge in our time of being together. The frightful tension of madness and falsity that has permeated this scene is overcome (for a charmed interval) by a soft-spoken pledge of faith in an all-but-invisible clemency.

Yet another way in which Blanche's words turn us around is in their unemphatic capture of power while seemingly giving it all away. Most simply, this power is the expression of her willingness to hazard her life, unafraid, by entrusting herself fully to another's keeping (rape, madness, exile notwithstanding). Power also accumulates in the savored ambiguity of the phrase "whoever you are," which seems, all at once, to say: "I do not need to settle the question of your identity. I am choosing not to come to a decision about where you are taking me, or for what purpose. By not naming you, I make you as large as my imaginative claim on your human-ity. If I survive this encounter, it will be in part because of what I have made you understand about me." The spectator—the other stranger that Blanche addresses here—is similarly challenged to destroy or save by her acknowledgment: "Do you now have some inkling of all I failed to make clear? Have you the empathy to harmonize with this moment of fuller knowledge? If it strikes you as one more delusion, then your place is here, with those in this room. Understand me, kind stranger, for this is the end." A passion can only be overcome by a stronger passion; the passion of terror is despoiled and undone by the shocking intrusion of a reverence born of clairvoyant fellow feeling.

What wisdom has always depended on is the compression of aphorism, and a felt kinship with oracle—as in these lines from Theocritus, radiantly austere in their effort to accept one's helplessness in the face of withdrawn love: "Now turn your horses seaward / And leave me to my longing which I must bear / As I have borne it. Goodbye, remote bright Goddess / Goodbye, you stars that crossed night's silent path." One cherishes the quality of sur-viving fragment here, conjuring up a lost fullness of nature and time. Wis-dom is both frank and teasingly elusive in the telling—a plainly whispered memory from a far-off place. The effect of wisdom in Blanche's parting line is owing in part to her unexpectedly solving the riddle (or the curse) of her isolation and invisibility. Until her discovery of this way of putting things, there seems to be an insurmountable set of obstacles to her shaking off her numbing confusion and reclaiming herself. She wanders aimlessly, enslaved to understandings more focused than her own, and lacking a language equal to their unspoken consensus. Where so much still needs to be explained to those grown expert in dismissal, and where there is no time left even to prop-erly begin, her only recourse would appear to be the martyr's teeming silence, crowned with the marks of defilement. But the twelve words she arrives at are, wondrously, just enough. She elects her fate, and inwardly grasps it, with a simplicity that feels comprehensive yet quietly compels us to ponder. Any further disclosure would return her to dishonor. Wisdom dissolves if it self-consciously lingers, and offers to elaborate. There is no clear, abstract space for it to repose in; there is only the remorseless flow of experience.

The cost of Blanche becoming present to herself (and us) at last is the reassertion of death. The doctor, her dark ministering angel, does not so much claim her existence as her full attention, and she passes out of view, into the din of the French Quarter streets. When Blanche has left the stage, it becomes apparent that her endlessly misjudged form of knowing, in its final absence, appears to be the only thing that is not a hiding place. Stella waits until there is no chance of a reprieve before helplessly sounding her sister's name. Stanley soothes her by luring her back into the broken sanctuary of "colored lights," the oblivion of sex. Mitch (in Elia Kazan's definitive image) buries his head in his arms at the poker table. The other players resume their game. Eunice makes her dim realist's peace with the way things inalterably are in the Quarter, and takes comfort in her judgment of the childish perfidy of men.

Since I have so strongly insisted throughout this discussion that our sense of closure is real and that endings matter, let me try out, for my own conclusion, an observation that will fittingly shift the balance. If a narrative ending properly completes its work of resolution, in which, as Meyer Schapiro once said of Cézanne, "opposed qualities are joined in a scrupulously controlled play," the ending seems, more often than not, to be something unnecessary to remember with any precision. Endings, when we think about them from a distance, typically acquire the pleasing vagueness of broad emotional effects, positive, negative, or bittersweet. The often imputed quality of inevitability in a "good" ending subdues the attendant force of surprise, and frees us to think about other things, things more pertinent to our experience of life than closure, which is surely more agreeable to crave than to contemplate, after the fact.

PHILIP C. KOLIN

"It's Only a Paper Moon": The Paper Ontologies in Tennessee Williams's A Streetcar Named Desire[1]

I

Paper, as product and inscription, is a proleptic dramatic force, Blanche's as well as Stanley's signifier, and Williams's own signature in *A Streetcar Named Desire*. Speaking of Belle Reve, Blanche DuBois immediately conjures up papers: "There are thousands of papers, stretching back over hundreds of years. . . ."[2] One gets the same impression of an endless stream of papers underlying the convoluted histories comprising the *Streetcar* script. Perhaps no other Williams play is so implicated in the physicality, temporality, and psychology of paper as *Streetcar*. Some of the papers are legal documents, visible and objective; others are invisible yet no less empirical, evidentiary and binding; and still others are occluded, imprisoned within the play. Almost every major signifier in *Streetcar* is (de)constructed out of paper—mortgages, foreclosures, directions, letters, poems, telegrams, newspapers, appraisals, songs, even moons. And these papers exist in various stages of (de)composition and in various colors. There are love letters "yellowing with antiquity," poems, a book of "colored comics," legal papers pressed into an envelope, a flimsy "colored paper lantern," an even more insubstantial "Kleenex" billet-doux, a "red stained" swatch of butcher's paper, Blanche's dialect notebook, and assorted slips and scraps of paper, some of them no larger than a bus ticket and others more ominous than a

From *Modern Drama* 40, no. 4 (Winter 1997): 454–467. © 1997 by University of Toronto Press.

lettre de cachet. Ultimately, *Streetcar* itself, which incorporates all these documents, is a paper script (or series of scripts) seeking ownership.[3]

Paper was Williams's metier, the sign of a compulsory *jouissance.* In *Something Cloudy, Something Clear* (1981)—"one of the most personal essays I've ever written," according to Williams[4]—he recounts the events of the summer of 1940, just before he launched his professional career. The playwright, August—Williams's name in the play—confesses that "I don't own anything here but the typewriter and the paper."[5] As the play opens, August is seated before a *"secondhand portable typewriter,"* and then at the appropriate entrance cue "snatches up some papers." Disliking what he has composed, *"He crumples it and tosses it fiercely away . . . and then inserts a clean sheet of paper in the typewriter, but does not profane it with a typed word for a considerable pause"* (1). In Williams's own words, paper, when properly inscribed, can be sacred, yet when it is subjected to corrupt or untruthful imprints it is "profane[d]," contaminated. Paper magically represented pain and power, script and Scripture for Williams. In *Something Cloudy,* paper was the playwright's signature, his emblem, linked inextricably to the discourse of his dramaturgy. In a postmodern analysis of Williams's life, Nicholas Pagan aptly observes: "Foucault argues that we can never complete the task of putting our sex, 'a universal secret, an omnipresent cause, a fear that never ends,' into words. This is precisely the task in which Blanche and Williams are engaged—it is the reason why she cannot stop speaking, and perhaps to some extent why Williams cannot stop writing."[6] Williams compulsively sexualized/textualized himself by emphasizing his mission as scribe, the signatory in, of, and through paper on which he could write and be read. *Streetcar* is inscribed with Williams's papers; collectively they may be regarded as one large inscription itself. Paper, then, becomes the reality that the text (re)presents. But, as I hope to show, paper is the *vestigium* of a realism sacrificed for the sake of a theatricality that revels in uncertainty.

No less for Williams than for his characters, paper acquires overarching cultural and sexual signification. Scribes—writers and their papers—are everywhere in *Streetcar.* A character's power or instability is tracked in paper, the medium through which *logos* or chaos, history or hysteria, determinacy or indeterminacy are expressed. Paper becomes the paradigm of performance in *Streetcar,* helping to create and destabilize fictions. Williams's characters fashion their rhetorical identities and construct their appropriate scripts in paper. Paper prepares a way to proliferate and to evaluate a character in his/her flight from or toward fictionality. How we read Williams or his characters, then, depends on their scripts, which in turn are vital to the characters' roles as contenders in what Anca Vlasopolos calls "the contest for textual authority."[7] Their rhetoric is empowered or silenced through paper. Paper maps desire.

II

Blanche is insistently associated with paper and writing. In many ways Williams metamorphosizes Blanche herself into paper. She has the complexion of paper—"her dominant color is spectral white" for William Kleb, and Calvin Bedient even refers to her as "Miss White attempting to dismiss Stanley's sexuality as apish."[8] Seemingly like a sheet of undefiled paper, not profaned with improper sentiments, Blanche is "Sculptural . . . bloodless" for Bedient. Her blanched face suggests the paper of a ghostly aesthetic, decadent yet distant. Even when "Miss White" dons Della Robbia blue, her associations with paper surface. "Blue is such a delicate piece of paper," Williams wrote in "Intimations," a poem from *In the Winter of Cities*.[9]

Blanche encapsulates herself in paper, her epistemology is limned in paper. The first time we see her it is with a *"slip of paper"* in her hand, and a trunk full of her papers follows her to New Orleans. She sends a telegram to Stella, though she "couldn't put all of those details" of her dismissal "in the wire" (21). She writes a letter on tissue paper, keeps a "notebook of quaint words" from New Orleans, hangs a paper lantern, sings of paper moons, and, when Mitch is less than gallant, she "gives him his walking papers" (126). She is deeply invested in the paper economy of the arts, teaching sacred texts of a "literary heritage" (56), quoting poetry, and preaching the sanctity (and snobbery) of literacy. Her universe is paper, bibliotechal.

When Blanche arrives at 632 Elysian Fields, *"She looks at a slip of paper, then at the building, and then again at the slip . . ."* (15). Realistic yet expressionistic, the stage business projects a *tableau vivant* of Blanche's cultural predicament and feminine anxiety in paper, a Williamsesque icon. Like the piece of paper she carries, Blanche has been fragmented, severed, torn from one world (Belle Reve to Laurel) and slipped into another (Stanley's New Orleans). The small piece of paper signifies the randomness, the disconnectedness of Blanche's life journey, and further intensifies her tragedy as woman, her reduction in the land of the minimalists. Violated by Stanley's masculine aggression, Blanche becomes isolated, ripped apart from the larger, more complex feminine scripts she textualizes for herself as sister, guardian of the arts, coquette and chatelaine, Aphrodite and Madonna. The slip of paper is her passport into this new deterministic, mechanistic world.

Imagistically, the slip of paper links Blanche to her trunk filled with "thousands of papers, stretching back hundreds of years, affecting Belle Reve as, piece by piece, our improvident grandfathers and father and uncles and brothers exchanged the land for their epic fornications . . ." (43). In that trunk, appropriately underneath the Belle Reve documents, is a "tin box" containing "love-letters yellowing with antiquity" (41). The trunk is the nexus where sexuality meets death, fornications embrace foreclosures. This paper trail ends with the death certificate of desire. Williams would later use paper signifiers in his collection of poems *In the Winter of Cities* to foreshadow death. In "Cortege,"

> The parlor was uncomfortable as the cellar,
> the attic was filled with rafts of legal papers,
>
> testimony at lawsuits
> stuffed the pillows,
>
>   "It's only a paper moon..
>
> dawn was judicial
> and noon made confiscations. (54)

And in "Androgyne, Mon Amour," a "ghostly little customs-clerk" demands "'Vos documents, Mesdames, Messieurs'" to separate one frontier from another—"a definition of the pure"[10]; papers signify the venal and the transitory, the pursuit of desire by death with documents in hand. The "rafts of legal papers" and documents are scripts in the decay of desire for Blanche as well. Nor were Allan Grey's love letters exempt from the documentation of death and desire in paper in other Williams scripts. In "Photograph and Pearls," a poem on the exhaustion of desire, a mother presents "the last of [her son's] letters . . . mailed from one of those islands where Paul Gauguin died painting . . . the formalized, purified images of the lust that diseased him."[11] Sealed in Blanche's mausoleum trunk, Allan's love letters paradoxically read of purity and disease; she becomes their clerk of record, the cataloguer and recipient, too, of their death-cold calamity.

Appropriately, too, the papers—legal documents and billet-doux—reveal the female consciousness, the ways in which Blanche chronicles history. Her trunk, as many critics have argued, is quintessential feminine space, feminine order. After Stanley's rummaging around in the trunk, Blanche exclaims: "It looks like my trunk has exploded" (38). When he violates that space—"*Stanley crosses to the trunk, shoves it roughly open, and begins to open compartments*" (41)—he betrays Blanche's intimacy. Rapaciously investigating the love letters, "*He rips off the ribbon and starts to examine them, Blanche snatches them from him, and they cascade to the floor.*" Furious, she shouts: "Now that you've touched them, I'll burn them" and then starts scooping "the floor, gathering them up" (42). This stage business reiterates the death and love connection imprinted through Blanche's papers. In a review of a 1988 production of *Streetcar* starring Blythe Danner as Blanche, Frank Rich insightfully remarked: "When, early on, Miss Danner scoops up the cherished papers, poems that a dead boy wrote, she does so with a tremulous delicacy, as if picking up their author's ashes."[12] The ultimate disposition of paper is ashes, the dissolvable commodity in Blanche's bankrupt economy of desire. Even more significant as a signifier of Blanche's feminine tragedy, these papers point to her instability, her indeterminacy. Nothing is settled, despite legal actions; closure is fissure. These scattered papers mock Blanche's desire "to breath quietly again" (81). Kind distinctions are illusory. As Anne Fleche emphasizes, events in *Streetcar* involve us in "seeing from outside what we cannot see from within . . . the outside keeps becoming the inside."[13] Blanche's scattered, violated papers dismantle any hopes for the comforting ministrations she seeks for her desires. The disruption outside her trunk allows us to see the disintegration—her own and her view of history—within.

The papers in the trunk also show how Blanche conflates history and hysteria. What playwright Joan Schenkar observed of her own dramaturgy can also be said of Williams's: we have to see "memory and history in relation to our psychic lives."[14] Blanche's psychic life filters and transforms public event into private crises. She reads history through these papers to circumvent detection by Stanley, yet her "historical revisionism boomerang[s] against her."[15] Historically, Blanche thinks she can dissociate herself from the larger events of DuBois history. She guards Allan's poems and letters but willingly, even condescendingly, surrenders the Belle Reve papers to Stanley, who wants "a lawyer acquaintance . . . [to] study these out" (43). "Present them to him with a box of aspirin tablets" (43), Blanche wryly retorts, as if she can readily eject herself from the DuBois debaucheries. Her view of history in reading the DuBois papers may be prejudiced against the patrilineal, but she is nonetheless incriminated in the epic fornications which deprived the family of its inheritance. Like her ancestors, Blanche has squandered the possibilities for love. In bequeathing the Belle Reve papers to Stanley, Blanche deeds him her inheritance of loss, a beneficence devoid of empowerment. Blanche, like the DuBois fathers and brothers, had fumed presence into absence; history becomes void, fornication foreclosure. Love poems and foreclosure notices, housed and sealed together in her trunk, disallow any audience to deny the admixture of death and desire that accompanies Blanche to New Orleans. Her psyche too easily bifurcates history and desire, dehistoricizing her role in the larger contours of intimacy.

Blanche's Kleenex note to Shep is one of the most important paper scripts in the play. It is written at a crucial juncture for Blanche and the *Streetcar* narrative—between scenes four and five. In the early scenes of *Streetcar*, Blanche has played the coquette with Stanley, thinking she could be the victor in their verbal games, but after scene four (and Stanley's eavesdropping), he decidedly emerges triumphant. Midway in scene four the stage direction reads, "*She goes to the dressing table, and grabs a sheet of Kleenex and an eyebrow pencil for writing equipment*" (68); and by the beginning of scene five "*Blanche is seated in the bedroom fanning herself with a palm leaf as she reads over a just completed letter*" (74). In terms of the paper texts in *Streetcar*, Blanche's Kleenex letter to her old beau Shep Huntleigh removes us even farther from the cruel realities of the Belle Reve papers into the insubstantial, the imaginary. Blanche has discarded the Belle Reve legalities and now writes a feminine narrative on stationery engendered of gossamer—Kleenex the perfect signifier of desire and of Blanche's infatuation with butterfly wings and moths. This delicate script identifies Blanche with individuals who must be "soft"; "Blanche is sensitive," insists Stella to Stanley (98). Freeing her from the world of harsh legalities, Blanche's Kleenex stationery provides her, if only temporarily, with a suitable liminal media for a spectral reader—Shep. Porous and easily decomposed, the sheet of Kleenex, appropriated into Blanche's paper universe, is nearly (in)visible, just like her lovers—Shep, Allan Gray, the soldiers who fall by the wayside like so many daisies. Fashioning herself like this sheet of tissue paper, she embodies the *mise-en-scène*.

Once again, Williams emblematizes through paper, taking advantage of the history of desire embedded in this insubstantial sheet of Kleenex. Fond of making metaphors with and about tissue paper in his poems from *In the Winter of Cities*, Williams associated the flimsy paper with desire/sex. In "The Angels of Fructification," inspired by his sister Rose, for example, he speaks of one of these angels from whose "vast umbilicus" "birds yellow as butter" were released and "each [angel] sorely buttered her puffed-up cheeks / with a childlike smile / and opened her pudgy pink palms on pink tissue paper, / lacily fluted and frilled, / for caps and aprons with French phrase books in the pockets / and cinnamon red hearts to sweeten their fluttering tongue-tips" (33). Emerging from the shades of Richard Crashaw and other Metaphysical Poets, Williams's "pink tissue paper" in this poem may have been foreshadowed in *Streetcar* where Blanche's Kleenex note to Shep invokes a compendium of romantic tropes, tastes, and sounds. Recall that Blanche, too, lives in a world that is "lacily fluted and frilled" and that she keeps a "phrase book." For Williams, the tissue paper in "Angels" and the Kleenex in *Streetcar* signal indulgent, even fetishistic, passion. In another poem relating back to his sister, "Recuerdo," Williams similarly talks of "love's explosion, defined as early madness" burning out his sister's heart like "a tissue-paper lantern" (*In the Winter of Cities*, 77). Interestingly, one of the earliest drafts of *Gentleman Caller* is about a brother and sister decorating a Christmas tree, presumably with such lanterns.[16] Memories of Rose can be found in Blanche's Kleenex note. Finally, in "The Jockeys at Hialeah," Williams imagines that "The Sunshine Special has deposited you under skies of pink tissue paper which little girls' scissors will cut into gap-toothed grins and triangular eyes" (74). The image of tissue paper in these three poems underscores the illusory romance attached to Blanche's Kleenex letter.

Williams may also have incorporated the Kleenex and the eyebrow pencil to portray Blanche as a self-reflexive reader of glamour/fashion magazines whose stories (and ads) abundantly provide the billet-doux material that a woman absorbed in such fantasies might easily encode. In the Mexican premiere of *Streetcar* in 1948, when Blanche finds Stella in bed in scene four, the younger DuBois sister is not in a state of "*narcotized tranquillity*" because she has been reading "*a book of colored comics*" (62), but, instead, the Mexican Stella has a well-endowed supply of glamour magazines in bed with her, the glossy narratives of desire spilling off her bedclothes and onto the floor.[17] We are in a world of m'lady's boudoir, the romanticized dressing room where Kleenex helps to fashion desire. Certainly the eyebrow pencil—ostensibly used for eye shadowing—is also a romance signifier advertised in such glamour magazine sources, an instrument used to invite and deny the male gaze. Blanche, however, after starting the letter, bites the pencil and then "smokes it" thinking "you never get anywhere with direct appeals" (68). The pencil is a wonderful instrument to notate a *trompe-l'oeil*, the sexual rapture that is—but that really is not—there. Finally, the Kleenex episode positions Blanche in radically different yet complementary states—as a romance-haunted schoolgirl writing a dreamy love letter or as a salacious barmaid or chorus girl using the most available writing materials to lure or respond to a john.

Regardless of its history in the annals of billet-doux, the Kleenex note is a site for and a fetishization of her romantic desires. Onomastically, the Kleenex points the way to a clean ex-boyfriend Blanche thinks she can reclaim. It is a significant record, too, of Blanche's visionary—and insubstantial—ontologies. Paper moons can only sail in skies of pink tissue paper, and assignations with imaginary lovers are appropriately arranged with/through flimsy Kleenex notes. The Kleenex fetishizes the feminine gaze. It both encodes and makes transparent Blanche's sexualized (fictive) identity, and perhaps Williams's too. If Blanche's totem animal is the mother, her glyph is best depicted in Kleenex.

The sacred hieroglyphs of Blanche's alphabet, though, are at best flimsy, transparent text that will not withstand a Kowalski-like scrutiny and that may last no longer than it takes to wipe off too much of an aging sister-in-law's makeup. When Stanley asks "Where are the papers?" he will tear such Kleenex notes to shreds. The Kleenex may well be the objective correlative of Blanche's desire—insubstantial, vulnerable, and visionary, or, in the parlance of Lacan, the Kleenex is the "*objet a*,"[18] of Blanche's desire—the note upon it the long-sought-after fulfillment of desire. Of course, as the sign of love's possible fulfillment, the Kleenex note is, though tantalizing, not worth the paper it is written on. The Kleenex is the contract on which

Blanche builds an epistemology of love; it is the non-concretized, non-specific, type of engagement that ultimately will be her undoing. The Kleenex is Blanche's new (and ominous) contract with an intangible future. Williams uses Kleenex to inscribe messages that are both seen and unseen, open and hidden simultaneously.

Like her Kleenex note, the paper Chinese lantern that Blanche hangs over the "naked" light bulb foregrounds her desire, her fate. This paper shade, which reveals more than it conceals, is another *desideratum* in Blanche's epistemology of fantasies. And like the Kleenex note, the paper lantern enables Blanche to script herself. She tries to redefine existence—for herself, Stella, Stanley, Mitch—with the paper lantern. Ostensibly, she wants to dilute and to neuter Stanley's harshness, the power of his glaring male gaze, by shadowing and thereby diminishing the intensity of the light bulb. Blanche seeks to modulate the physics of Stanley's desire through this paper script. An either/or Cartesian, Stanley wants to retain naked light bulbs or to smash them. Unlike her sister, who is subjugated to Stanley's male desire, Blanche with her flimsy paper lantern desires indeterminacy (and female ambiguity) to reign. The lantern is Allan's shroud in this new world, death never very far away from desire; it is also a costume for Blanche's costume; "wherever she is, Blanche is already in a play."[19] Death and desire again. The paper lantern—like the revealing slip Blanche wears in the famous Thomas Hart Benton painting of the play, or like the Kleenex note—lets in illusion, shadow, imagination, teasing opaqueness. Holding the lantern to the light allows Blanche to capture magic in paper, holding the liquor "bottle to the light to observe its depletion" Stanley sees realism through a paper cover (30). Blanche is, perhaps, dangerously "too transparent."[20] Stanley strips (scene two and scene ten); Blanche teases.

III

Like Blanche, Stanley lives in a world of paper. "Let's see the paper" is a frequent order issued by the former record-keeping master sergeant who served in the Engineers' Corps. Stanley's *nom de guerre* is written all over the photo—the glossy paper—of him in uniform, enshrining the war hero as Blanche's trunk commemorates desire's victim, Allan Grey. In point of fact, though, Stanley may refer to paper more frequently than Blanche does, but from a completely different registry. While Blanche escapes the cruel realities of documentation, Stanley revels in the evidentiary, a *modus operandi* of Luce Irigaray's "male system of representation."[21] Blanche fantasizes through paper magic; Stanley constructs paper empires and courts to legitimize the polity. He legislates a witch hunt against Blanche's paper ontologies.

Williams's theatre of (im)plausibilities establishes parallels and antin-
omies between these protagonists through a carefully crafted network of
paper. While Blanche entered the script with a slip of paper, Stanley's first
appearance is similarly announced in paper, with a "red stained package"
of meat tossed up to Stella, his paper emblem characteristically bloody in
tooth and claw. His "six number ticket" which he hopes will win him a
fortune, is contrasted with Blanche's bus ticket back to Laurel (111) at the
end of the play, her unlucky passport to the asylum. The bus ticket may
be Stanley's most lethal paper document As Dan Sullivan wittily reminded
audiences, "Blanche was destroyed not by the rape but with a bus ticket back
to Laurel."[22] Blanche enshrines the sacred texts of Hawthorne, Whitman,
Poe, Baudelaire, Chekhov, while Stanley valorizes the codified papers of
Napoleon and Huey P. Long, Napoleon's descendent in Faubourg-Marigny.
Stanley clarifies his association with Napoleon through paper. As I have put
it elsewhere, "In striving for dominion at home, Stanley uses Napoleonic
jurisprudence (the Code) to elevate his position and to ensure his rights. The
code is filtered to him through an intermediary archetype, the Louisiana-
styled Napoleon, Huey Long. Legitimizing his domestic reign of terror, he
invokes the power of the primal male as articulated by Long and buttressed
by Napoleonic law."[23] Blanche writes her paper texts with an eyebrow pencil or sends a wire through a hysterical voice; Stanley's ink is Napoleonic,
filtered through Huey P. Long, grease, blood, or fists upon the tablecloth.
Blanche's paper beguiles with desire and dreams while Stanley's paper asserts
with authority.

Paper helps to (in) and (de)scribe Stanley's masculinist imperatives.
Control over and through paper for Stanley justifies and entrenches his
power. In Stanley's ontology, paper establishes boundaries and empowers
containment, and the more invested he is through paper documentation, the
more control he believes he acquires. Stanley physicalizes paper (the text) to
protect his ideology of reproduction; he practices a rhetoric of instrumentality. Born under the sign of Capricorn, the paper-eating goat, Stanley ravages
anything paper. Recall Blanche's response when he picks up Allan's "love
letters": "the touch of your hands insults them" (42). Scene two reads like a
probate hearing with Stanley and his nameless experts hunting for letters
testamentary. Obsessed like a trial-mad attorney, Stanley ferrets through
Blanche's papers for the evidence he needs to indict—contain—her. He
fumes as he tells Stella, "Now let's have a gander at the bill of sale" for Belle
Reve. When Stella responds with a DuBois-like insouciance about paper
resolutions—"There weren't any papers, she didn't show any papers. I don't
care about papers" (34)—Stanley becomes incensed. Like her older sister,
Stella does not valorize disclosures on paper; earlier, she informed Blanche,
who was incredulous about the Kowalski home: "I'd tried to gloss things

over a little in my letters" (33). This is so unlike Stanley, who builds his case, his life, his epistemology of worth on the determinacy of paper. In rapid succession, he fires off a series of questions about paper: "Where's the paper? In the trunk? What's underneath" (41). "I'll have a look at them first." "What's all the rest of them papers" (43). And he finally thumbs through the stack of papers and "goes into the bedroom with the envelope and the box" (43), hoping to find the debentures of fault that will certify his sexual supremacy (inheritance) and Blanche's embezzlement. Paradoxically, the Belle Reve papers spin a judicative censure that silences Stanley about Blanche's crime to disinherit him and his progeny, for he does not refer to the Belle Reve papers again after scene two. Yet, ironically, he takes these legal documents to desire's reading room—the bedroom—to decipher them.

Stanley believes that paper speaks in a contractual, unilateral voice. Experts in reading/preparing papers—including supersleuth Kowalski himself—can unlock and proclaim a true, unambiguous meaning. For that reason he wants Blanche's jewelry appraised. "I have an acquaintance that works in a jewelry store. I'll have him in here to make an appraisal of this. Here's our plantation, or what was left of it here" (36). Believing that Blanche's "summer furs are worth a fortune," Stanley tells Stella: "I got an acquaintance who deals in this sort of merchandise. I'll have him here to appraise it. I'm willing to bet you there's thousands of dollars invested in this stuff here" (36). Sounding like a David Mamet denizen, Stanley smugly testifies that the appraisals uncontestedly validate true worth. His male importunity is based on worth certified in paper. While Blanche is content to spin (or conceal) airy nothings in her papers—or to deny that she has any papers that quantify at all—Stanley resists ambiguity and ends speculation and doubt through documentation. Stanley characteristically sees through the reality— if not the illusion—of Blanche's papers. He denies lace, poems, lanterns, anything transparent or indefinite. For that reason he tears the Chinese lantern off the light bulb. It is no act of brother-in-law kindness that motivates Stanley's gesture at the end of *Streetcar*. "You left nothing here but spilt talcum and old empty perfume bottles—unless it's the paper lantern you want to take with you. You want the lantern?" (143). That lantern is a reminder of Blanche's indeterminate world which, if left to signify in the Kowalski's household, would challenge his inscribed authority as king, as *pater familias*. The appraisal by the jeweler and the assessment by his lawyer friend are to bring swift, decisive closure. But "analysis imprisons desire."[24] Paper gives Stanley authority; it renders Blanche tentative.

Paper is history and law for Stanley. It energizes him as law maker and interpreter. Stanley finds out that "they kicked her [Blanche] out of high school before the spring term ended" (100–01) because, in Stanley's foregrounding of evidentiary paper, "it was practickly a town ordinance passed against her!" (101). Stanley likes the punitive certitude that the written record—the hypothetical but still applicable "ordinance"—provides. His references to the Napoleonic Code, Huey P. Long's popularist legislation, and all the other jurisprudential documents underlie Stanley's validations of paper historiography. "All we discussed was recent history," he brags to Stella, informing her about how he obtained damning news about Dame Blanche from the "supply man" (102), and in the process, Stanley banishes any past predicated on desire or longing. Branding Blanche as the dangerous Phallic Mother by adopting a Foucault-inspired pro-Stanley reading, Calvin Bedient maintains that "the play sacrifices Blanche, or 'feminine' abjection, however reluctantly, in favor of the transparent social system. When the cards are down, the playwright prefers identity-sustaining law to the engulfing archaic mother."[25] But not always. Other paper scripts deserve interrogation.

IV

Papers that are actually seen or mentioned in the text (Allan's love letters, Blanche's lantern, Stanley's call for appraisals) are not all there is. A variety of papers are suppressed from the audience's eyes and ears yet essential to the script life of the play. At the emotional center of *Streetcar*, these papers underneath the script are the forces behind the fictions perpetuated by the characters. These occluded papers are inside the text of the play coming outside; they are like seismic waves below ground that erupt in the magnitude of the quake's effect at ground level. We don't see or hear the waves yet we feel their force. So too with hidden papers in *Streetcar*. These papers—suppressed or imprisoned in the script—are very much incorporated into the denials or affirmations of love, the cycles of doubt and plausibility. "Oh, you can't describe someone you're in love with," fantasizes Stella in scene two and thereby voices the romantic ecstasy of intangibility. But, as she (and we) later learn, Stanley, as well as Blanche, hold defining papers they are not showing.

These hidden papers are significant to the contrapuntal allegiances in *Streetcar*. Opposing constituencies in *Streetcar*—Blanche-philes or Stanley-philes—want certain papers suppressed or publicized. In fact, *Streetcar* is a contract of negotiation between the forces mandating full disclosure and those demanding concealment. Blanche's/Stanley's (im)print is (in)visible. Choose your Derridian options. In the larger perspective of Foucault's reading of culture, society (or the *Streetcar* participants, including the audience) is often judged not so much by what it wants and shows but by what it does not want shown. The *Streetcar* script can only be fully realized, therefore, through a process of emancipating these suppressed papers.

The records of Blanche's promiscuity provide an aperture. Like so many of Williams's wanderers, Blanche, to use Stella's words, "didn't have any papers" (34), or the proper legal ones at any rate. In this respect she is vulnerable, dangerous to a prying status quo, as are Williams's other wanderers—Kip, the Canadian draft dodger, has no papers in *Something Cloudy* and Marguerite, the mistress of love, has hers stolen in *Camino Real*—and of course Williams himself. Too much documentation (or of the wrong sort) endangers a wanderer's invisibility, as Williams himself recognized. He had occluded his own papers in *Streetcar* by writing about what could not be written in the 1940s—a multiplicity of sexual identities. Williams may in fact, as he insists in the *Memoirs*, be Blanche wanting discovery, celebrating performance. "Given to continual self-creation, self-concealment, Blanche imitates her author."[26] But clearly Blanche, like Williams, is not paperless. In her "old maid, schoolteacherish" way even Dame Blanche had to keep papers and be aware of their import. In seeking sanctuary, though, she jettisoned them. Her previous seductions and dissolvable memories—her sexual scripts—have been inserted, if not promoted, beneath the text of *Streetcar*. Among her records in infamy and pain underlying the script are letters to Mr. Graves, the principal at the high school, complaining of Blanche's immoral conduct; her dismissal notice from Mr. Graves; and her eviction notice from the Flamingo Hotel. Alluding to the suppressed written record of the latter, Stanley uses an unintended paper/printing pun: "In fact they were so *impressed* [italics added] by Dame Blanche that they requested her to turn in her room key" (99).

Behind these documents lie even more papers: news of Blanche's marriage; Allan's suicide; a plethora of DuBois obituaries; auction sales. All of these are seemingly erased from—made (in)visible in—Blanche's sojourn in New Orleans. It seems appropriate that the young man collecting for *The Evening Star* carries no newspaper, but in his personification as *nuntius*/gallant amorist he knows of Blanche's previous history: "I'm not the lady of the house. I'm her sister from Mississippi. I'm one of those poor relations you've heard about" (83). The more we want to read these papers, the more we are embedded in the truth of Blanche's fictions.

Blanche is not the only one implicated through suppressed papers. The papers she wants hidden are matched by those Stanley (and Stella, too) are silent about. Undoubtedly the most notorious covered/concealed papers in *Streetcar* deal with Blanche's commitment to the asylum, all the complaints, testimonies, and orders. These documents are certainly part of the "supplice" that Kleb sees Stanley enacting to punish and contain his errant sister-in-law,[27] and they are necessary for the plot to propel itself toward uneasy closure. Eric Bentley is perhaps being too impressionistic when he speculates: "Can a sister send someone to an asylum without any medical advice? If so, which of us is safe?"[28] Not even in New Orleans in the fall of 1947 could a sister's worried phone call issue in Blanche's incarceration in a state hospital. The doctor—the Angel of Death as well as the empowered agent of the Law—did not come without papers.

The commitment papers—court order, if you will—occupy a strategic place in Williams's theatre of uncertainty, and in the paper ontologies unfolding and being dismantled in *Streetcar*. These papers may be buried in the script, but Williams engenders their presence in our sense of uneasiness about Blanche's fate. Bringing these commitment papers to our attention, Williams the scribe and we as audience assume the role of witness, our ultimate involvement in the paper ontology of *Streetcar*.[29] If Blanche cannot get away with anything, neither can Stella or Stanley: the commitment papers are the *coup de théâtre* of Stanley's undoing. Williams subverts one law to emancipate another.

Excavating these commitment papers and inserting them in the ongoing fictions, we see Stanley deconstructed, foiled by the very paper tactics he directed against Blanche. Stanley's signification throughout *Streetcar* has been voiced through the scrupulosity of record-keeping, the law of the Same against the Other, as Kleb maintains.[30] If he and/or Stella are sending Blanche to a madhouse, why not disclose the papers of the legal system empowering such action? But in the last scene of *Streetcar* Stanley is conveniently silent about the very legal documents enfranchising his conquest. The covert commitment papers intervene between his credibility and our bafflement. Exploiting the law to exonerate himself, Stanley is culpable (but with far graver consequences) of the type of deceptions in paper that Blanche was accused of at the start of the play. The instrumentality of discourse—Stanley's paper script—loses power in the disruption of legalistic causality that the absent commitment papers celebrate. The politics of Stanley's paper fictions indict him. In the greatest scandal about paper in *Streetcar*, Stanley's legalism is both hidden and revelatory, while at the same time, Blanche's history is fully disclosed yet commemorated in silence.

NOTES

1. An earlier, much abbreviated version of this article was read at the Tennessee Williams Literary Festival, March 1997, New Orleans. I am grateful to the University of Southern Mississippi, and especially to Vice President Karen Yarbrough, for a research grant that enabled me to prepare this article.

2. Tennessee Williams, *A Streetcar Named Desire* (New York, 1947). Subsequent references will appear parenthetically in the text.

3. In some productions, directors even add to the paper medley of *Streetcar*: at a 1994 production of the play by the South Coast Repertory, scene designer Michael Devine painted Stanley's "hothouse French Quarter setting" with "dark floral wallpaper that climbs up a high wall, appearing waterstained and ruined at

the top." Laurie Winer, "Strong Performance Fuels *Streetcar,*" *Los Angeles Times* (12 September 1994).

4. Quoted in Michiko Kakutani, "Tennessee Williams: 'I Keep Writing. Sometimes I am Pleased,'" *New York Times* (13 August 1981), C7.

5. Tennessee Williams, *Something Cloudy, Something Clear* (New York, 1995), 9.

6. Nicholas Pagan, *Rethinking Literary Biography: A Postmodern Approach to Tennessee Williams* (Rutherford, NJ 1993), 72. Pagan is quoting Michel Foucault, *The History of Sexuality,* Volume I, *An Introduction,* trans. Robert Hurley (New York, 1980), 69.

7. Anca Vlasopolos, "Authorizing History: Victimization in *A Streetcar Named Desire,*" *Theatre Journal,* 38 (1986), 333.

8. William Kleb, "Marginalia: *Streetcar,* Williams, and Foucault," *Confronting Tennessee Williams' A Streetcar Named Desire: Essays in Critical Pluralism,* ed. Philip C. Kolin (Westport, 1993), 36; Calvin Bedient, "There Are Lives That Desire Does Not Sustain: *A Streetcar Named Desire,*" ibid., 55.

9. Tennessee Williams, *In the Winter of Cities* (New York, 1956), 63.

10. Tennessee Williams, *Androgyne, Mon Amour: Poems by Tennessee Williams* (New York, 1977), 18.

11. Tennessee Williams, *In the Winter of Cities,* second printing (New York, 1964), 42.

12. Frank Rich. "Danner and Quinn," *New York Times* (11 March 1988), C1.

13. Anne Fleche, "The Space of Madness and Desire: Tennessee Williams and *Streetcar,*" *Modern Drama,* 38:4 (1995), 498.

14. Joan Schenkar, interviewed by Vivian Petraka, "An Interview with Joan Schenkar," *Speaking on Stage: Interviews with Contemporary American Playwrights,* ed. Philip C. Kolin and Colby H. Kullman (Tuscaloosa, 1996), 235.

15. Vlasopolos, 331. See note 7.

16. For a discussion of the manuscripts from which *The Glass Menagerie* emerged, see R.B. Parker, "The Composition of *The Glass Menagerie*: An Argument for Complexity," *Modern Drama,* 25 (1982), 409–22.

17. Philip C. Kolin, "The Mexican Premiere of Tennessee Williams' *A Streetcar Named Desire,*" *Mexican Studies/Estudios Mexicanos,* 10:3 (1994), 331.

18. Jacques Lacan, *The Fundamental Concepts of Psycho-Analysis,* trans. Alan Sheridan (New York, 1977), 112.

19. Bedient, 51. See note 8.

20. Pagan, 95. See note 6.

21. Luce Irigaray, *Speculum of the Other Woman,* trans. Gillian Gill (Ithaca, 1985), passim.

22. Dan Sullivan, "'Streetcar' On, Off the Track," *Los Angeles Times* (21 March 1977), IV, 1.

23. Philip C. Kolin. "Bonaparte Kowalski: Or What Stanley and Napoleon Have in Common (And What They Don't) in *A Streetcar Named Desire,*" *Notes on Contemporary Literature,* 24:4 (1994), 7.

24. Fleche, 504. See note 13.

25. Bedient, 56. See note 8.

26. Ibid., 51.

27. Kleb, 38. See note 8.

28. Eric Bentley, *In Search of Theatre* (New York, 1953), 62.

29. The indeterminacy of responsibility for Blanche's incarceration may have had even more serious implications for Williams and his family. The lack of documentation may be related to Williams's own bad conscience about the degree of his personal responsibility for institutionalizing his sister Rose, a decision he tried to blame on his mother but which he knew about and silently condoned. In a letter to her parents, Williams's mother Edwina wrote that when Rose's condition worsened, "Cornelius [Williams's father] got busy right away and had Dr. Satterfield and another [doctor] visit her and sign the necessary papers. They all agree that this is the only hope and that Farmington [the state mental hospital] is the best place, so there was nothing for me to do but consent" (quoted in Lyle Leverich's *Tom: The Unknown Tennessee Williams* [New York, 1995], 223). Williams's father's own culpability, too, may be one of the underlying forces behind Stanley's distancing himself from the documentation of which he has such a vital part. In his magisterial biography, Leverich comments on the Stanley-like role of Cornelius in Rose's commitment: "In signing the admission papers, Cornelius gave the power to the state hospital to make all determinations and decisions regarding Rose's therapeutic treatment" (224). Like Cornelius, Stanley takes himself out of the process his writing (paper) initiated.

30. Kleb, 31–3. See note 8.

GEORGE W. CRANDELL

Misrepresentation and Miscegenation: Reading the Racialized Discourse of Tennessee Williams's A Streetcar Named Desire

Audiences and readers familiar with the plays of Tennessee Williams recognize immediately in the voice, the inflection, and the idiom of characters such as Amanda Wingfield, Blanche DuBois, and Big Daddy Pollitt, a language variety that distinguishes the South from other regions of the United States. What is no less obvious, but seldom noted, is the apparent absence of African American voices from this otherwise realistically depicted discourse community.

In many of the Williams plays set in the South—*Battle of Angels, The Glass Menagerie, Summer and Smoke, The Rose Tattoo,* and *Suddenly Last Summer*—African American characters do not appear in the plays at all. Although C.W.E. Bigsby has remarked upon this absence—"scarcely a black face is to be seen in Williams's South"—Bigsby directs his attention to the more visible presence of the bigot in plays such as *Orpheus Descending* and *Sweet Bird of Youth* to illustrate Williams's "contempt for the racist."[1] The attention that bigots such as Jake Torrance and Boss Finley attract to themselves nevertheless obscures from sight and attention a group of African American characters whose menial roles, limited dialogue, and disparaging names (or namelessness) all attest to their marginal status in Williams's dramatic world.

From *Modern Drama* 40, no. 3 (Fall 1997): 337–346. © 1997 by University of Toronto Press.

With the exception of Chicken, a man of mixed racial heritage who plays a prominent role in *Kingdom of Earth* (*The Seven Descents of Myrtle*), the few African American characters who appear on stage in Williams's plays are relegated to peripheral positions, acting as servants or in subservient roles, for example, Lacey and Sookey in *Cat on a Hot Tin Roof*, Fly in *Sweet Bird of Youth*, and the hotel porter in *The Last of My Solid Gold Watches*. If these characters speak at all, it is to say only a few lines (as does the "Negro Woman" in *A Streetcar Named Desire*),[2] or to utter inhuman cries (for instance, the "barking sounds" of the Conjure Man in *Orpheus Descending*).[3] Contributing to the unflattering images of these characters, Williams ascribes to them names with negative connotations, "Chicken" and "Fly," for example, or—by refusing to name them—diminishes the importance of their personal and social identities. As Lionel Kelly observes, the "social identity" of "the unnamed Negro woman" in *A Streetcar Named Desire* "is predictably marginalized through her namelessness."[4]

The absence or underrepresentation of African American characters in Williams's drama nevertheless constitutes a meaningful "gap" or "blank" in the dramatic text that might be said to signify by means of its implicit presence.[5] These "gaps," Wolfgang Iser asserts, are what prompt readers "to supply what is meant from what is not said."[6] Such gaps, of course, are not limited to the dramatic form or to the works of Tennessee Williams. Writing about the novel, for example, Peter J. Rabinowitz remarks that "it is often more useful to look not at the assertions about the issues at hand but rather at those places where the novel is silent." By examining these silences, Rabinowitz suggests, by considering the assumptions about reality that author and audience share (and which for this reason are not stated explicitly in the text), we can discover "the implied audience's unspoken, perhaps unrecognized, beliefs about reality." Thus, he concludes, "in answering questions about the views held by this larger community [of which the author is also a part], what is not said is as important as what is."[7] Along similar lines, Wolfgang Iser argues that "[w]hat is said only appears to take on significance as a reference to what is not said; it is the implications and not the statements that give shape and weight to the meaning."[8]

The failure of Tennessee Williams to write explicitly about issues, such as "race" for example, should not be construed to mean that his works are silent about such matters. Toni Morrison recalls, in *Playing in the Dark: Whiteness and the Literary Imagination*, how she once believed that the paucity of fully developed black characters in American literature meant that "black people signified little or nothing in the imagination of white American writers."[9] After more careful deliberation, however, she concluded that the presence of Africans and African Americans had had a significant impact on the imagination of white American writers such that many of the "championed characteristics of our national literature" are "in fact responses to a dark, abiding, signing Africanist presence,"[10] a presence that has been largely ignored in critical studies, among them studies of Tennessee Williams. Along with Toni Morrison, Henry Louis Gates, Jr. champions the idea that "[i]n much of the thinking about the proper study of literature in this century, race has been an invisible quantity, a persistent yet implicit presence," yet "until the past decade or so," Gates writes, "even the most subtle and sensitive literary critics would most likely have argued that . . . race has not been brought to bear upon the study of literature."[11]

If, however, we turn our attention to the representations of blackness in works by white American writers, as Toni Morrison suggests we do, the effort, she says, repays itself in knowledge gained about the creating artists, for "[t]he fabrication of an Africanist persona" constitutes "a powerful exploration of the fears and desires that reside in the writerly conscious."[12] If we apply this method to the works of Tennessee Williams, we see that, in representing the relationships between blacks and whites, Williams exhibits a fascination with the fearful *and* desirable prospect of miscegenation. In some of his short stories, a number written in the 1930s and 1940s (but not published until 1985), Williams writes explicitly about miscegenation, but even in plays such as *A Streetcar Named Desire* he broaches the topic. Sensitive, however, to the limits of disclosure acceptable on the Broadway stage in the late 1940s, Williams employs a coded discourse, concealing an implicit but nonetheless discernable Africanist influence and presence. Masked beneath the ostensible class conflict between the aristocratic Blanche DuBois and the bourgeois Stanley Kowalski lies another struggle, one that may be explicated by considering the relationships among Williams's portraits of black men, the racialized discourse he uses to characterize them, and his depiction of ethnic characters such as Stanley Kowalski.

Although some of Tennessee Williams's most fully developed fabrications of Africanist personas appear in the short stories and thus may not be familiar to theatre audiences, they nevertheless provide a paradigm for later figurations that appear, in coded form, in *A Streetcar Named Desire*. In the stories Williams repeatedly draws upon a historical, if not stereotypical, model to represent his black characters, but in *A Streetcar Named Desire* he displaces this image, ascribing to a "white" character (Stanley Kowalski) the features of the racial Other. He thereby obscures and confuses the boundaries between ethnic and racial groups, at the same time debunking the notion that "race," ethnicity, and identity are unified, stable, and immutable features of the Self.

In the fictional renditions, the racial Other is most frequently depicted as a black male whose presence excites both fear *and* desire in the mind of an observing narrator or character. Performing a primarily functional role, this fearful and desirable Other serves not only to mirror the Self's ambivalent feelings about miscegenation but also to reflect the divided and incomplete nature of the observing Self. In the figure of the Other, the Self first recognizes its own incompletion, and then, desiring to unite with the Other, seeks to compensate for the inadequacy it perceives in itself. Moreover, Williams often associates this fearful and desirable black male character with the following characteristics (many of them derived from cultural or literary antecedents but also stereotypical): (a) great physical size or strength; (b) inability to communicate; (c) lack of intelligence; (d) uncontrollable desire; and (e) potent sexuality. Finally, employing a racialized discourse, Williams frequently associates this black character with an animal or beast as a means of suggesting one or more of these characteristics through a kind of verbal economy. By economy I mean to suggest, as Hans Robert Jauss has argued, "associations called forth by certain words." *Black* and *beast*, for example, "evoke in the reader a self-contained sphere of ideas which are often recognized when just one *single* element of such a system is presented."[13] In other words, as Aldon Lynn Nielsen similarly writes: "only a suggestion of blackness need appear for the entire structure to be articulated."[14]

To illustrate, in a short story composed in the early 1930s called "Big Black: A Mississippi Idyll," Tennessee Williams characterizes the black male protagonist in terms that emphasize his resemblance to a fearsome beast. Nameless, except for the de-humanizing designation "Big Black," he is "gargantuan" in size, "prodigiously, repulsively ugly" in appearance, and huge in strength, having "more lifting, and pounding, and dragging power than any two men."[15] "Strange, savage, inarticulate" (27), he is, Williams writes, "a black beast in grotesque human form" (29). In physical size and strength, Big Black resembles the masseur (in "Desire and the Black Masseur"), the "black giant" before whom Anthony Burns trembles in fear,[16] and also one of the black lovers of Miss Coynte (in "Miss Coynte of Greene"), who towers above the white woman by "almost two feet" in height.[17] Big Black is also distinguished from other men by "a huge, towering cry," an indicator of his inability to communicate as well as his inhumanity (27). Governed not by reason or intelligence but driven by instinct and desire, Big Black responds in characteristic animal-like fashion when he chances to find a young, white girl bathing in a river: "Like a great black animal, he crouched behind the bushes, peered at the naked girl bathing up there" (29). "Sick with desire of her" and unable to control his violent sexual impulse, he seizes the girl: "He swayed back and forth, clasping her, and uttered low, guttural sounds like a hungry animal tearing at a fresh kill" (30). Initially Big Black's "elemental" cry may be inexplicable to readers of the story, but following Big Black's violent attack on the girl, the cry becomes an expression of unfulfilled desire coupled with guilt (27).

Remembering his assault upon the white girl, Big Black later thinks of it as "Ugliness seizing upon Beauty—Beauty that never could be seized!" (31). Giving expression to his thought, "Big Black tore his blue shirt open to the waist, arched his huge black chest, flung his sweating arms above his head, and uttered a savage, booming cry" (31).

In many of his characteristic features and actions, Big Black resembles characters in American fiction that antedate Tennessee Williams's own portrait and attest to the pervasiveness and the longevity of cultural images that serve to degrade and dehumanize black men. Big Black's sexual assault on the white girl, for instance, recalls a scene from Thomas Dixon's antiblack novel *The Clansman: An Historical Romance of the Ku Klux Klan* (1905), in which Dixon draws upon animal imagery to depict the rape of a white woman by a black man: "A single tiger-spring, and the black claws of the beast sank into the soft white throat."[18] Similarly, Big Black's inarticulate cries bear a resemblance to those of an earlier, nineteenth-century character from J.T. Trowbridge's novel, *Cudjo's Cave* (1864): "Then throwing himself back upon a heap of skins, with his heels at the fire, and his long arms swinging over his head, in a savage and picturesque attitude, he burst into a shout, like the cry of a wild beast."[19] In size and savagery, Williams's Big Black likewise resembles Herman Melville's Daggoo, whom Melville in *Moby-Dick* (1851) describes as "a gigantic, coal-black negro-savage."[20]

As these selected examples illustrate, long before Tennessee Williams depicted the conflicting desires and fears associated with miscegenation or used images linking black men with animals and savagery, these emotions and stereotypical representations had currency in English and American culture and consequently in the literature of nineteenth-century America. According to George M. Fredrickson, the "stereotype of the 'Negro as beast'" was especially used during the last decade of the nineteenth century to explain or justify lynching. It suggested that "Negroes were literally wild beasts, with uncontrollable sexual passions and criminal natures stamped by heredity."[21] As Fredrickson also writes, the image of Negro as beast "had its origins in the proslavery imagination, which had conceived of the black man as having a dual nature—he was docile and amiable when enslaved, ferocious and murderous when free."[22] Similarly, in *White over Black: American Attitudes toward the Negro, 1550–1812*, Winthrop D. Jordan traces the cultural origin of this stereotype to the sixteenth century, when Englishmen first encountered Africans in Africa:

> English observers in West Africa were sometimes so profoundly impressed by the Negro's deviant behavior that they resorted to a powerful metaphor with which to express their own sense of difference from him. They knew perfectly well that Negroes were

men, yet they frequently described the Africans as "brutish" or "bestial" or "beastly."[23]

Like the mythology linking Negroes and beasts, the conflicting emotions associated with miscegenation have a long cultural history that extends to the period of first English settlement on the North American continent. By the time of the eighteenth century, Winthrop D. Jordan writes, "miscegenation was extensive in all the English colonies, a fact made evident to contemporaries by the presence of large numbers of mulattoes," but, he adds, "[n]o one thought intermixture was a good thing. Rather, English colonials were caught in the push and pull of an irreconcilable conflict between desire and aversion for interracial sexual union."[24]

In stories such as "Big Black: A Mississippi Idyll," the focus upon the fearful yet desirable prospect of interracial sexual union or miscegenation serves to illuminate not only the ambivalent feelings within the observing self, but also, the sense of incompletion that stimulates the desire for union, a process that once initiated ultimately leads, in Williams's fiction, to the objectification of the Other. As much, then, as Big Black is a source of fear, he is to the gazing narrator an object of wonder, admired by the storyteller for his strangely attractive, exotic qualities. Enjoying a kind of voyeuristic pleasure in the observation of Big Black, the narrator displays a type of behavior that closely corresponds to Henry Louis Gates, Jr.'s definition of "racism," one that does not depend, as Tzvetan Todorov defines the term, upon "contempt or aggressiveness toward other people on account of physical differences,"[25] but instead may include behaviors such as "benevolence, paternalism," and, as in this instance, "sexual attraction."[26] Depicted as a sexually fascinating object, Big Black lacks the individualizing features of personality that are generally afforded to fully developed characters. In this respect, Big Black is a paradigm for similar romantic renditions of black characters in Tennessee Williams's stories and plays whose metaphoric or symbolic value displaces their worth as human beings and diminishes their individuality as characters in his fiction and drama.

"Ten Minute Stop," a story in which Williams describes a "young Negro" boxer, provides yet another illustrative example.[27] In the ring, the fighter excites fear in the hearts of his opponents; outside the ring, riding on a bus from Chicago to Champaign, Illinois, he stirs the imagination of Luke, an impoverished drifter not unlike the young Tennessee Williams. Gazing in awe at the slumbering figure in the seat beside him, Luke regards the black pugilist with "admiration and envy," but as Luke continues to contemplate the image of the black man, the boxer undergoes a transformation in Luke's imagination, changing from man to metaphor: "The Negro represented, he thought, something splendid and heroic. Something that made life possible

under any circumstances. A kind of impregnable simplicity. A completeness. An undividedness" (55). Luke's imaginative reconceptualization of the
boxer, similar to the narrator's objectification of Big Black, has an interesting parallel in the ideas of certain nineteenth-century "benevolent reformers
[who] tended to see the Negro more as a symbol than as a person."[28] For
these "romantic racialists," according to George M. Fredrickson, "the Negro
was a symbol of something that seemed tragically lacking in white American civilization."[29] James Russell Lowell, for example, whom Fredrickson
includes on his list of "romantic racialists," believed that "the African race
was intended to introduce a new element of civilization, and that the Cau-
casian would be benefited greatly by an infusion of its gentler and less selfish
qualities."[30] Similar to the Negroes in the eyes of these benevolent reformers, the black men in Williams's fiction more often than not serve as symbols
of what their white counterparts lack rather than as fully developed characters in their own right. Luke's envy of the black boxer, for instance, stems
from a sense of incompletion, a sense shared by the insecure Anthony Burns
in "Desire and the Black Masseur," as well as the narrator in "Big Black: A
Mississippi Idyll." Likewise, the black men who satisfy the sexual needs of
Miss Coynte in "Miss Coynte of Greene" appear not as realistically depicted
characters but as the expressions of Miss Coynte's libidinous imagination,
sexual objects who serve to compensate for her own sexual inadequacies.

What is most remarkable about Tennessee Williams's fabrications of
Africanist personae is not that Williams employs a racialized discourse, or
that he depicts black men as fearful and desirable beasts, but that he uses a
similar discourse for both racial *and* cultural aliens. In *A Streetcar Named
Desire*, for instance, Blanche's fearful and desirable Other is Stanley Kowalski. Of Polish descent rather than African American, Stanley is nevertheless defined as the Other by means of an Africanist presence implicit in the
racialized discourse spoken by Blanche and Stella when comparing Stanley
to a beast. This racialized discourse, familiar to readers of Williams's short
stories, and also a part of Williams's cultural milieu, links Stanley Kowalski
to a group of black characters who are similarly characterized as physically
threatening, inarticulate, lacking intelligence, full of desire, and sexually
potent.

Like Big Black and other powerful black men in Williams's short
stories, Stanley poses a physical threat to Blanche. His imposing presence
prompts Blanche to tell Mitch: "The first time I laid eyes on him I thought
to myself, that man is my executioner!" (351). Stanley's indifference to things
such as art, poetry, and music constitute for Blanche both ignorance and an
inability to communicate. When Stella relates to Blanche what she finds
attractive about Stanley, Blanche labels it "brutal desire" (321). The words
"brutal" and "desire" link Stanley once more to black characters whose

fearful *and* desirable presences reflect the ambivalent feelings of the Self. Daniel Aaron's description of white extremists' prejudicial opinion of the Negro, in the latter part of the nineteenth century, might very well be used to summarize Blanche's first impression of Stanley Kowalski: viewed from her perspective, Stanley is "the concupiscent ape, the wild beast, the putative rapist dominated by uncontrollable sexual passion."[31]

Many of the characteristics that Stanley shares with black characters in the short stories of Tennessee Williams are expressed economically and covertly in metaphorical comparisons to animals. Stella, for example, observes to Blanche that Stanley belongs to a "different species" (258), which Blanche elaborates more fully following the poker night: "He acts like an animal, has an animal's habits! Eats like one, moves like one, talks like one! There's even something—subhuman—something not quite to the stage of humanity yet! Yes, something—ape-like about him." (323). The racialized discourse spoken by Stella and Blanche serves to define Stanley as the Other, a sexual, cultural, and by implication, racial alien. The specific comparison of Stanley to an ape is a means by which Blanche implicitly links him to the black population. Henry Louis Gates, Jr. notes that on "the metaphorical great chain of being . . . [b]lacks were most commonly represented . . . either as the lowest of the human races or as first cousin to the ape."[32] The hierarchical arrangement to which Gates makes reference is also reflected in *A Streetcar Named Desire* when Blanche and Stella discuss Stanley's ancestral origins. Following Stella's casual remark, "Stanley is Polish, you know," Blanche joking replies, "Oh yes. They're something like Irish, aren't they? [. . .] Only not so—highbrow?" (256). The immediate laughter of the two women at this ethnic joke points to the cultural assumptions they share but do not express explicitly. In the view of Blanche and Stella, Stanley occupies a rung on the ethnic ladder even lower than the Irish, a group of people whom, according to Jan Nederveen Pieterse, Americans frequently likened to blacks.[33]

In rejecting Blanche's characterization of him as an animal, however, Stanley responds, as many immigrants and children of immigrants did, by asserting his *American* identity: "I am not a Polack. People from Poland are Poles, not Polacks. But what I am is a one-hundred-per-cent American, born and raised in the greatest country on earth and proud as hell of it, so don't ever call me a Polack" (374). Describing how "[r]ace . . . functions as a metaphor . . . necessary to the construction of Americanness," Toni Morrison observes how "immigrant populations . . . understood their 'Americanness' as an opposition to the resident black population."[34] As the child of Polish forebears, Stanley struggles to assert his identity apart from both his Polish heritage and the black population with which he is associated by means of animal imagery. To assimilate successfully, to establish more than a provisional claim to a domain generally afforded only to "white" men, Stanley must deny his ethnic heritage and erase the traces of Otherness reinscribed by Blanche's unexpected and disrupting presence in New Orleans. Considering Morrison's suggestion that the word "American" is closely linked to the concept of "race," and that in the United States, "American means white,"[35] we can conclude that Stanley's attempt to define himself as "American" is also an attempt to assert himself as "white."

In the context of *A Streetcar Named Desire*, however, Stanley Kowalski defies classification in terms as diametrically opposed as those of gentleman (white) or beast (black). It may be that Stanley is offered as a solution to the seemingly irreconcilable opposition of black and white. Occupying what might be called "common" ground, Stanley may represent, in Williams's coded discourse, the fearful and desirable prospect of miscegenation. In a context already charged with racialized discourse, Blanche's reflection, "Maybe he's what we need to mix with our blood now that we've lost Belle Reve" (285) suggests the possibility of miscegenation, just as the prospect is more explicitly proposed in the short story "Miss Coynte of Greene." "Someday after our time," Miss Coynte predicts, "there is bound to be a great new race in America, and this is naturally going to come about through the mixing together of black and white blood, which we all know is actually red, regardless of skin color!" (499).

Perhaps a sensitivity to the expectations of Broadway audiences in 1947 and a fear of commercial failure prompted Williams to misrepresent the topic of miscegenation in the form of an ethnic rather than a racial liaison in *A Streetcar Named Desire*. But by means of a racialized discourse, linking a descendant of Polish immigrants with imagery traditionally associated with black characters, Williams nevertheless covertly broaches the topic of miscegenation in a play ostensibly without an Africanist presence. In a creative work in which no black characters appear it "would be ludicrous and dishonest," Toni Morrison remarks, "to situate black people throughout the pages and scenes . . . like some government quota."[36] In this respect, Tennessee Williams cannot be accused of dishonesty, but he might be guilty, as Blanche is guilty, of "misrepresent[ing] things" (385). The virtual absence of African American characters in his plays belies the significance of an Africanist influence on Williams's creative imagination. As Toni Morrison so astutely observes: "Even, and especially, when American texts are not 'about' Africanist presences or characters . . . the shadow hovers in implication."[37]

NOTES

1. C.W.E. Bigsby, *Modern American Drama, 1945–1990* (Cambridge, 1992), 37.

2. Tennessee Williams, *A Streetcar Named Desire*, in *The Theatre of Tennessee Williams*, vol. I (New York, 1971), 245. Subsequent references appear parenthetically in the text.

3. Tennessee Williams, *Orpheus Descending*, in *The Theatre of Tennessee Williams*, vol. III (New York, 1971), 240.

4. Lionel Kelly, "The White Goddess, Ethnicity, and the Politics of Desire," in *Confronting Tennessee Williams's A Streetcar Named Desire*, ed. Philip C. Kolin (Westport, CN, 1993), 123.

5. For a more detailed discussion of "gaps" and "blanks," see Wolfgang Iser's *The Act of Reading: A Theory of Aesthetic Response* (Baltimore, 1978), 163–231, from which I borrow the specific terminology.

6. Ibid., 168.

7. Peter J. Rabinowitz, "Assertion and Assumption: Fictional Patterns and the External World," *PMLA*, 96:3 (1981), 409.

8. Iser, 168. See note 5.

9. Toni Morrison, *Playing in the Dark: Whiteness and the Literary Imagination* (New York, 1992), 15.

10. Ibid., 5.

11. Henry Louis Gates, Jr., "Editor's Introduction: Writing 'Race' and the Difference It Makes," *Critical Inquiry*, 12: 1 (1985), 2.

12. Morrison, 17. See note 9.

13. Hans Robert Jauss, *Aesthetic Experience and Literary Hermeneutics*, trans. Michael Shaw (Minneapolis, 1982), 264.

14. Aldon Lynn Nielsen, *Reading Race: White American Poets and the Racial Discourse in the Twentieth Century* (Athens, GA, 1988), 6.

15. Tennessee Williams, "Big Black: A Mississippi Idyll," in *Collected Stories* (New York, 1985), 27. Subsequent references appear parenthetically in the text.

16. Tennessee Williams, "Desire and the Black Masseur," in *Collected Stories*, 209.

17. Tennessee Williams, "Miss Coynte of Greene," in *Collected Stories*, 495. Subsequent references appear parenthetically in the text.

18. Thomas Dixon, *The Clansman: An Historical Romance of the Ku Klux Klan* (New York, 1905), 304.

19. J.T. Trowbridge, *Cudjo's Cave* (Boston, 1895), 116.

20. Herman Melville, *Moby-Dick, or The Whale* (Evanston, 1988), 120.

21. George M. Frederickson, *The Black Image in the White Mind: The Debate on Afro-American Character and Destiny, 1817–1914* (New York, 1971), 279, 276.

22. Ibid., 276.

23. Winthrop D. Jordan, *White over Black: American Attitudes toward the Negro, 1550–1812* (Chapel Hill, NC, 1968), 28.

24. Ibid., 137.

25. Tzvetan Todorov, "'Race,' Writing, and Culture," trans. Loulou Mack, *Critical Inquiry* 13: 1 (1986), 171.

26. Henry Louis Gates, Jr., "Talkin' That Talk," *Critical Inquiry* 13:1 (1986), 204.

27. Tennessee Williams, "Ten Minute Stop," in *Collected Stories*, 55. Subsequent references appear parenthetically in the text.

28. Frederickson, 109. See note 21.

29. Ibid., 108.

30. James Russell Lowell, *The Anti-Slavery Papers of James Russell Lowell*, vol. 1 (New York, 1902), 22.

31. Daniel Aaron, "The 'Inky Curse': Miscegenation in the White American Literary Imagination," *Social Science Information* 22:2 (1983), 174.

32. Gates, Jr., "Editor's Introduction: Writing 'Race,'" 12.

33. Jan Nederveen Pieterse, *White on Black: Images of Africa and Blacks in Western Popular Culture* (New Haven, 1992), 214.

34. Morrison, 47. See note 9.

35. Ibid.

36. Ibid., 15.

37. Ibid., 46–7.

BERT CARDULLO

Scene 11 of A Streetcar Named Desire

Scene 11, the last scene of Tennessee Williams's *A Streetcar Named Desire*, occurs "some weeks" (131) after scenes 7–10, which take place on September 15, Blanche DuBois's birthday. I would like to suggest that "some weeks" could be six weeks or so, and that scene 11 occurs—in the largely (Franco-Spanish) Catholic city of New Orleans—on November 2, All Souls' Day. On this feast, Roman Catholics pray for the resurrection of those suffering in Purgatory, where souls destined for heaven are purified of all sin and imperfection. The evidence for my conclusion can be found in both scenes 9 and 11.

Scene 9 contains the short confrontation between Blanche and the Mexican Woman Vendor, who is clearly meant to be a kind of death figure, with whom Blanche comes face to face as she begins to experience the spiritual death that—paradoxically, on her birthday—will lead to her being committed to a mental asylum. However, the blind Mexican woman, wearing a dark shawl, is a symbol not only of death but also of potential resurrection. She carries "bunches of those gaudy tin flowers that *lower-class Mexicans display at funerals and other festive occasions*" (119; emphasis mine), and therefore can be seen as a harbinger of the Mexican Day of the Dead (All Souls' Day). This religious festival is the greatest single manifestation of the Mexican preoccupation with death[1] and is pervaded both by an atmosphere of gaiety,

From *ANQ* 10, no. 4 (Fall 1997): 34–38. © 1997 by Heldref Publications.

intemperance, and affirmation, and by an atmosphere of piety, reverence, and abnegation. The fact that the Woman Vendor is Mexican and is selling her wares on the anniversary of Blanche's birth, long in advance of November 2, is significant: first, September 15 falls under the sixth sign of the zodiac, Virgo ("Virgo is the Virgin," Blanche tells Stanley in scene 5 [77]), and it is the feast day of the Virgin Mary as Our Lady of Sorrows, the Mater Dolorosa;[2] second, the Blessed Virgin Mary, in her dark-skinned incarnation as the Virgin of Guadalupe, is the patron saint of Mexico; third, the feast commemorating the Assumption, Mary's ascension into heaven, is August 15, a month before the action of scene 9, and thus prefigures Blanche's own "assumption" (we know from the following statement by Blanche that scenes 5–6 of *Streetcar* take place in August: "Oh, my birthday's next month, the fifteenth of September" [77]); and fourth, as someone conceived without original sin, Mary, the virgin mother of Jesus Christ, is believed to be especially efficacious at petitioning God on behalf of supplicants and sinners—especially those sinners consigned to Purgatory but awaiting elevation to Paradise. That the Mexican Woman Vendor is a symbol not only of death but also of resurrection is further emphasized by the fact that she sells "corones para los muertos" in addition to "flores para los muertos" (119–20). *Corones* are wreaths for the dead, but a *corona* can also be a white or colored circle seen around a luminous body, hence a halo, or symbolic ring of radiant light encircling the head in pictures of divine or sacred personages such as the Virgin Mary. As used by the Mexican Woman, then, the word *corones* has a double meaning. It signifies crowns of victory, of ascent, as well as wreaths of death or decline.

Other events in the play pointedly suggest Blanche's potential resurrection, most notably the appearance of the Kowalski baby onstage for the first time in scene 11 (142) at the very moment Blanche DuBois is being led away to an asylum by the Doctor and the Matron. The baby's brief, symbolic presence contrasts with, as well as complements, that of the blind Mexican woman two scenes earlier. These two events, the birth of the boy and Blanche's incarceration in a mental institution, may not initially seem to be related, but in fact they are. Henry I. Schvey has argued that

> Stella's baby, born at approximately the same time as Blanche's violation by Stanley in the previous scene, is associated with Blanche in the final moments of the play.... Williams clearly suggests an identification between the tragic fall of one and the birth of the other. [He suggests] that Blanche's symbolic death has resulted in new life.... Thus Blanche's fall is actually part of a process that goes beyond death and hints at something like heroic transcendence, ... [at] spiritual purification through suffering. (109)

Schvey believes that this process of transcendence or purification, or what I am calling *resurrection*, is augmented by Blanche's changing in the final scene (significantly, after a bath) from a red satin robe (133)—in which she flirted with Stanley during scene 2 (37) and with Mitch during scene 3 (53)—into a blue outfit. "It's Della Robbia blue," declares Blanche, "the blue of the robe in the old Madonna pictures" (135), and thus a blue that associates her with both the Virgin Mary in Renaissance art and the Kowalskis' baby boy, whom Eunice brings onstage "wrapped in a pale blue blanket" (142) and who had been "sleeping like a little angel" (132). (Even the sky cooperates: it is more or less the same color that Williams described at the start of the play as "a peculiarly tender blue, almost a turquoise" [13, 131].) Blanche's anticipated transcendence or resurrection is further augmented by the cathedral bells that chime for the only time in *Streetcar* during scene 11 (136) and lend increased support to the idea that this scene occurs on All Souls' Day; by her fantasy that eating an unwashed or impure grape, let us say one that has not been transubstantiated into the wine/blood of Christ, has nonetheless transported her soul to heaven and her body into a deep blue ocean (136); and by the Doctor's raising Blanche up from the floor of the Kowalski apartment, to which she dropped after the Matron had pinioned her arms crucifixion-style (141), together with Blanche's spiritedly leading the way out of the hell of her sister's home (without looking back), followed by the Doctor and Matron instead of being escorted by them (142).

Blanche is being sent to a purgatory of sorts, a psychiatric hospital, a kind of halfway house between the heaven of lucidity and the hell of insanity, the renewed life of the mind and the final death of the spirit. And it is while Blanche is in "purgatory" that she will be cleansed of her sins, particularly the sin—which she herself admits and laments (95–96)—of denying her homosexual husband, Allan Grey, the compassion that would have saved him from suicide. Perhaps this cleansing will come through the intercession of the Virgin Mary herself whose own sorrow and suffering made her compassionate. Blanche's religious origins are Protestant, not Roman Catholic—she tells Mitch that her first American ancestors were French Huguenots (55)—and many Protestant denominations object to the veneration of Mary, but that would not prevent so independent or willful a spirit as Blanche DuBois from either appealing to Mary for help or receiving the Blessed Virgin's ministrations. Indeed, Blanche has long since strayed from her religious origins, and her errant ways together with her lapse into madness put her in special need of God's grace—a grace, the Catholic Church teaches, for which Mary is the chief mediatrix.

A number of commentators have pointed out the irony of Blanche's spending several months on a street in New Orleans named Elysian Fields— in Greek mythology the dwelling place of virtuous people after death—and the further irony of her having previously lived in Laurel, Mississippi (laurel wreaths, of course, were used by the ancient Greeks to crown the victors in athletic contests, military battles, and artistic competitions). These ironies are compounded in the play by the names of the people who surround Blanche, with the important exception of Stanley: Mitch (derived from Michael, meaning "someone like God" in Hebrew), Stella (from the Latin for "star"), Eunice (from the Greek for "good victory"), and Steve (from the Greek for "crown"). Critics regard these various names as ironic because in fact Blanche DuBois—"white woods"—finds herself, not in heaven, but in what amounts to hell ("Redhot!" the tamale Vendor cries out at the end of scene 2 [44]) in a conflict with stone-age Stanley the blacksmith (whose first name derives from the Old English "stone-lea" or stone meadow, while his last, Kowalski, is Polish for "smith"); and, these critics argue, this conflict will obviously not send her to an eternal life of bliss in any Elysian Fields, but rather to the misery of a living death without chance of redemption in the madhouse.

It seems possible, however, that these celestial or winning names are not ironic, but instead suggest what they appear to suggest: that Blanche, brutally defeated in her crucible with Stanley in New Orleans, will ultimately triumph on Judgment Day in the kingdom of God if not on treatment day in the realm of secular ministry—modern (psychiatric) medicine. Blanche's own name, which appears to be ironic in that it suggests a virginity which she no longer possesses in deed, attests to her virginity of spirit—her "beauty of the mind and . . . tenderness of the heart" (126), as she puts it. Thus her name links her not only to the purity of the Virgin Mary, but also to the reclaimed innocence of Mary Magdalene, who was cured of her sexual waywardness by Jesus (Just as Blanche was suddenly cured of hers when she remarked to Mitch, "Sometimes—there's God—so quickly!" [96]) and later saw Christ after he had risen from the dead.

Scene 11 of *Streetcar* can be regarded, then, as a scene of celebration as well as mourning, of eternal life as well as transitory death—like the Mexican Day of the Dead itself. Hence Williams not only introduces the Kowalskis' newborn child into the action precisely at the moment of Blanche's "passing," a child of whom Blanche said in scene 8, "I hope that his eyes are going to be like candies, like two blue candies lighted in a white cake!" (109). Williams also creates a combination festive-macabre atmosphere: Stanley, Steve, and the Mexican, Pablo, play cards, eat, and drink, while Mitch sulks, slumps, and sobs at the same table over the loss of Blanche (the same Mitch who contributed to the festive-macabre atmosphere of scene 9 by demanding sex from a drunken, distraught Blanche DuBois); and Williams weaves into the action the music of the "Varsouviana," the polka tune to which Blanche and Allan were dancing the night he committed suicide (137, 139), the simultaneously melancholic and inspiriting sounds of the "Blue Piano," (142), and the harsh cries as well as lurid shadows of the jungle (139, 141). Moreover, Williams concludes the final scene of *Streetcar* on a sexual note: after Blanche has departed, Stanley "voluptuously" kneels beside the weeping Stella and places his hand inside her blouse, as Steve opens a new round of cards with the words "This game is seven-card stud" (142). Clearly, life goes on for the Kowalskis and their friends ("Life has got to go on," Eunice admonishes Stella [133]), but life goes on for Blanche too—in "purgatory" and beyond.

NOTES

1. Williams himself was to be preoccupied with his own death for much of his life. Moreover, he had begun writing *Streetcar* in Chapala, Mexico (near Guadalajara), convinced that he was dying, that this would be his last play, and that therefore he should put his all into it. (Williams thought that the agonizing abdominal pains he had been experiencing were the result of lethal stomach cancer, but in fact they were caused by a ruptured appendix.) See Tischler 133.

2. See Kolin 81–87, for a detailed discussion of the striking parallels between Blanche DuBois and the Blessed Virgin Mary. Kolin builds on the work of Henry I. Schvey, who was the first critic to link Blanche to Mary in *Streetcar*. Here I am linking Blanche to the Virgin through the Mexican Woman Vendor, who, I have argued elsewhere, is a kind of fateful double for Williams's tragic heroine.

WORKS CITED

Cardullo, Bert. "The Blind Mexican Woman in *A Streetcar Named Desire*." *Notes on Modern American Literature* 71 (1993): entry 14.

Kolin, Philip C. "Our Lady of the Quarter: Blanche DuBois and the Feast of the Mater Dolorosa." *ANQ: A Quarterly Journal of Short Articles, Notes and Reviews* 4.2 (1991): 81–87.

Schvey, Henry I. "Madonna at the Poker Night: Pictorial Elements in Tennessee Williams's *A Streetcar Named Desire*." *Modern Critical Interpretations: Tennessee Williams's A Streetcar Named Desire*. Ed. Harold Bloom. New York Chelsea House, 1988. 103–09.

Tischler, Nancy M. *Tennessee Williams: Rebellious Puritan*. New York: Citadel P, 1961.

Williams, Tennessee. *A Streetcar Named Desire*. New York: NAL, 1951.

JOHN S. BAK

Wagnerian Architectonics:
The Plastic Language of Tennessee Williams's
A Streetcar Named Desire

One of Tennessee Williams's most distinguishing dramatic signatures is his use of music. This music may emanate from a jukebox, a Victrola, or a nearby bar or dance hall, wafting in to create a particular mood onstage; or it may ruminate inside the head of a principal character, heard only by himself or herself and those privy to either's thoughts. In both instances, music is used to enhance the play's action or theme, as was typical of most modern plays during his time. Yet Williams used so much music—from Polish waltzes to Mexican cancions, from German operas to American folk songs—that critics have often dismissed it, as they have many of his extraliterary techniques, as elements of pure expressionism.

Comments on music specifically in *A Streetcar Named Desire* have not fared much better, with most early interpretations reflecting what Irwin Shaw wrote in his 22 December 1947 review of the Elia Kazan production: "voices and music" break in "again and again with no reasonable justification but thunderous effect . . ." (Miller 46). A decade later, critics like W. David Sievers began to see that Williams had "orchestrated the sounds of the French Quarter" in *Streetcar* with this music but again failed to discern why (Miller 91).[1] More recently, however, criticism has sought to reexamine Williams's use of music, especially in *Streetcar*, with the hope of eradicating

From *The Tennessee Williams Literary Journal* 4, no. 1 (Fall 1997): 41–58. © 1997 by *The Tennessee Williams Literary Journal*.

earlier myopic scholarship and exploring uncharted territory pertaining to Williams's dramaturgy.

Mary Ann Corrigan and Joseph N. Riddel, for instance, contend that the music and aural effects in *Streetcar* make audible the internal contortions of Blanche's mind as she gradually digresses into madness ("Realism" 392; 425). Corrigan even makes the distinction between Williams's use of a musical theme and a musical motive:

> *The Glass Menagerie*'s musical themes . . . reflect not so much the characters' inner lives, as the author's ironic perspective on them. On the other hand, in *A Streetcar Named Desire*, the nightclub music and the Varsouviana convey the emotional states of the characters at each stage of the action. ("Realism" 394, see Tharpe 384)

In his 1982 dissertation on the function of music in the Williams canon, William J. McMurry claims that *Streetcar*, because its extramusical leitmotifs thematically (as opposed to structurally) accompany the onstage action, is "quasi-operatic" (803A). It is for this unique blend of music and poetry in the American theatre that Esther Merle Jackson associates Williams with the German Romantic tradition that employed what Wagner termed the plastic language of the arts. Making abundant use of art, poetry, lighting, dance, and music to help deliver a message that dialogue fails to accomplish alone, Williams is resuscitating what Jackson and Kenneth Tynan both recognize as Wagner's concept of the *Gesamtkunstwerk* (the Hellenic synthesis of the arts) ("Music" 295–96; Hurrell 124). Yet all of these critics, despite their cogent arguments, still regard music in *Streetcar* as an ornamentation to and not necessarily a structural ingredient of the play.[2]

Though Williams frequently displayed his passion for and knowledge of music in his interviews, letters, and *Memoirs* (1974), the extent of that knowledge, particularly of the composing processes of Richard Wagner, for these critics remained conjecture. Yet Williams's familiarity with Wagner is made explicit in his work. In his *Memoirs*, for instance, Williams paints an encounter he had with a German film company sent to New Orleans to interview him in the early seventies: "The crew was led with Wagnerian intensity . . ." (94). Later, he describes his anger at a party thrown for the pre-opening of *The Milk Train Doesn't Stop Here Anymore* (1964): "I flew into one of my Wagnerian tantrums" (196). Whereas both references allude only to Williams's understanding of Wagner the Man, as notorious for his megalomania as he was famous for his music, they help to support the contention that when Williams does refer to Wagner's art and artistry in his fiction, he is making a specific claim that should not be quickly discharged.

For example, in his novella, 'The Knightly Quest' (1966), Williams mentions Wagner's "Ride of the Valkyries" (435), the famous overture to act three of *Die Walküre*. It is probably to this music that Williams is alluding when he earlier wrote in his 1945 essay "The History of a Play (With Parentheses)" about *Battle of Angels*'s "Wagnerian experience" (114); both dramas conclude in an inferno (cf. Gassner 4). Moreover, in *Cat on a Hot Tin Roof* (1955), Williams notes in a stage direction early in act two, "*The room is suddenly blasted by the climax of a Wagnerian opera . . .*" (3.65). In *The Night of the Iguana* (1961), he again displays his knowledge of Wagner's style of composition: Wolfgang, Hilda's "*Wagnerian-tenor bridegroom*" (4.261), and his German party look on the storm which assails the Costa Verde "*as a Wagnerian climax*" (4.325) to the day.[3] Music, simply put, is an important element in the drama of Tennessee Williams and is, in fact, less an ornamentation or an expressionistic technique and more a vital ingredient to his dramaturgy. Although the extent of Williams's association with Wagner might appear to be limited to Wagner's life, it is not; for Williams, a music aficionado, was also well-versed in Wagner the Artist.

Those early critical studies that connect Williams to the Wagner tradition, however, do so on a strictly theoretical basis alone. Yet, as Williams's works attest to here, the Wagner influence is much more significant. No study to date, though, has examined as analog the Wagnerian elements of composition in Williams's plays, specifically the similarities in structure of both dramatists' masterpieces, *A Streetcar Named Desire* (1947) and *Der Ring der Nibelungen* (1876).[4] The Varsouviana, the jungle cries, the locomotive, the blue piano music and the hot trumpet from the Four Deuces—all appear to be external to the play and, therefore, insignificant to *Streetcar*'s structure. This, I believe, is not the case. Rather, the music and the aural accents provide an underlying structure to *Streetcar* which melds all the elements of the play together—literary, dramatic, and thematic—just as Wagner had attempted in the *Ring*. In other words, Williams builds *Streetcar* architectonically, adapting Wagner's use of webbing leitmotifs for his own purpose of reinforcing for the reader or audience the struggle that Blanche experiences with everyone in the play.[5] These leitmotifs create a metalanguage in *Streetcar* that subliminally works to tamper with our emotions and our feelings—all without any character uttering a single word.

Richard Wagner, a name as ubiquitous in the music world as Williams's is in theatre circles, also contributed a substantial body of prose work on music theory and musicology. His numerous essays—collected in eight volumes by W. A. Willis—range in topic from his views on the then current state of music and opera; the future of music; and the role of art, religion, and revolution in the theatre. In fact, a good portion of these book-length essays were written while Wagner was in Zurich, exiled for his role in the 1849 failed coup attempt in Dresden against the Prussians. During those eleven years in exile (1849–1860), Wagner wrote the most influential and, arguably, the most controversial prose works of his life. In *Oper und Drama* (1851), for example, a work which belongs to the former more than the latter of these two groups, Wagner outlined his revolutionary theory of the leitmotif. This single but complex idea alone has generated more secondary literature than all of that ever written on Williams, which is itself no small body of work. This theory, Wagner believed and was correct to assert, would revolutionize music and drama, creating, in a sense, the music of the future.

Although he never actually used the term *leitmotif* nor was the first to experiment with its use in his work, Wagner did write in a letter of 1867 to Heinrich Porges that he employed a "*Hauptmotif*" (principal motive) in structuring his music dramas and was the first to take full advantage of its plastic capabilities (Goldman and Sprinchorn 222). This motive, Wagner earlier described in *Oper und Drama*, is akin to a gesture—nonverbal in communication, having "the faculty of uttering the *unspeakable*" (2.316). Despite never using the term as we know it today, Wagner did describe precisely in this lengthy essay what this musical motive was and how it was to be used. Since "Music cannot think" but can "materialise thoughts," Wagner argued, a musical theme could be implanted in the audience's sub-conscious—whether first attached to a particular person, theme, or event or not mattered little—then used later to foreshadow events, as a motive of "*Ahnung*" (foreboding), or to flashback a history, as a motive of "*Erin-nerung*" (remembrance) (2.329, 335).

This "verse-Melody," as Wagner came to call it, contains "the non-present but *conditioning* emotion, as described from memory and thought" (2.327). In effect, it would suggest an idea or make privy a character's thoughts and feeling without the use of the spoken word. But, Wagner warned,

> A musical motive (*Motiv*) can produce a definite impression on the Feeling, inciting it to a function akin to Thought, *only* when the emotion uttered in that motive has been definitely conditioned by a definite object, and proclaimed by a definite individual before our very eyes. (2.329, emphasis added)

Therefore, a motive had to be attached to some idea, person, or concept, even if the audience was not yet certain what that connection was. But once the melody was "imparted to us by the actor" or "expressively delivered by the orchestra at an instant when the person represented merely nurses that emotion in his memory," it then "materialises for us this personage's Thought" (2.328). A leitmotif, then, operating in discrete isolation, equates a specific thought or emotion to a conditioned response.

Unlike his predecessors who experimented with a similar concept of the leitmotif, Wagner did not make his motives static or unduly repetitive. Once their meaning was confirmed on an individual basis, Wagner would then alter and intertwine them, giving his original motive new meaning or creating a new idea from the integration of established ones. Wagner continued in *Oper und Drama* to define how these original motives were to become this meshwork, or webbing structure, of leitmotifs that would weave its nonverbal language throughout his drama, that would not become a string of unrelated musical themes but rather would "mould themselves into a continuous artistic Form, which stretches not merely over narrower fragments of the drama but over the whole drama's self" (2.348). The beauty of this structure for Wagner was that all of the motives that are at work in his music drama would develop from a few "root-motives" (2.347), allowing for an unlimited variety of expressions while still retaining the music's and the drama's essence.

Once he described what a leitmotif (singular) was and how these leitmotifs (plural) were to function structurally together, Wagner added this caveat:

> These Melodic Moments—in which we remember a Foreboding, whilst they turn our Remembrance into a prophecy—will necessarily have blossomed only from *the weightiest motives* of the drama. . . . (2.347)

New motives cannot deliver extraliterary commentary unless they develop from the "root-motives" of the work. These "root-motives" are not to be "mere 'sentences'" but "plastic moments-of-Feeling" (2.347), filling the music drama not with limited and repetitive musical phrases but with themes that are altered from their parent motive enough to change the original motive's idea but similar enough to that parent motive so it could be recognized as evolving from such. But, Wagner additionally warned, "We ought never to hear these prophetic or reminiscent melodic-moments, except when we can feel that they are complementary to the utterance of the character upon the stage, who either will not or cannot just now expose to us his full emotion" (2.346). A motive unconditioned to a particular thought or feeling would be as ineffective as one developing from a secondary, as opposed to a primary, motive.

Although the unity of the work remains with these root motives, Wagner noted, the webbing structure of the drama comes when they "contrast, complete, reshape, divorce, and intertwine with one another" (Goldman and Sprinchorn 229–30), forming an entirely new motive. These root motives, then, may remain unaltered, reflecting a consistency in the person or idea which it represents; altered in rhythm or intervallic structure, harmony, or orchestration, promoting a sudden or gradual shift in direction of action or thought; or combined with or superimposed upon other motives, either suggesting that a new dramatic condition has emerged or commenting upon, ironically or not, the incongruous or harmonic mixture represented onstage. But the success of these leitmotifs still lay in this conscious "knitting" of music "with a *remembrance*" (2.368), a concern Wagner would voice elsewhere in his prose work.[6]

Wagner, then, used leitmotifs to provide extraliterary commentary on a particular theme, characteristic, or idea imperative to the dramatic action. That leitmotif may reflect a character's personality, or it may suggest the transference of a particular trait of one character onto another. For example, in Wagner's great tetralogy, the *Ring* (*Das Rheingold, Die Walküre, Siegfried,* and *Götterdämmerung*)—the dramatic rendering of his theoretical treatise, *Oper und Drama*—Fafner the giant has music which is slow and lumbering, suggestive of his thunderous steps; similarly, Loge, the Promethean figure, is characterized at the fiery end of *Die Walküre* by wispy strains of piccolos and staccato strings, mimicking in music the desultory licking of flames that surround him: it is the motive of fire as primal energy. The motive of the Rhinegold, played first in *Das Rheingold* as a motive of anticipation, becomes later associated with the motive of the three Rhinemaidens who protect the gold until Alberich, the king of the underworld, steals it from them to forge the omnipotent ring.

Whereas a motive may represent something tangible or descriptive, as it does above, it can also stand for a concept or an action. The spear motive, which is related to the stage property that Wotan (the ruler of the gods) brandishes, also implies several auxiliary concepts: the contract to which Wotan agrees with the two giants who build Valhalla—the gods' new castle—in return for the ring; the runes of the gods which are carved on the spear's shaft; and the balance of world power that shifts when Siegfried, the mortal hero, shatters Wotan's spear with his sword Nothung, an act which directly precipitates the gods' fall. As noted above, the motive may be singular in importance or pluralistic in the ideas it evokes.

The transference or superimposition of one character's leitmotif onto another became another important function for Wagner. This motive inversion may be portentous or ironic, depending on the context of the action. In other words, having an upbeat motive intermeshed with a dark and sinister motive may suggest a glimmer of goodness in an otherwise evil mind; or, conversely, it may mean that the evil character has assumed the good character's nature, indicative of the one leitmotif being subsumed into the other. When Siegfried professes his love to Brünnhilde at the end of *Siegfried*, for instance, the giant Fafner's motive is heard intermixed with Brünnhilde's, suggesting that, although now bereft of her divinity, she is still a powerful woman. But the motive also reminds the audience of the contract to which Wotan had entered with the giants in *Das Rheingold* that the earth goddess Erda professed would seal the doom of all the gods, of which Brünnhilde's will soon be the first.

Similarly, Wagner superimposed or intertwined several root motives together for varying effects, a prominent one being irony. For example, when Gunther and Siegfried consummate their blood-brotherhood in *Götterdämmerung*, several motives are intermixed and provide a heterogeneous blend of ideas that both support and contradict one another. During the swearing of blood loyalty, the Hagen motive is played sinisterly; at the height of the pledge, the curse motive is heard. Earlier in *Das Rheingold*, when Wotan and Loge had duped Alberich into relinquishing the ring, Alberich put a curse on the ring that promised death to its bearer. Now, Hagen, the son of Alberich and Gunther's half brother, reminds us of that curse through his actions and his motive.

Moreover, when Siegfried agrees to Gunther and Hagen's plan after this oath scene to rescue Brünnhilde from the ring of fire that Wotan (her father) had encircled her with at the end of *Die Walküre*, he does so only because they have drugged him. Hagen had earlier suggested to Gunther that he take Brünnhilde as his wife, so as to assure the survival of his Gibichung race. But only the hero Siegfried can brave the flames which surround her. So, under the spell of Hagen's magic potion, Siegfried agrees to wear the *Tarnhelm* (the magic helmet forged by Alberich which gives its bearer the power to assume any form), approach Brünnhilde in Gunther's form, and return with her so that Gunther can marry her. What is ironic here is that Siegfried had already professed his love to Brünnhilde at the conclusion of *Siegfried* and given her the ring as a token of his love; but now, because of the spell, he can no longer remember it or her. Hagen's intentions are anything but altruistic, however, for he arranged this entire scheme simply to get the ring for himself. Thus, during the whole scene in which Siegfried follows through with the plan, the accompanying music includes the *Tarnhelm* magic motive, the magic potion motive, and Gunther's motive. The twists in plot development become further entangled when the leitmotifs weave and meld their ideas as well.

This use of webbing musical phrases together is Wagner's architectonic method for all of his *Ring* cycle, and those music dramas which came after. The leitmotifs allowed him to say many things, delivering multiple impressions, that spoken language cannot fully realize. In fusing words with music, then, Wagner successfully blended two media of expression into one metalanguage. Tennessee Williams achieved a similar effect in *A Streetcar Named Desire*, in which music becomes an architectonic device by which he structured his operatic play. In drawing from Richard Wagner's plastic language of fusing word with music, Williams was able to make effective use of the extraverbal language of Wagnerian leitmotifs—an intricate webbing of musical phrases with ideas, themes, and character traits that allow for the flexible reordering of the original meaning without the need for additional spoken or written words. Although there are many lesser motives at work in *Streetcar*, the most prominent are for Blanche, Stanley, and Allan and the gossamer thread of their interconnectedness.

As Blanche's character assumes two roles—one living, one dead—so is her leitmotif twofold. The first is the music of the blue piano which "*expressed the spirit of the life which goes on*" in New Orleans (1.243). Whereas Elia Kazan correctly asserts that the blue piano "catches the soul of Blanche" (Cole and Chinoy 371), Constance Drake wrongly attributes this music to Stanley Kowalski (59). Although Stanley *is* the way of life in the Quarter—vibrant, vulgar, blues-esque—the music is actually Blanche's, for it first plays when she enters and continues throughout *Streetcar* when she is onstage, either in person or as the topic of discussion.

The blue piano music plays, for instance, when Blanche reveals to Stella that Belle Reve was lost: the "*music of the 'blue piano' grows louder*" (1.261). It also plays under her seduction scene with the paper boy collecting for *The Evening Star* (1.339). Williams later colors it with a "*hectic breakdown*" (1.368) when Blanche fears that something sinister has taken place between Stella and Stanley before her birthday party. The music returns again in scene eight when, Stanley now gone, Blanche asks Stella what Stanley had said about her. The piano also enters "slow *and blue*" with Blanche and Mitch's break-up at the end of scene nine (1.390). The blue piano is Blanche, and Williams reaffirms this association when the "*perpetual 'blue piano'*" (1.269) is heard around the corner even when she is not present but is the locus of Stanley and Stella's conversation in scene two. Through these several allusions, Williams provides Blanche with her musical motive; it takes on ironic overtones when we begin to see Blanche objectively and recognize that she is the antithesis of her "*joie de vivre!*" (1.344), becoming anything but the spirit of life in the Quarter.

As paper is clearly established as Blanche's literary motive, Williams draws from it Blanche's second musical motive.[7] Like paper, Blanche is artificial and susceptible to decay. The distant band, for example, plays "Paper Doll" "*slow and blue*" (1.305) after Stanley's violent outburst during the poker party; it will serve as a motive of anticipation for Blanche when, in the very next scene, she attempts to turn Stella against Stanley with her "*Don't—don't hang back with the brutes*" speech (1.323). Furthermore, Blanche sings her "paper moon" ditty "*contrapuntally with Stanley's speech*" (1.359) to Stella about Blanche's sordid past. Williams pits her motive against Stanley's to show the irony of Blanche's words as she sings that her future will indeed be a false "Barnum and Bailey world" if no one will believe in her; and no one, in fact, does. Bert Cardullo finds this song serving, in addition to its comical juxtaposition, as a thematic commentary on Blanche's future: while she looks to Mitch to believe in her, he will not, and her world will be the "honky-tonk parade" she fears (12). Cardullo correctly asserts that Blanche's fate is sealed when, during the rape scene, this honky-tonk music is prevalent (12).

Stanley's music is that of the honky-tonk.[8] *The New Grove Dictionary of Music and Musicians* describes honky-tonk music as being "associated with uprooted rural people, and the words dealt increasingly with their social problems" (8.682). With Blanche present, Stanley's marital harmony with Stella is in question. For example, when Stella leaves him at the end of scene three after he strikes her, a peal of "*Dissonant* brass" reflects his state, dominated by a moaning "*low-tone clarinet*" (1.305, 307). This same motive is heard when Stanley reenters in scene five, accompanied by the "*Trumpet and drums*" (1.335), and again in scene ten as "*Stanley appears around the corner of the building. . . . As he rounds the corner the honky-tonk music is heard*" (1.391). The connection with Stanley to the honky-tonk is finally solidified at the peak of the rape scene, in which his "*hot trumpet and drums*" (1.402) triumph over the blue piano just as he does over Blanche.

Stanley has two other lesser motives that figure into *Streetcar*'s structure as well, both describing not so much him but his identity with raw violence: the jungle cries and the locomotive. When he introduces us to Stanley, Williams writes that implicit in him is an "*Animal joy*" (1.264). He is an ape (as Williams portrayed him in earlier draft, scratching under his armpits) and a brute, which Blanche herself calls him. He is, to be sure, the "survivor of the Stone Age! Bearing the raw meat home from the kill in the jungle!" (1.323). Thus, when the cacophonous jungle cries irritate Blanche in scene ten, Williams, with Stanley's leitmotif, foreshadows his more serious attack upon her. Then after this rape, while Blanche is being led away, Stanley asks her if she forgot something. She cries "Yes!" but never continues; Williams does so for her as Stanley's jungle-cry motive rises up in the wings. Indeed, she has either forgotten the rape in her madness (doubtful) or is afraid to say anything, fearing that no one will believe her anyway (as is the case). Regardless, her thoughts about Stanley are made implicit with the musical motive.

Williams similarly portrays Stanley's raw power and dominance over Blanche with the locomotive motive. In scene four, for instance, when Blanche is describing Stanley's brutishness, he enters "*under cover of the train's noise*" (1.322), then later exits "*stealthily*" as "*Another train passes outside*" (1.323). Williams alerts us to Stanley's motive here, preparing us later for when the locomotive sound has more of an adverse effect upon Blanche. A further connection comes when, as Blanche tells Mitch about the story of Allan's suicide,

> *A locomotive is heard approaching outside. She claps her hands to her*
> *ears and crouches over. The headlight of the locomotive glares into the*
> *room as it thunders past. As the noise recedes she straightens slowly and*
> *continues speaking.* (1.354)

Although Stanley is not present in this scene, his presence is surely felt, Williams having already established his identity with the train in scenes one (with the L & N tracks) and four. Lastly, the locomotive sound is played again moments before the rape, again to foreshadow Stanley and Blanche's violent confrontation.[9]

Allan is the last character to have a principal leitmotif in *Streetcar*. Although he never appears in the play, he is vital to this thematic and dramatic development. Therefore, Williams includes him first from Blanche's story, and second from the Varsouviana, the Polish waltz which was playing at the time of his suicide. Furthermore, when Blanche makes several references to Allan, all are accompanied by the Varsouviana, further confirming his connection with it. For instance, when Stanley asks Blanche if she ever married, "*The music of the polka rises up, faint in the distance*" (1.268). In typical Wagner fashion, Williams establishes the association in anticipation first, before we understand its intent, then reconfirms our suspicions later with motives of remembrance. For example, when Blanche is discussing Allan's death with Mitch, the polka music is present, even breaking into a minor key, a coloring technique that further alters the leitmotif's message. This coloring is a technique Wagner called chromaticism, in which a musical phrase is altered in key or syncopation to suggest a change from the phrase's original meaning. Allan has indeed changed for Blanche, and Williams accentuates this by distorting his leitmotif. The mixing of leitmotifs to produce an array of contradictions, much the way Blanche's vital blue piano music contradicts her true nature, is uniquely Wagnerian as we have seen. Williams attempts a similar technique in *Streetcar*, in which the motives that he established for certain characters are subsequently distorted or intertwined in order to create a new meaning. Some of these parallels are expressed in the altered leitmotif, as in the case of Allan's Varsouviana's being "*filtered into a weird distortion, accompanied by the cries and noises of the jungle*" (1.414). As Blanche can no longer distinguish time—is she in the past with Allan or in the present with Stanley?—the result is a combination of the two male characters' motives. It is, after all, only fitting that Allan's Polish waltz should bleed into the Polish Kowalski's "one-hundred-per-cent American" (1.374) music, for Stanley's locomotive motive had earlier mixed with Allan's Varsouviana (1.354–55). From this juxtaposition, an incongruous brotherhood is achieved, from which Blanche is ostracized.

In the rape scene, as in the "paper moon" scene, Williams uses counterpoint to combat Stanley's hot trumpet with Blanche's blue piano, with the former drowning out the latter by the end. Williams had earlier established the blue piano's counterpoint to Stanley's leitmotif, as both were played softly at the conclusion of scene four: "*the music of the 'blue piano' and trumpet and drums is heard*" (2.324). The harmony of these two motives here served to foreshadow the disharmony of their pairing during the rape scene, where the two musical motives contend as strongly offstage as Blanche and Stanley do onstage. In fact, just before Blanche is confronted by Stanley, so too is her motive being subsumed into his: "*The barely audible 'blue piano' begins to drum up louder. The sound of it turns into the roar of an approaching locomotive*" (1.400). Then, as Stanley increases his aggression toward Blanche, so too does his leitmotif dominate her: Blanche's blue piano "*goes softly*," and Stanley's "*inhuman jungle voices rise up*" (1.401). Finally, just before he picks up her "*inert figure*" and carries her to the bed, Stanley's "*hot trumpet and drums . . . sound loudly*" (1.402). The celebration is short, however, as in the closing moments of the play Stanley's trumpet is "*muted*" (1.419); as is he, so goes his leitmotif.

Though Signi Falk calls this motive juxtaposition "a good stage trick" (Miller 100), Blanche, acknowledging to herself that it will be "a honky-tonk" (1.361) world if Mitch repudiates her love, is forced into Stanley's world—cold, heartless, callous. Williams described this truism not only in the dramatic rendering onstage but also in his use of Wagner's "Verse-Melody" offstage. The music in *Streetcar*, then, is a seemingly contradictory architectonic webbing of leitmotifs which provides both a structure to and metalanguage in the play. John Deathridge and Carl Dahlhaus describe this Wagnerian technique of meshing motives as "a means . . . of linking what is seen and spoken with what is not seen and not spoken" (146).

After establishing different leitmotifs for characters in the beginning of the play—Blanche's blue piano, Stanley's honky-tonk, and Allan's Varsouviana—Williams then distorted, mixed, juxtaposed, or superimposed many combinations of these several musical phrases onto one another, thus changing the original motives' discrete meanings. The effects achieved may be intentional, as with the clumsy Mitch's rumba music; or ironic, as with the moribund Blanche's vigorous blue piano. Williams also made an absent character present onstage in word or thought simply by playing his or her leitmotif behind the dialogue. Williams also used counterpoint, combating one character's motive with another's, thereby accentuating or foreshadowing through the resultant harmony or dissonance the accompanying action onstage.

Because of Williams's attention to music and form in his drama, Esther Jackson contends that "Williams scores his middle dramas with elaborately orchestrated compositions, with intricate patterns of songs, voices, music, noises, and cries" (*Broken World* 100; "Music" 299). In *Streetcar* specifically, Jackson finds that Williams "develops a fabric of sound" (*Broken World* 100) in his dramaturgy which adheres to the edicts of Wagner's theory of plastic language, for he describes his dramatic text as a series of notation—a score— set down by a composer. . . . Like Wagner, he suggests that much of the significant content of drama is suprarational in nature and, in consequence, extra-verbal in form (*Broken World* 89).

In short, the leitmotifs in *Streetcar* become an additional character: the omniscient and intrusive narrator that prods us, confuses us, and deceives us—all with its subliminal manipulations of our emotions and feelings. Williams described, after all, in a September 1943 note about his early intentions in *Streetcar* (two years before these playlets began to take the play's final form), precisely what Jackson has noted:

> The influence of modern music and surreal art . . . could be used . . . in a poetic stage play. The passionate restraint, the sculptural effect noted in the film [Eisenstein's *Alexander Nevsky*], became the artistic tone of this play as I began to conceive it.
>
> In my dramatic writing prior to this I have always leaned too heavily on speech, nearly everything I have written for the stage has been overburdened with dialogue. In working on this new project I determined to think in more plastic or visual terms. . . .
>
> Written in verse, with a surrealist influence and a background of modern music, it would have to be independent of nearly all dramatic conventions.
>
> . . . Win, lose, or draw, the following play, the story of the disintegration of a land-owning Southern family, emerges from a desire to *synthesize* these elements I have noted . . . (qtd. in Bigsby 56–57, emphasis added)

It is, therefore, incorrect to consider Williams's choice of music flippant or his placement of it in the text haphazard. Music in *Streetcar* is a vital ingredient to the play's overall structure and provides for us a metalanguage by which all subtle deviations in both theme and character are elucidated without a spoken word. We must, then, reconsider the structures of his other plays as well, especially those like *Camino Real* that appear to have little or no form to them. Intuitive in Williams is a dramaturgy that relies as strongly on form as it does on sense, and we must be cognizant of this structure in his plays as we are of their poetry and lyricism.

Notes

1. For a recent analysis of Kazan's interpretation of Williams's use of music in *Streetcar* during its 1947 Broadway premiere, see Brenda Murphy, pp. 28–31.

2. Several other critics have also connected Williams to the Wagnerian tradition. In addition to Esther Jackson, who believes Williams was influenced by the German Romantic literary tradition (*Broken World* 89, 93–94, and 101; "Music" 294 ff.; "Problem" 17), June Bennett Larsen argues that Williams's plastic language is the product of Wagnerian aesthetics. Along with Jackson, Tynan, and Corrigan, Larsen finds Williams employing Wagner's theory of the *Gesamtkunstwerk*, where word is fused with "music, poetry, and all areas of design" (Tharpe 416, Though William J. McMurry devotes an entire chapter of his dissertation on music in Williams to *Streetcar*, only in his concluding chapter does he suggest that there are "Wagnerian leitmotifs" in *Streetcar* but then never proffers any analysis to defend this assertion, 132–33). Even Albert E. Kalson, sans the Wagner label, writes that music in Williams plays an important role, "establishing atmosphere as well as providing leitmotifs for various characters" (Tharpe 786); like the others, however, Kalson examines only the music's thematic function.

3. All citations from Williams's dramatic and fictional work are taken from the two standard editions: *The Theatre of Tennessee Williams* (New Directions, eight volumes to date) and *The Collected Stories* (Ballantine paperback). The number preceding the period in a citation corresponds to the volume in which that particular play is found. An identical system is used for W. A. Ellis's translation of Wagner's prose works.

4. I did analyze the Wagnerial leitmotifs at work in *The Glass Menagerie* but only as a thematic, as opposed to a structural, element in the play. See John S. Bak, "'Celebrate her with strings': Leitmotifs and the Multifaceted 'Strings' in Williams's *The Glass Menagerie*," pp. 81–87.

5. I am using the term *architectonic* in its strict literary sense: that is, a foundation of a fictional work built on symbols, motives, or other identifiable recurring images, here fragments of music. Wagner would eventually renounce the term because its musical connotation suggested a work built on elements of the aria, with insignificant recitative dialogue filling the space between songs. Wagner believed, in what he would later define in his essay *Zukunftsmusik*, that music dramas should be constructed on the idea of the '*unendliche Melodie*,' in which the area and the recitative would be replaced by the arioso, a continual singing that combined both the musical desire for the aria and the dramatic need for the recitative. See Deathridge and Dahlhaus, pp. 98–99 and 126–27.

6. Wagner repeated this sentiment years later in his 1870 essay *Beethoven*, in which a "meshwork" of "tones" should be used "to net" the audience (5.75).

7. She tries, for example, in scene five to seduce a paperboy; she places a Chinese paper festoon over a naked light bulb; her trunk is filled with *billet-doux* from Allan and legal papers from the Belle Reve foreclosure; she cries when Stanley rips the paper lantern off at the end "*as if the lantern was herself*" (1.416).

8. Mary Ann Corrigan has already made this connection, when she writes, "normally, the uncomplicated obtrusive rhythms of the honky-tonk express Stanley's personality. This music dominates the rape scene" ("Realism" 388, Tharpe 384).

9. No irony is lost on Stanley's locomotive leitmotif when in his famous letter to Audrey Wood, dated 23 March 1945, Williams suggested three possible endings to *Streetcar*, the last of which finds Blanche throwing herself "in front of a train in the freight-yards, the roar of which has been an ominous under-tone throughout the play" (Johns 203).

Works Cited

Bak, John S. "'Celebrate her with strings': Leitmotifs and the Multifaceted 'Strings' in Williams's *The Glass Menagerie.*" *Notes on Mississippi Writers* 24.2 (July 1992): 81–87.

Bigsby, C. W. E. *A Critical Introduction to Twentieth-Century American Drama.* Vol. 2. London: Cambridge UP, 1984. 15–134.

Cardullo, Bert. "The 'Paper Moon' Song in *A Streetcar Named Desire.*" *Notes on Contemporary Literature* 13.3 (May 1983): 11–12.

Cole, Toby, and Helen Krich Chinoy, eds. *Directors on Directing: A Source Book of the Modern Theatre.* 2nd rev. ed. New York: Macmillan, 1988.

Corrigan, Mary Ann. "Beyond Verisimilitude: Echoes of Expressionism in Williams' Plays." *Tennessee Williams: A Tribute.* Ed. Jac Tharpe. Jackson: UP of Mississippi, 1977. 375–412.

———. "Realism and Theatricalism in *A Streetcar Named Desire.*" *Modern Drama* 19.4 (Dec. 1976): 385–96.

Deathridge, John, and Carl Dahlhaus. *The New Grove Wagner.* New York: Norton, 1984.

Drake, Constance. "Blanche Dubois—A Re-Evaluation." *The Theatre Annual* 24 (1969): 58–69.

Falk, Signi. "The Southern Gentlewoman." *Twentieth Century Interpretations of A Streetcar Named Desire.* Ed. Jordan Y. Miller. Englewood Cliffs: Prentice-Hall, 1971. 94–102.

Gassner, John. "Tennessee Williams: Dramatist of Frustration." *College English* 10.1 (Oct. 1948): 1–7.

Hurrell, John D. *Two Modern American Tragedies: Reviews and Criticism of Death of a Salesman and A Streetcar Named Desire.* New York: Scribner, 1961.

Jackson, Esther Merle. *The Broken World of Tennessee Williams.* Madison: U of Wisconsin P, 1966.

———. "Music and Dance as Elements of Form in the Drama of Tennessee Williams." *Revue d'Histoire du Théâtre* 15.3 (1963): 294–301.

———. "The Problem of Form in the Drama of Tennessee Williams." *CLA Journal* 4.1 (Sept. 1960): 8–21.

Johns, Sarah Boyd. *Williams' Journey to Streetcar: An Analysis of Pre-Production Manuscripts of A Streetcar Named Desire.* Diss. U of South Carolina, 1980. Ann Arbor: UMI, 1981. 8102773.

Kalson, Albert E. "Tennessee Williams at the Delta Brilliant." In Tharpe, *A Tribute*, 774–94.

Kazan, Elia. "Notebook for *A Streetcar Named Desire.*" *Directors on Directing: A Source Book of Modern Theatre.* 2nd rev. ed. Eds. Toby Cole and Helen Krich Chinoy. New York: Macmillan, 1988. 364–79.

Larsen, June Bennett. "Tennessee Williams: Optimistic Symbolist." In Tharpe, *A Tribute*, 413–28.

McMurry, William J. "Music in Selected Works of Tennessee Williams." *DAI* 43.3 (1982): 803A. East Texas State U.

————. *Music in Selected Works of Tennessee Williams*. Diss. East Texas U, 1982. Ann Arbor: UMI, 1982. 8219476.

Miller, Jordan Y., ed. *Twentieth Century Interpretations of A Streetcar Named Desire*. Englewood Cliffs: Prentice-Hall, 1971.

Murphy, Brenda. *Tennessee Williams and Elia Kazan: A Collaboration in the Theatre*. Cambridge: Cambridge UP, 1992.

New Grove Dictionary of Music and Musicians, The. 20 vols. Ed. Stanley Sadie. London: Macmillan, 1980.

Riddel, Joseph N. *"A Streetcar Named Desire*—Nietzsche Descending." *Modern Drama* 5.4 (Spring 1963): 421–30.

Shaw, Irwin. "Masterpiece." In Miller, *Twentieth Century Interpretation of A Streetcar Named Desire*, 45–47.

Sievers, W. David. "Most Famous of Streetcars." In Miller, *Twentieth Century Interpretations of A Streetcar Named Desire*, 90–93.

Tharpe, Jac, ed. *Tennessee Williams: A Tribute*. Jackson: UP of Mississippi, 1977.

Tynan, Kenneth. "American Blues. . . ." *Two Modern American Tragedies: Reviews and Criticism of Death of a Salesman and A Streetcar Named Desire*. Ed. John D. Hurrell. New York: Scribner, 1961. 124–30.

Wagner, Richard. *Richard Wagner's Prose Works*. 8 vols. Trans. and Ed. William Ashton Ellis. London: Routledge & Kegan Paul, 1893; rpt. New York: Broude Brothers, 1966.

————. *Wagner: On Music and Drama*. Trans. H. Ashton Ellis. Eds. Albert Goldman and Evert Sprinchorn. New York: Da Capo Press, 1964.

Williams, Tennessee. *Collected Stories*. New York: Ballantine, 1989.

————. "The History of a Play (With Parentheses)." *Pharos* 1–2 (Spring 1945): 110–21.

————. *Memoirs*. Garden City, NY: Doubleday, 1975.

The Theatre of Tennessee Williams. 8 vols to date. New York: New Directions, 1971–1992.

RACHEL VAN DUYVENBODE

Darkness Made Visible: Miscegenation, Masquerade and the Signified Racial Other in Tennessee Williams' Baby Doll and A Streetcar Named Desire

> Through significant and underscored omission, startling contradictions, heavily nuanced conflict, through the way writers peopled their work with the signs and bodies of this presence—one can see that a real or fabricated Africanist presence was crucial to their sense of Americanness.[1]

Two men wolf-whistle at Baby Doll during the play of the same name: both of these men are positioned in the shadows. We see the one, Silva Vacarro, skulking around the dilapidated Plantation house in ghostly pursuit of Baby Doll, and the other as an anonymous male on Tiger Tail Road, part of a group of "White an' black mixed."[2] Both of these men represent an encroaching dark threat to the sexual and property rights of Archie Lee. It is no coincidence that Silva's forced intrusion into Archie's house is mirrored by the sexual trespassing of the anonymous whistler, and Archie himself challenges the invisible agitator: "trespass across my property . . . [and] I'll blast . . . [you] . . . out of the Bayou with a shotgun . . . Nobody's gonna insult no woman *of mine*!!" (*BD*, 74) Neither Archie nor Baby Doll can see the identity of the invisible menacing man, and so the threat from the shadows is communicated through implicit rather than explicit dialogue. Interestingly, these shadows, hovering amidst the domestic and sexual spaces, allegorize a deeper instability permeating Southern discourse: that of the blurring of racial identities and the threat of miscegenation.

From *Journal of American Studies* 35, no. 2 (2001): 203–215. © 2001 by Cambridge University Press.

133

Silva Vacarro, and Stanley Kowalski in *A Streetcar Named Desire*, perform the dastardly role of the "dark" male. Williams not only assigns these
men the dark tasks of rape and psychological terror, but also superimposes
their dramatic identity upon that of the contemporary racially marginalized.
This superimposition is realized through masquerade, since, although we
see/read Silva and Stanley as European immigrants, they regard themselves
as Americans.[3] However, my reading not merely illuminates the marginality
of Silva and Stanley due to their foreign origins, but sees these two men as
conduits for Williams' own veiled fantasies of the dark Africanist other. Toni
Morrison's epigraph suggests that these masqueraded or signified bodies of
racial others play an instrumental role in defining white "Americanness"
through divorcing it from what it is not. The distinction of such otherness is
created through Williams' manipulation of racially laden stereotype, especially concerning black male sexuality and his crude use of the black–white
binary to disseminate colour-coded symbols as "carriers" of ideology.

The virtual absence of African American characters within Williams'
plays disguises the significance of an Africanist influence on the playwright's
creative imagination.[4] The Africanist presence is not only visible in the bodies of signified dark deviant males, but also implied through the mediation
of silent yet significant black overseers. For example: a black "boy" cutting
the grass mediates the climax of Silva's and Baby Doll's frenzied sexualized dialogue. The critic George Crandell notes that Williams' own sense of
desire and terror is displayed most visibly within the "fearful and desirable
prospect of miscegenation."[5] Acknowledging the deep significance of miscegenation in the South's psychosocial history and the fetishization of blood,
Blanche's postulation that the old South can only be saved "through mix[ing]
our blood" heralds an overt eroticism throughout Williams' dramatic world.[6]
This overt eroticism threatens to destabilize the discourse due to Williams'
persistent conflation of the erotic with the dark deviant male. The typology
of blood mixing and contamination links Williams' work to a tradition of
Southern Gothic fiction, which "speaks to the dark side of domestic fiction
. . . [and is] obsessionally connected with contemporary fears."[7] Williams,
like Edgar Allan Poe, William Faulkner and Flannery O'Connor, captures a
sense of cultural disorientation through representing, often implicitly encoding, the desire to express that which is deviant, violent and socially repressed.
Morrison, amongst others, reads the inscription of dark Gothic fantasy as
evidence of the desire to connect with the shadowed life of African Americans. Hence, Gothic literature may deploy the figurative and the phantasmagoric to suggest the interrelationship between "darkness" and "white."
Finally, Williams' use of masquerade supports the notion of "race as a performance," as evident in minstrelsy, whereby the mask of blackness provided
the white actor with an opportunity to indulge his own sublimated desire for

the "lusty life of black folk" under the protection of otherness. The creation of textual masks not only subverts "racial privilege and disrupt[s] binary oppositions" but also importantly deconstructs Williams' work.[8] Williams, mirroring African American oral and folk tradition, manipulates within his plays the Trickster figure whose goal is to convince the audience that it has seen his/her face when in fact it is only encountering another mask.[9] Seeing race as performative also valorizes the visual realm, championing a subjective and plural reading of the text.

This article seeks to illuminate the dark shadows in two of Tennessee Williams' plays. I will show that Williams creates a distinction between racial and non-racial others through invoking symbols and sounds which relate directly to a historicized and racialized discourse. Through the contradictory distinction and blurring of racial boundaries, Williams visualizes his own contemporary fears of cultural degeneration, censorship and deviancy which are most evident in his overriding attraction to and repulsion by the prospect of miscegenation.

The Stiffening of Black–White Sexual Difference

The perception of black–white sexual difference was formulated through the European colonialization of the Americas, whereby a vindication of conquest demanded a broad typology of difference. The subordination of black men was ritualistically reanimated through the sex act where white men might indulge in fornication with black women, whilst black men were stringently barred from sex with white women. From its slaveholding inception, the zealous use of castration as a mode of punishment in the colonies reified the assumption that the white man's insecurity vis-à-vis the black man derived from a sexual origin.[10] The notion that black men were particularly virile, promiscuous and lusty was not particularly new to the English colonists in America, but the ornamental function of white women within plantation culture added to a specific corollary between the asexuality of white women and the "natural" lust of black men towards white women.[11] With this in mind, the protection of white women and the construction of white femininity (particularly in the slaveholding South) became crucially related to and intertwined with the notion of the uncontrollable sexuality of black males. This perception of black male potency was generated by assumptions regarding anatomical prowess since the interracial sex complex did not relate to Native Americans (also subject to justifying ideologies of conquest), simply because European commentators from 1770 popularized the myth that Native Americans were less well endowed and virulent than Europeans.[12] Philip Cushman, like Toni Morrison, postulates that the insecure, increasingly diverse American nation had to develop a consensus as to what the American was, through constructing a sense of what the self was not—the supposedly lazy or stupid Negro or the supposedly heathen, savage Indian.[13] According to Cushman, the configuration of the white American self was thus shaped through the mediums of popular theatre (the minstrel stage) and political discourse (intellectual conceptions of the "Wild West"). Furthermore, the fun-loving and sexual behaviour of African Americans as played on the stage evidenced the schism in moral sanctioning which disallowed such behaviour characteristics from being "owned" by whites. Powerful sexual and racial tropes not only informed the early visible representation of African Americans on the stage, through minstrelsy and musicals, but also submerged these tropes into invisible and self-reflexive properties. Eugene O'Neill in *All God's Chillun Got Wings* (1925) anticipates such reflexivity through using the presence of African Americans to mirror the gulf between America's rhetoric and reality, and so challenges American democratic idealism. However, O'Neill's play also draws upon the binaries of racial difference (especially sexual) through the inflection and encoding of "innate" difference between blacks and whites as evidenced in the contrast between idiom, phonetics, dialogue, music, characterization and sexual typecasting. Such polarity both informs and is challenged by the work of Tennessee Williams through the playwright's reliance upon racially laden symbols, on the one hand, and a bifurcation of identities, on the other. Williams disguises his dark deviants either through anonymity or through masquerading them as others (the mask of the immigrant), and these deviants (Silva, Stanley and the dark, unnamed children in *Suddenly Last Summer*) simultaneously affirm racial typecasting and seek to break down the permanence of racial boundaries. The suspension of these two contradictory impulses predominates in Williams' work and mirrors the playwright's personal fear of fragmentation, political conflict and sexual alienation.

The Signification of White Women as (White Male) Property

That prevailing fears of psychic or cultural disintegration should be encoded within the bodies or shadows of racial others subverts the independence and integrity of white characters. Similarly to the Gothic landscape in which a "demonized and malevolent human nature coexist," the fantasy of whiteness relies upon its darker mirror-image to affirm meaning.[14] Blanche DuBois in *Streetcar* represents Williams' dialectical response to the "problem" of defining white identity, and through verbal and physical symbols she poses as the "zodiacal virgin," on the one hand, and death, sterility and debased/perverted sexuality, on the other.[15] Equally, her name "Blanche" signals an association with her white, French Huguenot forefathers and a mythic association with the old colonial South. This blanched dreamland is dominated by the overbearing symbols of mythical purity and modern mourning, allegorized in Blanche's final exit when she is dressed in her red satin robe and Della Robbia blue jacket and fantasizes that her dead body is dropped into the ocean.[16] Blanche, the white one, shrouded in the colours of the American flag affirms her Americanness against the ascending sexual and social threat of Stanley, the dark other.[17] Blanche reiterates that the blue of her jacket is the "blue of the robe in the old Madonna pictures" (*SND*, 219), and this iconographic image of womanhood is destroyed in favour of Stella, the new modern mother who will reject her "clean white sack" (*SND*, 220) and bear the child of the dark "*gaudy seed-bearer*" (*SND*, 128).

The representation of Baby Doll incorporates a binary concept of white womanhood which manipulates the combination of voluptuousness and sexual innocence embodied within the symbolic white woman. Williams' explicit use of child imagery overstates the paedophilic connotations of Baby Doll's and Archie Lee's relationship. The collapsing Plantation house transforms into a doll's house during Silva and Baby Doll's perverse game of hide-and-seek, and the infantile doll's house replicates Williams' own anxieties apropos the South's history. Archie Lee's sense of white emasculation is evidenced in the threat posed by the "foreign wop" (*BD*, 27). Archie Lee conflates Baby Doll's symbolic status as wife and property when he declares: "This is my baby. This is my little girl, every precious ounce of her is mine, all mine" (*BD*, 38). Silva's wolf-whistling at Baby Doll whilst creeping through Archie Lee's house masks the white woman as signified sexual and spatial (white male) territory. Characteristically, Archie Lee asserts his property rights and/or position of white privilege in response to the threat posed by the foreign other. In two other instances, Archie Lee invokes his "natural" (read racial) male rights: the first during the conspiratorial white male silence during the fire, and the second when Archie Lee threatens to call his "long-standin' *bus'ness* associates" (*BD*, 84) to dispossess Silva at the end of the play. Baby Doll, having previously been "gobbled" by Archie Lee in an episode which balances a valorization of male appetite with child's play, is embraced by the property laws of white patriarchy. White female property is thus active property shaping the social and sexual relations of America, and Silva's intrusion into the dramatic discourse reifies the body of Baby Doll as the site and exchange of male entitlement.[18] Silva, dispossessed by the fire, reclaims his property rights through the "robbery" of Baby Doll, and once again the interchange between (dis)possessed males is communicated through non-verbal, Gothic signifiers. The Gothic and the surreal transmit the implicit understanding of difference between the white male community and the dark other. Silva sees reflected in the "*distorted angle, lit by the victorious flames* [. . .] *a circle of faces which are either indifferent or downright unfriendly. Some cannot control a faint smile*" (*BD*, 28). The unfriendly faces, illuminated by the glow of the fire, communicate their unified defiance through the faintest of smiles. The stage directions show that the fire represents far more than a signal of economic rage; it also satisfies *"some pro-found and basic hunger and left the people of that community exhilarated"* (*BD*, 31). Silva's burnt body, surrounded by the grotesque and misshapen faces and flames of the white male community, surely signifies an historical allegory with black male lynching. Williams links the sexual context of the fire with the body of the dark male through this implicit link with lynching as a dem-onstration of white socio-sexual regulation. Williams, through the figure of Silva, resurrects the persecuted dark male and reconciles him to the white woman, thus signifying the inevitability of miscegenation.

Implicit Racial Signifiers and the Trickery of Racial Masquerade

Tennessee Williams, like Eugene O'Neill, utilizes implicit signifiers such as black music to show the presence of African Americans within the text. In *Streetcar*, the *"blue piano . . . played with the infatuated fluency of brown fingers . . . expresses the spirit of life which goes on here"* (*SND*, 115), and this blue music provides a musical chorus to the play. The melancholy of the blues exemplifies the struggle of African Americans, and, whilst lamenting the dispossession of blacks, Williams unmasks the violence of (coloured) males over (white) women's bodies. In *Baby Doll*, the musical chorus is provided by the mechanized sound of the Syndicate Cotton Gin, which pulsates like a *"gigantic distant throbbing heart-beat"* (*BD*, 13). Cotton, the pagan god of the South, is the tainted bargain of this story-turned-film and evokes, symbolically, images of African American enslavement. Baby Doll herself is described as *"humming a little cakewalk tune . . .* [which] *she walks in sympathy to"* (*BD*, 16), and the importation of an African American dance reflects the syncretism of musical and cultural form within the South.

The use of African American characters (albeit that they are normally nameless and/or silent) as "reference points" illustrates the symbolic func-tion of the Africanist presence within the text. In *Streetcar*, the reference to "this ole nigger [joke]" (*SND*, 144) during the poker match between the four "bucks" exhibits the defence of masculine Americanness against impotent otherness. The notes on lighting suggest that these men are transformed into a *"spectrum,"* and this sense of fractured light instantly conveys the notion of multi-colouredness or an intracultural meeting of men defining their iden-tity against the textually invisible but explicitly coloured other.

The shadows of the text also hide the lurking omniscient black overseer, and in *Baby Doll* the mediating presence of the "Negro Boy" between scenes 65 and 67 concelebrates Silva's sexual advances upon the white woman. The anonymous but significant "nigger who's cuttin' the grass across the road" (*BD*, 51) self-reflects the destabilizing threat of extramarital and interracial sex posed by Silva Vacarro. Miscegenation symbolizes the threat of degen-eracy and of a sexualized white woman, debased and corrupted by her desire for a dark other. Baby Doll's desire is expressed with reference to her insatiable thirst which cannot be satisfied by a drink from the doll's house but only by the watercooler "across the road to the gin" (*BD*, 54). Silva's retort succinctly articulates the "danger" implied by white women sating their desire for deviant oral satisfaction:

> The watercooler's for colored. A lady, a white lady like you, the wife of the big, white boss, would place herself in an undignified position if she went over the road to drink with the hands! They might get notions about her! Unwholesome ideas! The sight of her soft white flesh, so smooth and abundant, might inflame their—natures. (*BD*, 54)

Silva perpetuates the myth of black "natural" sexual desire for white women and alludes to his own sense of dark violent desire. Throughout the play, Silva twitches Baby Doll with his riding crop and draws attention to the whiteness of Baby Doll's flesh only to fantasize that: "I might whip you with it [the crop] and . . . leave red marks on your—body, on your—creamy white silk—skin" (*BD*, 66). Baby Doll's body becomes, therefore, a sacred tableau upon which dark males can inscribe their sense of manhood and ownership. Envisaging the dark deviant proves to be a difficult task for the bumbling Archie Lee as he is blinded by the outer mask of Silva Vacarro. Archie Lee, fixated upon the perceived threat of the field hands, cannot see the trickery performed literally on his own doorstep. Silva, in the tradition of the Trickster, disguises his dark sexual threat, and between scenes 69 and 71 an interesting non-verbal discourse emerges that valorizes the importance of the visual terrain. In scene 69, Baby Doll flees from Silva across the road to the cotton gin, looking for protection from her husband. Archie Lee responds characteristically: he "*smacks BABY DOLL. Good and hard*" (*BD*, 56). Between scenes 70 and 71, Silva enters the action and watches Baby Doll being beaten and the two men exchange stares. Baby Doll entreats Archie to see what he has left her with, but as Archie looks to Silva for the second time, Baby Doll sees him and clams up. The triangular stare illustrates the subjectivity of the visual realm since Baby Doll sees Silva as a dark sexual threat, whilst Archie merely dismisses him as a foreign other, impotent in the South for want of long-standing "business associates and friends."

Archie Lee's inability to see Silva as a sexual threat not only supports the notion that race can be performed, disguised and passed through, but also illustrates the potency of historical allegory in conjuring images of deviance. Toni Morrison cites the following fictional, linguistic strategies as examples of evoking the presence of an Africanist other: economy of stereotype, metonymic displacement, metaphysical condensation, fetishization, dehistoricizing allegory, and patterns of explosive, repetitive language.[19] The deployment of colour coding and the collapsing of human behaviour into animal imagery can be found vividly in the depiction of Stanley in *Streetcar*. In *Streetcar*, features of the racial other displace Stanley's whiteness, thereby confusing the boundaries between racial and ethnic groups.[20] George Crandell notes that the five main stereotypical and cultural antecedents which represent the black male other comprise: great physical size or strength, inability to communicate, lack of intelligence, uncontrollable desire, and potent sexuality.[21] Through a verbal economy or compression of imagery, Stanley's association with bestial behaviour affirms Blanche's declaration: "There's even something—subhuman—something not quite to the stage of humanity yet . . . something—ape-like about him" (*SND*, 163). Blanche's comment, incidentally endorsed by Stella, affirms the black stereotype, and the character notes supplement the sexualized representation of Stanley: "*animal joy in his being is implicit in all his movements and attitudes . . . the centre of his life has been pleasure with women . . . emblem of the gaudy seed-bearer*" (*SND*, 128). An animalistic pleasure in procreative sex echoes the phobia of white males with regard to black male potency, and reflects the fundamentally contradictory narrative response to Stanley, oscillating as it does between desire and revulsion. Stanley is described in biological terms that separate the co-conspiring white women from the darker "different species" (*SND*, 124), and Stanley's identity is conflated with all other alien ethnicities: "something like the Irish . . . only not so high-brow" (*SND*, 124). Blanche reduces Stanley to the status of animal or predator, surmising that: "What such a man has to offer is animal force . . . the only way to live with such a man is to—go bed with him" (*SND*, 161). The overt eroticism of the play suggests that such desire binds men and women together, and yet that desire is expressed in racially explicit language. Colour imagery is closely associated with sexual climax, and the expression of white male frigidity/emasculation is typified in Stanley's assertion to Stella that: "I pulled you down off them columns and how you loved it, having them coloured lights going" (*SND*, 199). Significantly, the DuBois male ancestors had spoiled the riches of the family through their "epic fornications" (*SND*, 140), and Stella, now driven wild by the desire of the dark male, is dragged off the pedestal of white Southern womanhood and allows herself to colour her life with a sexual and erotic appetite. Historically, this sense of female sexual desire was largely expressed through coloured women (note the sexual licentiousness of black women as depicted through the minstrelsy genre and Hottentot Venus), and so Stella's overt sexual desire inverts racial and sexual gender roles. The destabilization of the black–white binary with regard to women's sexual identity mimics Williams' own fear that race cannot be clearly distinguished. This nightmare of blacks and whites beginning to look alike surely highlights the dilemma (inherent from its inception) within the minstrel show.[22]

Silva Vacarro performs the role of the dark male, and Williams superimposes upon the image of the dark impostor contemporary phobias about black domestic and sexual trespass. The stage directions point to a specifically animalistic depiction of Silva, exacerbated during the "Trail'o'blood" (*BD*, 62) when he gnaws at the remains of chicken bones and hurls the lemon rinds "SAVAGELY AWAY" (*BD*, 62) before sucking Baby Doll's spilt blood (the breaking of the hymen). The implication of violation is evident since the audience is aware that Baby Doll is a virgin, and the sticking of the ice pick into the wall "*as if he were stabbing an enemy*" (*BD*, 62), suggests that rape of a white woman would be an act of retribution against the white man.[23] Once again, the overt use of blood as a signifier of sexual contamination and rape links Williams' discourse to the broader tradition of the Southern Gothic. Silva's desire to avenge his "loss of property" entails the body of white women as collateral. Silva "*grins evilly*" (*BD*, 47) as he ascends the staircase, and whilst creeping through the house he is transmuted into a ghostly ancestral spirit, resurrected from the bodies of dark others who were enslaved and died on the Plantation. Silva's representational status as an embodied slave is also made evident in the hiding of Baby Doll and Silva (from the lynched-crazed Archie Lee) in the branches of a Plantation tree at the close of the play. The provocative symbolism of the tree, which was a place both of refuge and terror for black slaves, suggests that Silva's "othering" draws upon cultural motifs of African American history. Equally, Silva identifies himself in explicitly racial terms, declaring: "I am a Sicilian. They're an old race of people, an ancient race" (*BD*, 66). Though he acknowledges and celebrates his foreignness, his sense of regionalism and neighbourly duty imply an inclusive relationship to the American community. Although Silva always remains an outsider within the Bayou, his economic success compels him to identify, to some extent, with American democratic ideals.

Conversely, despite Stanley's narrative equation with racial other, Stanley defines himself as explicitly American but in terms that exclude ethnic participation. Stanley declares "I am not a Polack . . . what I am is one hundred percent American, born and raised in the greatest country on earth and proud as hell of it, so don't ever call me a Polack" (*SND*, 197). Stanley and Silva therefore represent mirroring responses to the "problem" of foreign integration, though importantly they are both equally identified with the dark deviant other. Crucially, the contemporary notion of multicultural Americanism is at odds with the foundations of American thought which presupposes an innate universalism, and Stanley affirms this sense of inclusiveness through consciously relinquishing his ethnic/racial signifiers.[24] This excessively hegemonic perception of Americanism indicates that in order for

Stanley to achieve integration he must deny his ethnic heritage and "claim" whiteness. Silva, too, isolated and marginalized within the community, cannot integrate into Archie Lee's world because his attachment to otherness is too strong. Considering Morrison's contention that the word "American" is closely linked to the concept of race, it appears that Stanley's attempt to define himself as American is also an attempt to assert himself as white.[25] Ironically, despite the implied cosmopolitanism of New Orleans where there is "*a relatively warm and easy intermingling of races in the old part of town*" (*SND*, 115), Stanley's house does not "admit blacks, artists, marginals and those refusing democratic equalization."[26] Incidentally, judging by his last name, Hubbel, the owner of the Kowalskis' house is German, and Stanley's other friends include a Mexican (Pablo Gonzales) and only one Anglo-Saxon (Harold Mitchell) who is considered by Blanche to be superior to the others (*SND*, 146).[27] Inside, 632 Elysian Fields is a "microcosm of America in the forties and fifties," and, arguably because Blanche does remind Stanley of his fixed inferior, denigrated status and social difference, he vengefully destroys her.[28] The implied interculturalism of Stella and Stanley (typified by miscegenation), and Blanche's fear of the bastardization of culture, reflects Williams' own contradictory response to the survival of the South in the context of the fledgling Civil Rights movement of the 1950s. Equally, Williams' attempt to capture a "cultural disorientation that was as much political as it was aesthetic" is realized through the bodies of dark deviant males who express their own angry voices through the bodies of white women.[29]

Conclusion

The dark designs of Silva and Stanley illustrate the fear of predatory dark others who, disguised and shadowed, threaten to destabilize Southern sexual and social relations. Williams draws upon a tradition of Southern Gothicism which holds in suspension the oppositions of submerged and explicit/natural desire. Unmasked, we see that this suppressed desire manifests as the desire for racial otherness whilst the shadows of the text illuminate the fear of cultural fragmentation. Williams conflates the image of the foreign other with that of the racial marginal in order to censor his discourse for his profoundly "closed" Southern society. However, the compression of racial metaphor abuses the long history of meaning that attaches to colour imagery and suggests that racial signification remains a consistent feature of white American self-definition and the masquerade of Southern discourses. The prospect of miscegenation appears to Williams as at once a frightful and an inevitable consequence of multiculturalism, exacerbated by the expansion of urban landscapes and a technological revolution. (All the same, the ambiguous gender of Stanley and Stella's baby maybe points to a less defined, more fluid future based on nondifferentiation of gender and race.[30]) Williams' presentation of whiteness, and particularly white women, rests upon static cultural and historical tropes of sexual and racial isolation, yet this isolation is always mediated by the signified and explicit presence of dark, racial others.

NOTES

1. Toni Morrison, *Playing in the Dark: Whiteness and the Literary Imagination* (New York: Vintage Books, 1992), 6.

2. Tennessee Williams, *Baby Doll, Something Unspoken* and *Suddenly Last Summer* (London: Penguin, 1968), 74. Subsequent page references for *Baby Doll* will be given as *BD* in parentheses in the text.

3. Toni Morrison in her seminal work *Playing in the Dark* asserts that the word "American" is an exclusive term, closely related to assumption of white homogeneity.

4. George W. Crandell, "Misrepresentation and Miscegenation: Reading the Racialized Discourse of Tennessee Williams' *A Streetcar Named Desire*," *Modern Drama*, 40 (Fall 1997), 345.

5. Ibid., 339.

6. Tennessee Williams, *A Streetcar Named Desire and Other Plays* (London: Penguin, 1962), 140. Subsequent page numbers are given as *SND* in parentheses in the text.

7. *Gothic Horror: A Reader's Guide from Poe to King and Beyond*, ed. Clive Bloom (Basingstoke: Macmillan Press, 1988), 2.

8. Craig Werner, "The Framing of Charles W. Chestnutt: Practical Deconstruction in the Afro-American Tradition," in *Southern Literature and Literary Theory*, ed. Jefferson Humphries (Athens: The University of Georgia Press, 1990), 351.

9. Ibid., 351.

10. Winthrop D. Jordan, *White Over Black: American Attitudes towards the Negro, 1550–1812* (New York: W. W. Norton & Co, 1968), 137–54.

11. Ibid., 154.

12. Ibid., 154.

13. Philip Cushman, *Constructing the Self, Constructing America: A Cultural History of Psychotherapy* (Reading: Addison-Wesley Publishing Company, 1995).

14. Bloom, *Gothic Horror*, 11.

15. Gerald M. Berkowitz, *American Drama of the Twentieth Century* (London: Longman, 1992), 90.

16. Georges-Michel Sarotte, "Fluidity and Difference in Three Plays by Tennessee Williams: *The Glass Menagerie, A Streetcar Named Desire* and *Cat on a Hot Tin Roof*," in *Staging Difference: Cultural Pluralism in American Theatre and Drama*, ed. Marc Maufort (New York: Peter Lang, 1995), 151.

17. Ibid., 152.

18. Cheryl Harris, "Whiteness as Property," *Harvard Law Review* (1993), reprinted in *Black on White: Black Writers on What it means to be White*, ed. David R. Roediger (New York: Schocken Books, 1998), 103–12.

19. Morrison, *Playing in the Dark*, 67–69.

20. Crandell, "Misrepresentation and Miscegenation," 339.

21. Ibid., 339.

22. Werner, "The Framing of Charles W. Chestnutt," 344.

23. Jordan, *White Over Black*, 154.
24. Maufort, *Staging Difference*, 2.
25. Crandell, "Misrepresentation and Miscegenation," 344.
26. Sarotte, "Fluidity and Difference," 146.
27. Ibid., 146.
28. Ibid., 146.
29. Bloom, *Gothic Horror*, 11.
30. Sarotte, "Fluidity and Difference," 146.

MICHAEL PALLER

A Room Which Isn't Empty:
A Streetcar Named Desire *and*
the Question of Homophobia

In recent years, *A Streetcar Named Desire* has been the subject of considerable criticism for its treatment of homosexuality. As the play concerns the
loves and cruelties of heterosexuals, this might strike one as odd. *Streetcar*
is a prime example, in the view of John Clum, of Williams's taste for "heterosexist discourse" (166). As Clum's comment suggests, *Streetcar*, for all
of our supposed familiarity with it, often has been misunderstood and its
meanings misconstrued since its opening night—December 3, 1947. This
misperception particularly obtains concerning the role of Allan Grey, the
offstage and dead homosexual husband of Blanche DuBois. To understand
Allan Grey's centrality to *Streetcar* and to appreciate the extent to which
the play is not any kind of "heterosexist discourse" require both backtrack-
ing and untangling. A full understanding would require examining the
situation of gays and lesbians in America in the years before and following
World War II, Williams's own activity after the war, the legal threats sur-
rounding the portrayals of gays and lesbians in the New York commercial
theatre, the response to the play by its first-night critics[1]—and a close reading of the play itself. For the purposes of this article, we'll look only at the
initial critical response to the first production of the play and at the text.

John Clum's work follows, if not intentionally, in the tradition of the
first critics who reviewed *Streetcar*. The response of the earliest reviewers to

From *The Tennessee Williams Literary Journal* 5, no. 1 (Spring 2003): 23–37. © 2003 by *The
Tennessee Williams Literary Journal*.

a play is crucial to the popular understanding, or misunderstanding, of it even years later. Preconceptions harden into misconceptions, and what goes unrecognized about a play at the beginning of its public life largely remains unrecognized. What is said about a play's first production tends to get carved in stone about the text. That Allan Grey is at the very center of everything that happens in *Streetcar* eluded the critics who saw it on opening night; forty-five years later, in his book, *Acting Gay*, Clum accuses Williams of "dramatizing the closet" in *Streetcar* by banishing its one gay character to a place offstage and off the earth (149).

In the 1940s, critics were no more likely than anyone else to assume that a character might be gay if not specifically told so through dialogue or stereotypical action. In *Streetcar*, Blanche trenchantly spells out Allan's gayness in scene six. Still, only three of the New York daily critics mentioned that she had been married to a gay man, and none connected her actions in the play to the events that occurred at Moon Lake Casino on the night when Allan shot himself to death. Allan's gayness and its implications were erased from public consciousness by the opening night critics in two ways. First, they mentioned Allan only tangentially, if at all, in the plot summary and elided the details of Blanche's past, not detecting the direct line from the way she treated her late husband to her behavior once she arrived in New Orleans. Second, the critics normalized the behavior of the heterosexual characters as boys will be boys, whether they are playing poker, humiliating vulnerable women, beating their pregnant wives, or raping their sisters-in-law. With these devices, Allan was effectively expunged from the play and has largely remained so to this day.

So we must remind ourselves of the facts of Blanche's past. In scene one, with a bitterness concealed only with effort as she throws herself on her sister's mercy, Blanche recalls the solitary battle that she fought to hold onto the ancestral home, Belle Reve. The DuBois family had fallen on hard times long before Blanche's marital problems occurred, and she is quite specific about the vice that bled the estate dry. "There are thousands of papers," she tells Stanley in self-defense as he rifles her trunk in scene two, "stretching back hundreds of years affecting Belle Reve as, piece by piece, our improvident grandfathers and fathers and uncles and brothers exchanged the land for their epic fornications—to put it plainly! The four-letter word deprived us of our plantation til finally all that was left was the house itself [. . .]" (284). A gruesome parade of illnesses and death wiped out what remained of the family savings, and once Blanche lost her teaching job (which would have produced little more than a pittance), there was nothing left to pay the mortgage. The fact that a woman of Blanche's background was forced to find employment at all speaks volumes about the family's finances: a long-established aristocratic family with a grand estate like Belle Reve would not consider sending a daughter to work short of dire need.

In scene six, Blanche describes to Mitch the way she treated her husband. By doing so, she hopes to prove that they are two of a kind, for Mitch, whom she would very much like to marry, has also lost someone he loved. The adjectives Williams uses to describe Allan have been criticized for enforcing a stereotype of a certain kind of gay man. But given the mores of 1948, which applied to Broadway producers perhaps even more than they did to the general public, such stereotypes were necessary shortcuts to create an image Williams could not state directly. Blanche characterizes Allan in terms as explicit as they could be in 1948: "There was something different about the boy, a nervousness, a softness and tenderness that wasn't like a man's, although he wasn't the least bit effeminate looking—still—that thing was there. [. . .] He came to me for help. I didn't know that" (354). Williams might well have imagined Allan privately as less effeminate, more "straight-acting." But then the audience, largely unaware that gay men could be anything but "nellie," would not have understood him to be homosexual—and then the danger to Allan in a small southern town would have been considerably less, which would alter the play in significant ways.

Blanche tells how she surprised Allan and an older man during a sexual encounter. She saw, and they saw that she saw, but all three pretended that no one had seen anything. They go for a drunken ride to Moon Lake Casino, that place of passion and death that stands as a geographical and spiritual landmark in many of Williams's plays. There, on the dance floor, Blanche confronted her husband: "I saw! I know! You disgust me . . ." (355). Moments later, a gunshot rings out at the edge of the lake. As Blanche comes running, the crowd keeps her away from the sight of her husband, who has blown away the back of his head with a revolver. Haunted by guilt, Blanche returns to Belle Reve. She seeks comfort and escape in a jungle of arms: first those of soldiers bivouacked near the former plantation, and later, after it was lost amidst the orgy of illness and death, those of strangers in an infamous room in the Flamingo Hotel.

These, then, are the circumstances under which Blanche arrives in the French Quarter. Although Williams makes all of this exposition quite clear, virtually none of the critics who saw the first performance of the play in New York mentioned it accurately in their reviews or understood its centrality to the rest of the play. *Streetcar* was "a tale of two sisters, well born, whose plantation was lost in debt [. . .]" (Morehouse 250); "After her marriage's sordid ending, she has struggled to keep up the remnants of an ancestral Southern estate. Her existence meant constant association with old age and death [. . .]" (Hawkins 251); "Williams' (sic) portrait of a boozy prostitute, who gradually loses her mind in the Vieux Carré of New Orleans, is a looming figure in the modern theatre" (Barnes 252); *"A Streetcar Named Desire* is a history of a gently reared Mississippi young woman who invents an artificial world to mask the hideousness of the world she has to inhabit" (Atkinson 42); "Blanche was a broken remnant of an aristocratic Mississippi family [. . .] (Coleman 252); "Living with dying and decadent relatives made Blanche more than a little touched in the head" (Garland 251); "Blanche is a Mississippi schoolteacher who broods over an unfortunate marriage and the loss of caste that she suffered when the family estate went the way of all mortgaged estates [. . .]" (*"Streetcar"* 16); "Once the girls had a fine house but it has slipped from Blanche's hands—just how is never made clear, for Blanche is not one for facts" (Chapman 249).

Only three of the critics for the daily papers made any allusion to Allan Grey: Blanche's "own marriage ended in a revolting tragedy" (Morehouse 250); Blanche's husband was "a degenerate" (Barnes 252); and, most curious of all, "When a tiny tot, back on the old plantation, her boyfriend acted kind of odd, and ran away with an odder sort of rival. From then on, the furies consistently pursued her" (Garland 251). Thus did the play's first-night critics render Allan degenerate or invisible and marginal to the play's action. Then, they normalized, to the extent they could, the behavior of the play's straight characters. They described Stanley as "a warm-hearted but violent and no-nonsense redneck" and a "simple, hardworking brute of a boy [. . .]" (Kronenberger 250); Stella as "the better balanced of the two who is married to a toughly tender American whose name is Stanley Kowalski" (Garland 251) and as "easygoing," married to a "stalwart Polish-American whose enthusiasms run to bowling, beer, poker and whiskey" (Chapman 249). Mitch, whose treatment of Blanche in scene nine is gratuitously cruel and includes a fumbling rape attempt, is called "the mother's boy who almost succumbs to Blanche's efforts to marry him" (Garland 251), "a good boy," and a "nice friend of the family" (Barnes 252).

Other factors blinded the first night critics and then those that followed to Allan's posthumous destruction of Blanche, one of the true dynamics of *Streetcar.* One is a curious notion that has entered the canon of conventional Williams knowledge: "There is," Ward Morehouse wrote in *The Sun*, "quite a good deal of Amanda out of *The Glass Menagerie* in the character of Blanche, the faded, shattered daughter of the South" (250). Williams Hawkins agreed in the *World-Telegram* that Blanche "springs from the same source as The Mother in *The Glass Menagerie*" (251), while Richard Watts, Jr., writing in the *Post,* concurred: "In his latest work to reach Broadway, the dramatist is telling the story of a doomed Southern girl who seems startlingly like what the foolish old mother of his previous drama, *The Glass Menagerie*, might well have been at a similar age" (249). The notion that Amanda and Blanche have much in common beyond the geography and class of their birth and an underlying, if overlooked strength, is superficial, at best. Amanda is a puritan who revolts at the mention of anything sexual; Blanche is scarcely that. In the face of a tormented conscience and a guilty past, Blanche gradually loses her mind; Amanda, who is certainly no fool and seemingly feels guilt for nothing, is a woman of the present who recognizes the dangerous world for what it is and strives to protect her children from it. This series of confusions regarding Amanda and Blanche would not matter much if the doubly-mistaken impression that Blanche resembled a foolish Amanda did not mask Blanche's cruelty toward her husband as well as the connection between that behavior and the price she pays for it once she enters the French Quarter in New Orleans. Blanche is more soiled than faded; and, like so many of Williams's protagonists, she fights for her sanity with a jungle cat's ferocity.

Only *The Nation's* Harold Clurman came close to understanding Blanche's true nature as it manifested itself in her treatment of her husband and then to relating that behavior to her fate in the play. But Clurman could not, finally, make the connection, either. Ironically, his sophisticated interpretation, more nuanced and knowing than those of the other critics, and his romanticized view of Blanche, made it impossible for him to admit her brutality toward Allan. To Clurman, *Streetcar* pits the alienated soul and lover of beauty and refinement—Blanche—against the crueler, cruder instincts inherent in much of American life—Stanley.

"Tennessee Williams," Clurman wrote, "is a poet of frustration, and what his play says is that aspiration, sensitivity, departure from the norm are battered, bruised and disgraced in our world today." He added:

> It would be far truer to think of Blanche DuBois as the potential artist in all of us than as a deteriorated Southern belle. [...] Her lies are a part of her will-to-beauty; her wretched romanticism is a futile reach toward a fullness of life. She is not a drunkard, and she is not insane when she is committed to the asylum. She is an almost willing victim of a world that has trapped her and in which she can find "peace" only by accepting the verdict of her "unfitness" for normal life. (12)

She is, he says, in short, a poet, a superior person done in by her intense realization of her experiences. Opposed to her is Stanley, whom Clurman describes as "a rather primitive, almost bestial person (12)."

Clurman views Blanche as a symbol for all the finer impulses that are scorned in American life. This notion of her, compelling as Clurman makes it, does not allow for her treatment of Allan Grey and subsequently for the way he, through her own conscience, destroys her. Although Clurman's view of Blanche as a symbol of embattled sensitivity does reflect Williams's own beliefs about the larger patterns of American culture, at the same time it turns the play into a Manichean battle between Good (Blanche) and Evil (Stanley) that Williams, in this play at any rate, avoided. But Clurman was a man of great perception and deep sensibilities, a lifelong champion of Williams who directed the first national company of *Streetcar* and the Broadway production of *Orpheus Descending*. He points out that Blanche is neither whore nor drunkard and that, if her soul had been without sensitivity, she would not suffer the guilt that her own mind wills upon her. If she were merely the crackpot that other critics considered her, or a drag queen, as later ones would characterize her, she would not carry in her trunk the letters Allan wrote her, letters that only accuse and condemn her for her moment of cruelty. Clurman's Blanche is sincere when she tells Stanley that "Deliberate cruelty is not forgivable," (397), and, although she would like to be able to, she has neither forgiven nor forgotten the cruelty she practiced on her husband.

Unlike most critics then and now, Clurman was a thorough student and expert practitioner of the art he criticized. As such, he could identify in his review of *Streetcar* another, subtle reason that the critics were likely to normalize, even idealize, Stanley's often thuggish behavior, further disguising Allan's centrality—the personal qualities and performance of Marlon Brando. Clurman understood that, in addition to whatever talent actors possess, they also bring to their work certain qualities of personality: those elements of emotion, intellect, sensibility, and spirit that together form "presence," a force that makes an audience want to watch them onstage, whether they are speaking or simply being still, and that makes them fascinating to us before they utter their first word. Actors either have or do not have presence; it cannot be taught. Clurman knew Brando well, having directed him in Maxwell Anderson's *Truckline Cafe* two years before *Streetcar* and writing in his *Streetcar* review:

> Brando's quality is one of acute sensitivity. None of the brutishness of his part is native to him: it is a characteristic he has to "invent." The combination of an intense, introspective, and almost lyric personality under the mask of a bully endows the character with something almost touchingly painful. Because the elements of characterization are put on a face to which they are not altogether becoming, a certain crudeness mars our impression, while something in the nature of the actor's very considerable talent makes us wonder whether he is not actually suffering deeply. [. . .] When he beats his wife or throws the radio out the window, there is, aside from the ugliness of these acts, an element of agony that falsifies their color in relation to their meaning in the play: they take on an almost Dostoyevskian aspect. (15–16)

In other words, the personality and presence of Brando and of Jessica Tandy as Blanche, who, Clurman wrote, was "fragile without being touching" (10), as well as the critics' heterosexual assumptions and prejudices which normalized Stanley's behavior, caused the audience to identify more with him than with Blanche and to be unaware, no matter how clear Williams tried to make them, of Blanche's guilt and Allan's crucial relation to the action of the play.

Four interlocking critical tactics, then, effectively erased Allan Grey's presence from the play and his enormous influence on the play's action: ignoring the specifics of Blanche's past and disconnecting her past behavior from her actions once she arrives in the French Quarter, negating the existence of Allan Grey, highlighting the supposed similarities between Blanche and Amanda Wingfield, and normalizing the behavior of the play's straight characters. It is not Tennessee Williams who rendered the offstage and dead gay figure invisible and impotent; it was, first, the opening night critics and, more recently, gay critics of the 1990s who have inherited and embraced that early point of view.

The argument about the "heterosexist" character of *Streetcar* is easy to grasp. Allan Grey in the play which Clum calls "the quintessential closeted gay play" (150) is offstage and dead, one proof that Williams was unsuccessful at "presenting a coherent, affirming view of gayness" (149–50). Whether Williams ever took this as his own brief, or whether it is an after-the-fact criterion imposed by a critic writing forty-five years after the fact Clum does not discuss. For that matter, there is no evidence that Williams was interested in presenting a coherent, affirming view of humanity in general. In order to dismiss *Streetcar* as an example of homophobic discourse, Clum must rely almost entirely on Blanche's famous monologue in scene six, in which she describes the pivotal events of her life. Clum writes that, when the subject of homosexuality comes up in the dramas of the forties and fifties,

> it is usually linked to the brutal exposure of a sensitive man who is often a writer. [. . .] Blanche DuBois tells of "coming suddenly into a room that I thought was empty—which wasn't empty but had two people in it [. . .] the boy I had married and the older man who had been his friend for years." Typically, this extremely discreet description tells us nothing. What room? What were Blanche's husband and his older friend doing? The unspeakable remains unspoken in *Streetcar*, and the audience is expected to infer a sexual encounter from Blanche's judgmental language: "I saw! I know! You disgust me. . ." [. . .] Blanche, typical of Williams' [sic] characters, cannot exactly name what Allan is. But she can articulate her clear response. [. . .] Once made public, the sensitive

> poet's homosexuality becomes unbearable for him, and he commits
> suicide. The audience can accept Allan's self-destruction as poetic
> justice: there is no place onstage for homosexual behavior, and
> Allan's story encapsulates the problem-play resolution for fallen
> women and homosexuals—disappearance and, frequently, death.
> (149–50)

Williams, in other words, is guilty of an inability to provide a "positive image" of a gay man, falling back, instead, on rigid, homophobic Victorian patterns of morality. There is much material for an indictment of Williams in this paragraph, but there is confusion as well. It is indeed important for actress and director to ask, "What room? What were Blanche's husband and his older friend doing?" There is nothing any more mysterious, however, in Williams's failure to provide any answers than in Shakespeare's indifference to what Romeo and Juliet do between scene three and scene five in Act III, or in Chekhov's failure to tell us why Solyony is so disturbed and unhappy in *The Three Sisters*, or why it is, in *Happy Days*, that Beckett neglects to spell out in words why Willie cannot stand his wife. The playwrights chose not to fill in these details because these details are not what the plays are about. These are the quotidian particulars that playwrights skip over to get to the serious matters at hand; *A Streetcar Named Desire* is not about the nature of Allan's desire, although his desire plays a central role. It is the job of the actors and directors, not playwrights, to fill in these gaps.

Why does Allan Grey kill himself? One goes out on distant limbs dealing with the motivations of characters who do not actually appear in a play, so it is best to rely on common sense, which tells us that Allan Grey did not kill himself solely because he suddenly disgusted his wife, cruel though her treatment of him might have been. Moon Lake Casino had its origins in a gambling joint in Lula, near Williams's boyhood home of Clarksdale, near the northwest corner of Mississippi. Lyle Leverich describes it as a rough river port in which a minister like Williams's grandfather would find plenty of reforming to do (40). In *Orpheus Descending*, Moon Lake Casino is in Two River County, the small, xenophobic town ruled by Jabe Torrance and Sheriff Talbot where the eccentric, the creative, the sensitive—such as the Sheriff's painter wife, Vee—stand out and are regularly put down and humiliated. Allan Grey—nervous, soft, tender, and, worse still, a poet—could not easily conceal himself in such a town in the 1930s, even in a town less overtly hostile, even with a wife obtained in desperation.

Imagining this scene, an actor and director (and playwright) create circumstances which are not only possible but probable and dramatic, in which the stakes are high. So imagine it is a Saturday night in summer, not unlike the evening on which scene six, when Blanche tells her story to Mitch, occurs. Blanche, Allan, and his older "friend" are driving out to Moon Lake, laughing and drinking as they go. The casino is filled with couples gambling, dancing, smoking, drinking. The dance floor is crowded. There, in front of dozens of others, most of whom, we may assume, know the couple and have long been smirking about the sensitive young poet, Blanche—drunk, hurt, in shock—tells Allan she knows and that he disgusts her. Does she whisper it in his ear? No, it bursts out of her ("unable to stop myself—I'd suddenly said [. . .]" loud enough to be heard over the music by everyone around them. Allan and his secret are unmasked. He rushes from the dance hall to the edge of the lake. Moments later, a shot rings out. Why, one wonders, was Allan carrying a gun? Surely not against just such an occurrence. Even in a culture where many men owned guns, why would the nervous, soft young poet carry one? Perhaps for the same reason he is nervous, perhaps for the same reason he married: self-protection.

It is up to playwrights to suggest and to actresses, directors, and even critics to tease out the circumstances in which dramatic action occurs. One can imagine vivid circumstances, plausible both historically and psychologically, in which Allan Grey did not kill himself because his wife knew he was a homosexual but because, thanks to her, everyone in their small, insular town now knew. The danger for gay men in such small towns in the South was not theoretical but very real. Williams himself felt this way about the South. According to Elia Kazan, he refused to stay on in Benoit, Mississippi (forty miles south of Clarksdale) during the filming of *Baby Doll* because he was certain that people knew he was gay and looked at him threateningly (562; Murphy 131–132). Even given Williams's occasional paranoia and his bent for self-theatrics, he knew small Southern towns and their hostility towards outsiders and difference. Allan killed himself out of panic and fear. Blanche, who exposed him in the cruelest possible way, was responsible.

Clum also suggests, following Roger Boxill, that, as a "faded belle," Blanche is Tennessee Williams himself in drag; that she can be understood as a kind of gay subtext. Transforming Blanche into a drag queen ("I don't want realism. I want magic!" [385]) is the only way in which Clum can salvage anything "positive" in this play. Even if one holds nothing against drag queens, the tactic is strained: the only way to rescue the play and make it worthy is to turn the central character into an unflattering, stereotypical drag queen who preys on young, innocent newsboys, whose every utterance is laced with leering irony, who hates reality and who retreats into a dream world of fabulous performance. "*A Streetcar Named Desire*," Clum writes, "suggests that those who 'aren't straight' must act in order to survive and that they must imaginatively transform a world in which they are rejected into a bearable place. Allan Gray (and how his gray name contrasts with the lurid colors of Stanley's world) and Blanche cannot exist after they have been exposed. Their world is off the heterosexual stage, if they are allowed any world at all" (154). Clum depicts Blanche as the most stereotypical of drag queen vamps, although he says she is seen thus because it was the only way in which homosexuals were allowed to be portrayed in popular drama. While some critics may see homosexuality in drama this way, there is nothing to suggest that Williams did.

There is not much an actor or director can do with the notion that Blanche is actually a drag queen, unless the intent is parody. All one can do, faced with the task of playing Blanche or directing the play, is to ask, what is it that the character wants? What does she do to get what she wants? What are the circumstances in which she finds herself? What, in other words, actually happens in the play and prior to it, as opposed to what critics have said happens in the play? Asking these questions, one quickly discovers that, while Allan Grey is offstage and dead, he is hardly marginal to the action. In Williams's hands, Allan Grey is an Ibsenite figure. One of Ibsen's most significant innovations to the well-made play that he inherited from Eugène Scribe was to transform the secret around which the plot revolved from something essentially trivial and mechanical into something life-changing and organic. In Ibsen's middle and late plays, the past looms as large and plays as crucial a role as any major character, its power all the more terrible and potent for being invisible and seemingly absent. The presence and influence of Allan Grey on the characters of *Streetcar* are as palpable and irrevocable as Rebecca West's in *Rosmersholm* or Little Eyolf's in that eponymous play.

For some time before the play's action begins, Blanche has been fleeing Allan's ghost, doing everything she can to elude the memory of his face. Before losing Belle Reve, she seeks consolation in the arms of the young soldiers training nearby. So often did she seek—and find—comfort that the army declared Belle Reve off-limits. When the estate is lost, Blanche takes up residence in the Flamingo Hotel, where she continually seeks to lose herself—and Allan—in the arms of strangers, until, in her desperation, she seduces a seventeen-year-old boy. Perhaps he reminds her of her sensitive, young husband; perhaps loving him will atone for her brutal treatment of the other young man. Alas, her method of penance cannot be kept quiet in a small town (perhaps that is why she chose it), and, like Allan, she is exposed. Blanche, at least, manages to leave town alive.

In the play proper, it becomes obvious that the memory of Allan pursues Blanche like a Fury. From her first line of dialogue, Williams makes it clear that Blanche acts out of guilt for having driven her husband to suicide. To put it more actively, what Blanche wants is to find relief from her tremendous burden of conscience. "They told me to take a street-car named Desire, and then transfer to one called Cemeteries and ride six blocks and get off at—Elysian Fields!" (246) she says in her famous entrance line (246). Already, Allan is active in her unconscious: Blanche's exposure of his desire is what led him, if not to Elysian Fields, then to the cemetery. Her flight to New Orleans is also an unconscious calculation to punish herself, for she arrives in a condition unlikely to make her welcome to her self-absorbed sister. She arrives in New Orleans without money or plans for making any; in her flight from Allan, she has given little thought to the future. She comes, too, with a certain bitterness toward Stella for leaving her to deal single-handedly with the nightmare of death and loss at Belle Reve; it does not take even the length of the first scene for her to express her anger. Unconsciously, in her guilt, Blanche's own behavior becomes an instrument of Allan's vengeance; on the conscious level, Allan is the Fury she is seeking so desperately to escape. One can consider Blanche's guilty conscience as evidence of her sensitivity (and thus, her superiority). On the other hand, it may also reveal the depth and intensity of her need to escape Allan's ghost. It is *her* shame and guilt, not Allan's, on which the play turns. Williams never mentions Allan's shame for being a homosexual; only critics do.

Through which of her actions do we know of Blanche's obsession with Allan, and her need to escape his image? She drinks, early and often, and she denies it. She tells Stella in scene one that the reasons she will not go to a hotel (beyond the one, unmentioned, that she has no money) is desperation: "I want to be *near* you, got to be *with* somebody, I *can't* be *alone!* Because—as you must have noticed—I'm—*not* very *well* [. . .]". The stage direction that follows reads, *"Her voice drops and her look is frightened"* (257). Blanche's hesitations reveal her inner turmoil. She goes on at length, at once defensive and mildly accusatory, about the deaths and losses she faced without the aid of her sister. All that Blanche says here is true and truly felt. Her barely suppressed hysteria while telling the story, however, is also a reflection of the tale of death and loss and cruelty that she cannot speak, let alone face. "I, I, *I* took the blows in my face and body!" she declares. "All of those deaths! [. . .] You just came home in time for the funerals, Stella. And funerals are pretty compared to deaths." Describing any number of the deaths of Belle Reve, she could be describing Allan's: "Unless you were there at the bed when they cried out, 'Hold me!' you'd never suspect there was the struggle for breath and bleeding." Prefiguring the way she will describe the incident leading up to Allan's death, she goes on, "You didn't dream, but I saw! *Saw! Saw!*" (261–2). That she will use the same language in scene six suggests the link in her mind between these deaths and Allan's and the depths of her guilt and shame. Similarly, in scene two, as Stanley tosses the contents of her trunk around the room, he finds a pack of letters, which he promptly tears open:

[*He rips off the ribbon and starts to examine them. Blanche snatches them from him, and they cascade to the floor.*]

>   BLANCHE. Now that you've touched them, I'll burn them!
>   STANLEY [*staring, baffled*]. What in hell are they?
>   BLANCHE. Poems a dead boy wrote. I hurt him the way that you would like to hurt me, but you can't! I'm not young and vulnerable any more. But my young husband was and I—never mind about that! Just give them back to me! (282–3)

It takes little prompting to summon Allan's image to Blanche's mind. Once there, it is likely to trigger horrible memories, unless Blanche consciously attempts to banish it.

Scene four presents us with a replay of Blanche's seduction of the Laurel schoolboy. As she sits alone in the house, a teenage boy (Williams actually calls him a Young Man) calls, collecting for the newspaper. While one may view this scene as an opportunity for Blanche to play the campy drag vamp leering at the package of new meat, it can also be seen as another attempt, however sad, to find—and give—tenderness and kindness with a young man, to exorcise the image of Allan through an act of love. In scene five, as Blanche dresses for a night out with Mitch, Stella asks her, "Blanche, do you want *him*?" Blanche responds, "I want to *rest*! I want to breathe quietly again! Yes—*I want Mitch . . . very badly!*" (335). Mitch, she hopes, will provide a place where she can rest, where she can breathe, having found in the love of another man—and in loving him—escape from the sound of Allan's implacable tread.

That sound is the sound of the *Varsouviana*, the polka the band played that night, long ago but ever-present, at Moon Lake Casino. More than anything else, this sound that Allan's ghost whispers in her ear drives Blanche to madness. Silencing it would mean peace. We hear it first in scene one, when it is explicitly linked with Allan. Stanley says to her, "Stella's spoken of you a good deal. You were married once, weren't you?" Williams's stage direction reads, "*The music of the polka rises up, faint in the distance.*" Blanche responds, "Yes, when I was quite young." When Stanley asks what happened, Blanche responds with a pause, concealing and revealing: "The boy—died" (268). The music is heard again in scene six, as Blanche risks tremendous rejection by telling Mitch her story, sensing wrongly that he is kind. After all, he, too, lost someone he loved, a young woman who died of an unnamed illness but not before leaving Mitch with a remembrance far more benign than any Allan has left Blanche. It is a cigarette case with a sentimental Browning inscription: "And if God choose, / I shall but love thee better—after—death!" (297). That, with ominous pauses, is the way Blanche reads it by the light of a match. The stage direction says she reads with "*feigned dif-*

ficulty" (297). She may be feigning difficulty to conceal another feeling, irony or even envy: it is not the way Allan is loving *her* after death. As Blanche describes the terrible night at Moon Lake Casino, the polka sounds again, only to stop abruptly with the sound of a gunshot. The silence, however, is momentary; almost immediately, the music returns. The stage direction says that Blanche sways and covers her face, as if trying to push the music out of her ears. For the moment, Mitch is sympathetic. He takes her in his arms as the music increases, saying, "You need somebody. And I need somebody, too. Could it be—you and me, Blanche?" (354–6). They kiss, and the music fades away. This is what Blanche has hoped for.

The ghost of Allan, however, is only briefly silent. In scene eight, the music rises again as Stanley hands Blanche a one-way bus ticket back to Laurel—a reminder for her, and for us, that this is a punishment for a specific crime. In scene nine, the music returns for a sixth time. Mitch has learned from Stanley the details of Blanche's sordid life in Laurel and stands her up at her birthday party. Stella, about to give birth, has been taken to the hospital; Blanche is alone in the house. She is drinking when Mitch arrives. Now, Williams's stage direction is explicit: "*The music is in her mind; she is drinking to escape it and the sense of disaster closing in on her*" (379). The polka rises and recedes in her mind as she tries to elicit from Mitch the reason for his deliberate insult. The explosive sound of the gunshot brings silence but now Blanche's guilt and growing fear take another shape. As Mitch accuses her of lying to him about her past, a street vendor comes around the corner, a blind Mexican woman clutching bunches of "gaudy tin flowers" and crying her wares: "Flores. Flores. Flores para los muertos. Flores. Flores." Blanche reacts as if she is seeing Allan himself coming after her: "No, no! Not now! Not now!" (388). Not, that is, with Mitch, with salvation, just within reach. The old woman repeats her cry, as the polka tune takes up again in Blanche's head. Now Blanche herself makes the connection clear: "Crumble and fade and—regrets—recriminations . . . 'If you'd done this, it wouldn't've cost me that!'" (388). Now, there is only one escape route left.

Her crime and the consequent guilt and self-loathing cost Blanche her sanity. The intensity of her need for refuge drives her beyond hysteria into madness. She sinks deep within the recesses of her mind, the last place she thinks she can finally elude Allan's voice, the gunshot, and the *Varsouviana*. Even madness, however, cannot conceal her from Allan. In scene eleven, convinced that she is about to embark on a voyage with her new savior, Shep Huntleigh, she imagines her death at sea:

> BLANCHE. I can smell the sea air. The rest of my time
> I'm going to spend on the sea. And when I die, I'm going to die
> on the sea. You know what I shall die of? [*She plucks a grape.*] I

shall die of eating an unwashed grape out on the ocean. I will
die—with my hand in the hand of some nice-looking ship's doctor, a very young one with a small blond moustache and a big
silver watch. "Poor lady," they'll say, "the quinine did her no good.
That unwashed grape has transported her soul to heaven." [*The
cathedral chimes are heard.*] And I'll be buried at sea sewn up in a
clean white sack and dropped overboard—at noon—in the blaze
of summer—and into an ocean as blue as [*chimes again*] my first
lover's eyes! (410)

Even now, in madness, Blanche feels Allan's gaze burning in her.

The memory of Allan, then, and of her deliberate cruelty toward him, is
one motor that powers the play's action. An actress might well find in them
the details such as a reason for Blanche's constant—and to Stanley, increasingly annoying—singing of popular songs, anything to drive *The Varsouviana* out of her head. Beneath even this superficial gaiety lies desperation.
Allan's presence is felt from the beginning as an avenging angel, and Stanley
becomes his ironic instrument. About to rape Blanche, he says to her, "We've
had this date with each other from the beginning!" (402). In this sense, Allan
is hardly at the play's margins; he occupies the center with as much force as
any of the play's living characters. Williams himself told an interviewer that
the force propelling Blanche through *Streetcar* was her guilt. In 1973, he told
Playboy, "Blanche in *Streetcar* was at it like knives from the time of the death
of her husband, fucking those soldiers at camp. She had to expiate her feeling responsible for killing him. When he told her about his relations with an
older man [sic] she called him disgusting; then she just went out and solved
her problems with a continuous orgy" (qtd. in Jennings 228). Thus, she is no
more a faded belle than is Amanda. She is a fighter, fighting for her life.

Blanche's need to escape the memory of Allan is not the play's only
motor, of course. If one wishes to criticize *Streetcar* for not presenting a
"coherent, affirming view of gayness" while it has no living gay characters
in it, then it is reasonable to ask if it presents an affirming view of straightness, since its onstage characters are all heterosexual and driven by the
play's other very potent engine: desire. How well do the straight characters
in *Streetcar* behave?

Stanley can be viewed as Clurman saw him: a brute, a man with no
appreciation of culture or sensitivity. He distrusts Blanche from the beginning, accusing her of selling Belle Reve and keeping the proceeds for herself. He crassly presents his obviously fragile sister-in-law with a one-way
bus ticket home; he humiliates her in front of her sister. He has a temper
he cannot control which causes him to strike his pregnant wife and trash
their apartment. He is, as Williams writes, "*the gaudy seed-bearer*" (265)

and proud of it. He has no qualms about raping Blanche. As for Mitch, conventional wisdom about the play instructs us to consider him a gentleman, but his behavior toward Blanche is anything but gentlemanly. What is his reaction after she confesses her deeply painful role in Allan's death? In scene nine he fumblingly embraces her and in response to Blanche's alarmed "What do you want?" replies, "What I been missing all summer." "Then marry me, Mitch!" Blanche says (389–90). Marriage, after all, is what they both wanted three scenes earlier. Mitch's response: "You're not clean enough to bring in the house with my mother" (390). Marriage is now out of the question; sex is not.

In what is perhaps the play's cruelest moment, Stella tells Eunice in scene eleven that she cannot believe Blanche's story that she was raped by Stanley. Stella would rather see her sister locked away for life in a mental institution than entertain even the possibility that her tale of rape is true. Stella's behavior is at least consistent: this is the same young woman who left Belle Reve and allowed Blanche to struggle with the banks, doctors, and undertakers while she frolicked with her husband beneath their colored lights. This is the same Stella who returns to Stanley after he strikes her. Today, we would call her an enabler. As role models, as images of affirmative straightness, the characters of *Streetcar* are a sorry lot. They are, in fact, a prime example of "heterophobic discourse."

Williams did not view any of the characters this way. If he was judgmental, he was judge and executioner of Blanche, meting out punishment for her cruelty toward her gay husband. But unlike critics, who judge, Williams, as playwright, simply showed. What saves Stanley, Stella, Mitch, and Blanche, and, for that matter, Allan, from the reductionist treatment above is the intensity of their desires. If Stanley distrusts and then dislikes Blanche, it is because he views her as an intrusion into his previously happy life. One gets the sense that, prior to Blanche's arrival, Stanley was perhaps the most content character in all of Williams's work. He loves everything about his life, from his American citizenship and Polish heritage to coming home in the evening and, playing the role of provider, flinging his wife a package of meat. Blanche is right to say that Stanley is not cultured, but neither is he affected. He is vital, earthy, true to himself and, despite imperfections in temperament, deeply in love with Stella. Stella, for her part, intensely loves Stanley. She loves the nights beneath the colored lights as much as he does: "But there are things that happen between a man and a woman in the dark—that sort of make everything else seem—unimportant" (321). Mitch may be a Milquetoast and finally a hypocrite, but, like Blanche, he is desperately lonely and longs to change his life, and, like her, he has lost someone he loved. His cruelty toward Blanche is in exact proportion to the hopes he had that she would be the wife for whom he has longed. As much as Blanche needs a cleft in a rock, he needs tenderness and companionship far more than he needs another poker night with the boys. The depth of his cruelty in scene nine indicates the degree of hope and yearning underlying his last line in scene six: "You need somebody. And I need somebody, too. Could it be—you and me, Blanche?"

We may not necessarily endorse the view of life that Williams presents in *A Streetcar Named Desire*, but Williams is not interested in our approval. He is interested only in showing us what is true in the lives of these characters. In his plays, Williams is almost never directly interested in politics or sociology. It is the behavior of individual humans that concerns him. This dedication to human action, and his skill at portraying it, makes Williams's plays especially resistant to post-structuralist and post-modern criticism, more interested as it is in constructions and theories than in human beings behaving in concrete circumstances for specific reasons. One can easily agree with Clum when he writes, "To ignore the homosexual subtext of *Streetcar* is to reduce the play, but to see it as the only text is even more reductive." However, he continues, "Yet, *Streetcar* is a gay play in its theatricalization, not merely dramatization, of experience; its awareness of the power inherent in understanding the slipperiness of language; its playfulness within scenes of impending entrapment and destruction. It is, in short, about the theatricalization of experience as an act of liberation. Such theatricalization does not destroy the closet, but makes the closet bearable" (152). Perhaps. But one can take this tack only if one believes that Blanche is always acting. If she is always acting, then she is never sincere. If she is never sincere, then she is simply a campy drag act. If she is a campy drag act, then the role is unactable. An actress confronted with the text cannot go far along this line and produce a picture of a woman coping with a desperate situation as best she can, surrounded by characters who just as deeply desire their own happiness. The power of the kind of theatre to which Williams belonged still arises from a very simple formula: from opposed desires comes conflict which causes characters to behave in ways they might not otherwise. Blanche rejected Allan Grey in the cruelest way that could be imagined. By haunting her imagination, by stalking her into madness, Allan has his posthumous revenge.

Notes

1. For gays and lesbians in the military, see Allan Bérubé, *Coming Out Under Fire: The History of Gay Men and Women in World War Two* (New York: Plume, 1991). For social and political history involving gays and lesbians, see, for example, John D'Emilio, *Sexual Politics, Sexual Communities: The Making of a Homosexual Minority in the United States, 1940–1970* (Chicago: U of Chicago P, 1983); *Making Trouble: Essays on Gay History, Politics, and the University* (New York: Routledge, 1992); Jonathan Katz, *Gay American History: Lesbians and Gay Men in the U.S.A.* (New York: Crowell, 1976); and *Gay/Lesbian Almanac: A New Documentary* (New

York: Colophon, 1983). For Williams's activities during the war, see Donald Spoto, *The Kindness of Strangers: The Life of Tennessee Williams* (New York: Ballantine, 1986); Lyle Leverich, *Tom: The Unknown Tennessee Williams* (New York: Crown, 1995); and Tennessee Williams, *Memoirs* (New York: Anchor Press, 1983). For portrayals of homosexuals on Broadway, see Kaier Curtin, *"We Can Always Call Them Bulgarians": The Emergence of Lesbians and Gay Men on the American Stage* (Boston: Alyson, 1987).

Works Cited

Atkinson, Brooks. "At The Theatre." *New York Times* 4 Dec. 1947: 42.

Barnes, Howard. "A Long-Run Trolley." *New York Herald Tribune* 4 Dec. 1947. *New York Theatre Critics' Reviews 1947*, 252.

Chapman, John. *"Streetcar Named Desire* Sets Season's High in Acting, Writing." *Daily News* 4 Dec. 1947. *New York Theatre Critics' Reviews 1947*, 249.

Clum, John. *Acting Gay: Male Homosexuality in Modern Drama.* New York: Columbia UP, 1992.

Clurman, Harold. *The Divine Pastime.* New York: Macmillan, 1974.

Coleman, Robert. *"Desire Streetcar* In for Long Run." *Daily Mirror* 4 Dec. 1947. *New York Theatre Critics' Reviews 1947*, 252.

Garland, Robert. "Williams' New Play Exciting Theatre." *New York Journal American* 4 Dec. 1947. *New York Theatre Critics' Review 1947*, 251.

Hawkins, William. *"Streetcar* a Fine Play of Clashing Emotions." *New York World Telegram* 4 Dec. 1947. *New York Theatre Critics' Reviews 1947*, 251.

Jennings, C. Robert. *"Playboy* Interview: Tennessee Williams, 1973." *Conversations with Tennessee Williams.* Ed. Albert J. Devlin. Jackson: U of Mississippi P, 1986.

Kazan, Elia. *A Life.* New York: Anchor, 1989.

Kronenberger, Louis. "A Sharp Southern Drama by Tennessee Williams." *PM* 5 Dec. 1947. *New York Theatre Critics' Reviews 1947*, 250.

Leverich, Lyle. *Tom: The Unknown Tennessee Williams.* New York: Crown, 1995.

Morehouse, Ward. "New Hit Named *Desire.*" *The New York Sun* 4 Dec. 1947. *New York Theatre Critics' Reviews 1947.*

Murphy, Rosemary. *Tennessee Williams and Elia Kazan: A Collaboration in the Theatre.* Cambridge: Cambridge UP, 1992.

New York Theatre Critics' Reviews 1947. Vol. 8. New York: *New York Critics' Theatre Reviews,* 1947.

"Streetcar on Broadway." *Newsweek* 15 Dec. 1947: 16.

Williams, Tennessee. *A Streetcar Named Desire.* 1947. *The Theatre of Tennessee Williams.* Vol. 1. New York: New Directions: 1971.

Chronology

1911	Thomas Lanier ("Tennessee") Williams born March 26 in Columbus, Mississippi, to Cornelius Coffin and Edwina Dakin Williams, one-and-a-half years after his sister Rose Isabel was born.
1911–1918 or 1919	Family moves often, then settles in St. Louis, Missouri. In 1919, brother, Walter Dakin, is born.
1929	Graduates from University City High School and enters the University of Missouri.
1935	Suffers nervous breakdown. Play he collaborated on, *Cairo! Shanghai! Bombay!*, is produced.
1936–37	Enters and is later dropped from Washington University, St. Louis. Enters University of Iowa. First full-length plays, *The Fugitive Kind* and *Candles to the Sun*, are produced. Sister Rose undergoes lobotomy.
1938	Graduates from University of Iowa with a degree in English.
1941–43	Takes various jobs in different cities.
1944	*The Glass Menagerie* opens in Chicago.
1945	*The Glass Menagerie* opens in New York and wins New York Drama Critic's Circle Award.
1947	*Summer and Smoke* opens in Dallas. *A Streetcar Named Desire* opens in New York and wins the New York Drama Critic's

Circle Award and the Pulitzer Prize. Meets Frank Merlo, who becomes his longtime companion.

1948   *Summer and Smoke* opens in New York. *One Arm and Other Stories* published.

1950   *The Roman Spring of Mrs. Stone*, a novel, published. *The Rose Tattoo* opens in Chicago.

1951   *The Rose Tattoo* opens in New York, wins the Antoinette Perry (Tony) Award for best play.

1953   *Camino Real* opens in New York.

1954   *Hard Candy: A Book of Stories*, published.

1955   *Cat on a Hot Tin Roof* opens in New York. Wins New York Drama Critic's Circle award and Pulitzer Prize.

1956   First collection of poems, *In the Winter of Cities*, published. *Baby Doll*, a film, is released and nominated for Academy Award.

1957   *Orpheus Descending* opens in New York.

1958   *Garden District* (*Suddenly Last Summer* and *Something Unspoken*) produced Off-Broadway.

1959   *Sweet Bird of Youth* opens in New York.

1960   *Period of Adjustment* opens in New York.

1961   *The Night of the Iguana* opens in New York.

1962   Awarded a lifetime fellowship by the American Academy of Arts and Letters.

1963   *The Milk Train Doesn't Stop Here Anymore* opens in New York. Frank Merlo dies. Williams falls into depression.

1966   *Slapstick Tragedy* opens in New York.

1967   *The Two-Character Play* opens in London.

1968   *The Seven Descents of Myrtle* opens in New York.

1969   *In the Bar of a Tokyo Hotel* opens Off-Broadway. Converts to Catholicism. Nervous collapse causes him to stay hospitalized for three months in a hospital in St. Louis.

1970   *Dragon Country: A Book of Plays* published.

1971   Revised version of *Two-Character Play*, called *Out Cry*, opens in Chicago.

1972	*Small Craft Warnings* opens Off-Broadway.
1974	*Eight Mortal Ladies Possessed*, a collection of short stories, published.
1975	*Memoirs* and a second novel, *Moise and the World of Reason*, are published. *The Red Devil Battery Sign* opens in Boston.
1977	*Vieux Carré* opens in New York.
1978	*Where I Live*, a book of essays, published.
1980	*Clothes for a Summer Hotel* opens in Washington, D.C. Mother dies.
1981	*A House Not Meant to Stand* opens in Chicago. *Something Cloudy, Something Clear* opens in New York.
1983	Dies in February at the Hotel Elysée in New York City.

Contributors

HAROLD BLOOM is Sterling Professor of the Humanities at Yale University. He is the author of 30 books, including *Shelley's Mythmaking*, *The Visionary Company*, *Blake's Apocalypse*, *Yeats*, *A Map of Misreading*, *Kabbalah and Criticism*, *Agon: Toward a Theory of Revisionism*, *The American Religion*, *The Western Canon*, and *Omens of Millennium: The Gnosis of Angels, Dreams, and Resurrection*. *The Anxiety of Influence* sets forth Professor Bloom's provocative theory of the literary relationships between the great writers and their predecessors. His most recent books include *Shakespeare: The Invention of the Human*, a 1998 National Book Award finalist, *How to Read and Why*, *Genius: A Mosaic of One Hundred Exemplary Creative Minds*, *Hamlet: Poem Unlimited*, *Where Shall Wisdom Be Found?*, and *Jesus and Yahweh: The Names Divine*. In 1999, Professor Bloom received the prestigious American Academy of Arts and Letters Gold Medal for Criticism. He has also received the International Prize of Catalonia, the Alfonso Reyes Prize of Mexico, and the Hans Christian Andersen Bicentennial Prize of Denmark.

GULSHAN RAI KATARIA is the head of the department of English at Punjabi University, Patiala, India, where he is also a professor. He has published extensively in the field of modern drama, and his other primary areas of academic interest include twentieth-century literature as well as Elizabethan drama.

CALVIN BEDIENT is a professor at the University of California at Los Angeles. Among his books are *Eight Contemporary Poets*, which was nominated for a National Book Award, and *Architects of the Self: George Eliot, D.H. Lawrence, and E.M. Forster*.

167

SUSAN KOPRINCE teaches at the University of North Dakota. She is the author of *Understanding Neil Simon*.

GEORGE TOLES is chairperson of the film department and a distinguished professor at the University of Manitoba in Winnipeg. Aside from his work in film and theater, Toles has written *House Made of Light: Essays on the Art of Film*.

PHILIP C. KOLIN is a distinguished professor at the University of Southern Mississippi. He is a founding coeditor of *Studies in American Drama, 1945–Present*. He has written extensively on Tennessee Williams, including *Undiscovered Country: The Later Plays of Tennessee Williams* and *Williams: A Streetcar Named Desire*. He is the editor of the *Tennessee Williams Encyclopedia*. Additionally, Kolin is general editor for the Routledge Shakespeare Criticism Series and a poet.

GEORGE W. CRANDELL is head of the English department and a professor at Auburn University. In addition to articles on modern drama and American humor, he has published *The Critical Response to Tennessee Williams* and *Tennessee Williams: A Descriptive Bibliography*.

BERT CARDULLO has taught at the University of Michigan in the theater department. An editor and translator as well as a critic and dramaturg, he has published more than twenty books, among them *Theater of the Avant-Garde, 1890–1950: A Critical Anthology* and *Screening the Stage: Studies in Cinedramatic Art*. He is professor of media and communication at İzmir University of Economics in Turkey.

JOHN S. BAK has been a *maître de langue* at the Université de Nancy II, where he presents and publishes articles on American and British drama. He has been published in several journals.

RACHEL VAN DUYVENBODE teaches at the University of Sheffield in the United Kingdom. She was published in the *Journal of American Studies* and coedited a special edition of *U.S. Studies OnLine*. Additionally, she has been a reviewer of post–1945 American literature for *Year's Work in English Studies*.

MICHAEL PALLER is director of humanities in the M.F.A. program at the American Conservatory Theater in San Francisco. He has been consulting dramaturg for the Roundabout Theater Company in New York City, as well as literary manager and dramaturg at other locations. In 1997, he served as Richard Corley's dramaturg for the Russian premiere of Tennessee Williams's *Small Craft Warnings*.

Bibliography

Bak, John S. "'May I Have a Drag . . . ?': Mae West, Tennessee Williams, and the Politics of a Gay Identity." *Journal of American Drama and Theatre* 18, no. 3 (2006): 5–32.

———. "'Stanley Made Love to Her!—By Force!': Blanche and the Evolution of a Rape." *Journal of American Drama and Theatre* 16, no. 1 (Winter 2004): 69–97.

Cafagna, Dianne. "Blanche DuBois and Maggie the Cat: Illusion and Reality in Tennessee Williams." In *Critical Essays on Tennessee Williams,* edited by Robert A. Martin, pp. 119–31. New York, N.Y.: G. K. Hall, 1997.

Firenze, Paul J. "The Social Mask and the Dionysian Figure in Pirandello's *Liolá* and Williams' *A Streetcar Named Desire.*" *Neohelicon* 24, no. 2 (1997): 327–39.

Fleche, Anne. "The Space of Madness and Desire: Tennessee Williams and *Streetcar.*" *Modern Drama* 38, no. 4 (Winter 1995): 496–509.

Fordyce, Ehren. "Inhospitable Structures: Some Themes and Forms in Tennessee Williams." *Journal of American Drama and Theatre* 17, no. 2 (Spring 2005): 43–58.

Foser, Verna. "Desire, Death, and Laughter: Tragicomic Dramaturgy in *A Streetcar Named Desire.*" In *New Readings in American Drama: Something's Happening Here,* edited by Norma Jenckes, pp. 227–37. New York, N.Y.: Peter Lang, 2002.

———. "Desire, Death, and Laughter: Tragicomic Dramaturgy in *A Streetcar Named Desire.*" *American Drama* 9, no. 1 (1999): 51–68.

Gates, Jonathan. "T. William's Language of the Soul in *Glass Menagerie, Streetcar Named Desire,* and *Cat on a Hot Tin Roof* (October 10-12, 1996, Regis Col-

lege, Weston, Mass.)." In *Proceedings: Northeast Regional Meeting of the Confer-
ence on Christianity and Literature*, edited by Joan F. Hallisey and Mary-Anne
Vetterling, pp. 38–43. Weston, Mass.: Regis College, 1996.

Griffin, Alice. *Understanding Tennessee Williams*. Columbia: University of South
Carolina Press, 1995.

Han, Byungho. "Korean Productions of *A Streetcar Named Desire.*" *Journal of American Drama and Theatre* 13, no. 1 (2001): 36–51.

Harrington, Gary. "The Smashed Mirror: Blanche in *A Streetcar Named Desire.*" In
Staging a Cultural Paradigm: The Political and the Personal in American Drama,
edited by Barbara Ozieblo and Miriam López-Rodríguez, pp. 67–78. Brus-
sels, Belgium: Presses Interuniversitaires Européennes (P.I.E.)–Peter Lang,
2002.

Hovis, George. "'Fifty Percent Illusion': The Mask of the Southern Belle in Tennessee Williams's *A Streetcar Named Desire, The Glass Menagerie*, and 'Portrait of a
Madonna.'" *Tennessee Williams Literary Journal* 5, no. 1 (Spring 2003): 11–22.

Isaac, Dan. "No Past to Think In: Who Wins in 'A Streetcar Named Desire.'" *Louisiana Literature* 14, no. 2 (Fall 1997): 8–35.

Jones, David Richard. *Great Directors at Work: Stanislavsky, Brecht, Kazan, Brook*.
Berkeley: University of California Press, 1986.

Kazan, Elia. *A Kazan Reader*. New York: Stein and Day, 1977.

Kolin, Philip C. *Williams:* A Streetcar Named Desire. Cambridge, England: Cambridge University Press, 2000.

Londré, Felicia Hardison. "A Streetcar Running Fifty Years." In *The Cambridge
Companion to Tennessee Williams*, edited by Matthew C. Roudané, pp. 45–66.
Cambridge, England: Cambridge University Press, 1997.

Miller, Jordan Y., ed. *Twentieth Century Interpretations of* A Streetcar Named Desire:
A Collection of Critical Essays, edited by Jordan Y. Miller. Englewood Cliffs,
N.J.: Prentice-Hall, 1971.

Pagan, Nicholas O. "Tennessee Williams's Theater as Body." *Philological Quarterly*
27 (1993): 97–115.

Schlueter, June. *Dramatic Closure: Reading the End*. Fairleigh Dickinson University
Press: Madison, N.J.; London and Cranbury, N.J.: Associated University
Presses, 1995.

Shackelford, Dean. "Is There a Gay Man in This Text?: Subverting the Closet in
A Streetcar Named Desire." *Literature and Homosexuality*, edited by Michael J.
Meyer, pp. 135–59. Amsterdam, Netherlands: Rodopi, 2000.

Tischler, Nancy M. "Sanitizing the Streetcar." *Louisiana Literature* 14, no. 2 (Fall
1997): 48–56.

Vlasopolos, Anca. "Authorizing History: Victimization in 'A Streetcar Named
Desire.'" *Theatre Journal* 38, no. 3 (October 1986): 322–38.

Yamaguchi, Nahoko. "D. H. Lawrence, Tennessee Williams, and the Male Body."
In *D. H. Lawrence: Literature, History, Culture*, edited by Michael Bell,

Keith Cushman, Takeo Iida, and Hiro Tateishi, pp. 387–96. Tokyo, Japan: Kokusho-KankoKai, 2005.

Zelinsky, Mark. "'Oh, Well, It's His Pleasure, Like Mine Is Movies': The Film and Television Adaptations of *A Streetcar Named Desire*: New Orleans in Mass Culture." *Humanities in the South* 88 (2001): 59–78.

Zhang, Xin. "A Comparison between the Two Tragic Heroines: Miss Emily Grierson in William Faulkner's 'A Rose for Emily' & Blanche DuBois in Tennessee Williams's *A Streetcar Named Desire*." In *Re-Reading America: Changes and Challenges*, edited by Weihe Zhong and Rui Han, pp. 88–94. Cheltenham, England: Reardon, 2004.

Acknowledgments

Gulshan Rai Kataria, "The Hetairas (Maggie, Myrtle, Blanche)." From *The Faces of Eve: A Study of Tennessee Williams's Heroines.* © 1992 by Gulshan Rai Kataria. Reprinted by permission.

Calvin Bedient, "There Are Lives that Desire Does Not Sustain: *A Streetcar Named Desire.*" From *Confronting Tennessee Williams's* A Streetcar Named Desire: *Essays in Critical Pluralism*, edited by Philip C. Kolin. © 1993 by Philip C. Kolin. Reproduced with permission of Greenwood Publishing Group, Inc., Westport, CT.

Susan Koprince, "Domestic Violence in *A Streetcar Named Desire.*" From *Southern Studies: An Interdisciplinary Journal of the South* 7, nos. 2 and 3 (Summer/Fall 1996): 43–55. © 1996 by the Southern Studies Institute and Northwestern State University of Louisiana. Reproduced with permission of Northwestern State University of Louisiana in the format other book via Copyright Clearance Center.

George Toles, "Blanche DuBois and the Kindness of Endings." From *Raritan* 14, no. 4 (Spring 1995): 115–143. © 1995 by Rutgers University. Reprinted by permission.

Philip C. Kolin, "'It's Only a Paper Moon': The Paper Ontologies in Tennessee Williams's *A Streetcar Named Desire.*" From *Modern Drama* 40, no. 4 (Winter 1997): 454–467. © 1997 by University of Toronto Press. Reprinted by permission of the University of Toronto Press Incorporated (www.utpjournals.com) and the Graduate Centre for the Study of Drama at the University of Toronto.

George W. Crandell, "Misrepresentation and Miscegenation: Reading the Racialized Discourse of Tennessee Williams's *A Streetcar Named Desire*." From *Modern Drama* 40, no. 3 (Fall 1997): 337–346. © 1997 by University of Toronto Press. Reprinted by permission of the University of Toronto Press Incorporated (www.utpjournals.com) and the Graduate Centre for the Study of Drama at the University of Toronto.

Bert Cardullo, "Scene 11 of *A Streetcar Named Desire*." From *ANQ* 10, no. 4 (Fall 1997): 34–38. © 1997 by Heldref Publications. Reprinted by permission.

John S. Bak, "Wagnerian Architectonics: The Plastic Language of Tennessee Williams's *A Streetcar Named Desire*." From *The Tennessee Williams Literary Journal* 4, no. 1 (Fall 1997): 41–58. © 1997 by *The Tennessee Williams Literary Journal*. Reprinted by permission.

Rachel Van Duyvenbode, "Darkness Made Visible: Miscegenation, Masquerade and the Signified Racial Other in Tennessee Williams' *Baby Doll* and *A Streetcar Named Desire*." From *Journal of American Studies* 35, no. 2 (2001): 203–215. © 2001 by and reprinted with permission of Cambridge University Press.

Michael Paller, "A Room Which Isn't Empty: *A Streetcar Named Desire* and the Question of Homophobia." From *The Tennessee Williams Literary Journal* 5, no. 1 (Spring 2003): 23–37. © 2003 by *The Tennessee Williams Literary Journal*.

Every effort has been made to contact the owners of copyrighted material and secure copyright permission. Articles appearing in this volume generally appear much as they did in their original publication with few or no editorial changes. In some cases, foreign language text has been removed from the original essay. Those interested in locating the original source will find the information cited above.

Index